Education Priorities and Aid Responses in Sub-Saharan Africa

Report of a Conference at
Cumberland Lodge, Windsor
4–7 December 1984

Edited by
Hugh Hawes and Trevor Coombe
with
Carol Coombe and Kevin Lillis

Overseas Development Administration
University of London Institute of Education

ISBN 0 11 580248 7

Foreword
by the Rt Hon Timothy Raison MP

Not all that many conference reports mean much to anyone other than the participants themselves. The writers of this report are aiming at a much wider audience, and they have worked hard to draw out the general principles that surfaced during this unique meeting. I should like to thank the Director and staff of the University of London Institute of Education for all the energy which was put into the organisation of the Conference and the writing of this report.

It was a very successful Conference, and I am only sorry that the unforeseen Lomé signing ceremony which I had to attend that week took me away from what were clearly absorbing discussions. Naturally I do not agree with all the views expressed at the Conference or in the report, but I am glad that distinguished educationists were able to put them forward so freely at such a lively and stimulating forum.

The strength of the Conference and its report lies in the stress they put on the importance of the relationship between education and the key problems of food production, population increase and the environment in general. While the crisis of food shortages in Africa stares us in the face, we need to look beyond it to the longer term. That is why the British aid programme emphasises the development of Africa's manpower and looks to the strengthening of key institutions as the basis for future development.

I am sure that readers of this report will find for themselves that once again something new has come out of Africa.

TIMOTHY RAISON
Minister of State for Foreign and
Commonwealth Affairs and Minister
for Overseas Development

Editorial note

This report attempts to synthesise bodies of information and opinion from a number of sources:

1 Verbatim transcripts from the Conference itself
2 Lead papers submitted by the four theme speakers
3 Reports of working groups submitted during the Conference on two sets of discussions: Theme I — Priorities, and Theme II — Aid
4 Background documents commissioned for and submitted to the Conference
5 Individual views ('think pieces') submitted prior to the Conference by the majority of participants.

Selection and omission from this wealth of material are bound to reflect the particular viewpoints of the editors, however impartial they have tried to be. Moreover, the report does not merely record the proceedings, because from time to time the editors have attempted to interpret and extrapolate from what was said.

There was never any intention of presenting this report as a document officially sanctioned by the British Government. That would have run quite contrary to the whole intention of the Conference. As was agreed from the outset by the Conference Steering Committee, the report has been compiled by a group of editors from the Department of Education in Developing Countries of the University of London Institute of Education. Various people have kindly read through and commented upon the draft. As Editor-in-Chief, I have been responsible for all final decisions of what to include and what to leave out.

HUGH HAWES

Introduction

Origins

The idea of the Windsor Conference originated, as many ideas do, over a meal. Sir William Ryrie, then Permanent Secretary of the Overseas Development Administration (ODA), was visiting the University of London Institute of Education with Roger Iredale, his Principal Education Adviser. Over lunch with Denis Lawton, the Director, and with Peter Williams and Hugh Hawes, conversation turned predictably to the role the Institute would play in helping ODA in its task of making informed choices on educational aid.

Two issues were talked through. One was the need to achieve a better sense of educational requirements and priorities, especially in relation to the urgent and conflicting demands for educational assistance in Africa. The second was the need to achieve a deeper and more widely shared understanding of aid policies and priorities, and what was later referred to as the 'ecology' of different aid agencies.

There had been attempts in the recent past to get people together to share their experience of these issues. Such meetings had often been narrowly focused and attended only by particular categories of decision-makers such as vice-chancellors of universities, ministers of education, permanent secretaries, or heads of curriculum centres. Aid agencies also commonly met together, often inviting experienced educational executives from Africa to participate, but the purpose of these meetings was normally to present and discuss current programmes and projects. All such meetings tended to be official in tone and status. Participants came as delegates, spoke as delegates and reflected official positions. Many meetings ended with a set of resolutions, often carefully worded after much debate.

No one questioned the value of such gatherings, but was there not, perhaps, a need for a different sort of conference, something that the London Institute was particularly well suited to offer: a forum

1 Where politicians, academics and executives could meet with aid agency representatives in an open and relaxed atmosphere, and talk over the hard choices which faced all parties in providing assistance for education in Africa in these difficult times

2 Where people were invited on a personal basis and not as delegates of their countries

3 Where the emphasis would be on the sharing of ideas and experience across a very wide field, in an attempt to see problems and choices in perspective

4 Where no resolutions would be passed but certain areas of consensus might be identified?

ODA agreed to meet from the British aid programme all costs for this Conference except those for participants from other aid agencies. The

Institute, for its part, would undertake a substantial part of the considerable preparation involved. In fact the greater part of the organisation was done jointly by a steering committee from the University and ODA. The British Council kindly assisted with communications and travel arrangements for participants. The experience of working together, very harmoniously as it transpired, was a valued by-product of the Conference.

Selecting the participants

One of the first tasks to be faced by the steering committee was the selection of participants. Inevitably, many wise men and women were left out, though the Conference amply demonstrated that all who did participate had a wealth of experience to offer. In order to serve the purposes of the Conference, the following guidelines were used in deciding whom to invite:

1 About 50 participants should be invited. The Conference was to be residential, and the importance of generating an atmosphere conducive to discussion was paramount. This could not be achieved if the numbers were large or if there were too many 'day visitors'.

2 The majority of members should be from Africa and should represent a cross-section of experience: ministers, government executives and academics from a wide geographic and developmental range of countries. As far as possible, the participants should be recognised as opinion leaders in their own countries and internationally.

3 University representation should be kept relatively modest. The bulk of the participants from Africa and elsewhere should be people who took decisions about priorities rather than those who wrote and talked about them, however wisely.

4 Aid agencies should be represented by senior officials who would be able to present a wide and informed picture of their own policies, and the historical and political pressures under which they evolved.

5 Lastly, the Conference membership should reflect a wide interpretation of education, both formal and non-formal, linking with manpower planning on the one hand and, on the other, with non-governmental groups and agencies.

A glance through the list of participants (p. 176) suggests that the composition of the Conference observed all but the last of these initial guidelines. The relative absence of specialists from outside the formal education system was a serious omission.

Take-up of invitations exceeded the expectations of the Conference organisers. Only a handful of those approached were unable to come and the total fund of accumulated experience from Africa was impressive. Aid agencies released their senior executives. One agency, in the throes of a major programme review, lifted a temporary travel ban in order to allow its officer to come to Windsor. However, one sad gap in agency participation needs to be recorded and explained: UNESCO was not represented, the head of the regional office in Dakar having had to withdraw at a very late stage. His absence was greatly regretted, especially since no one of suitable experience was available at the time to take his place.

Preparation

Members of the steering committee visited the aid agencies which had been invited, to discuss with them the purpose and expectations of the Conference, and to collect up-to-date information of their policies and activities. Thereafter, a background paper for the Conference was prepared by Ian Clifton-Everest, which analyses and reflects on the policies of selected aid agencies, and provides an annotated bibliography of documents on aid to education in Africa. Extracts from this paper are reproduced in Part II of this report.

We also made a valiant attempt to collect the most recent statistics of education relating to countries from which participants came. Richard White's compilation draws on data from the statistical bureau of UNESCO, supplemented from other sources, the most important being the World Bank.* As in all similar compilations, the data vary in currency and credibility, but they were useful to participants and, in particular, chronicle the enormous efforts which have been made by nations to provide increasing amounts of formal education to their citizens over the past decades.

These two background documents and others were made available to Conference participants. They have proved to be valuable resources for aid administrators and universities in Britain, and are likely to prove equally valuable elsewhere.

The programme of the four days divided naturally into two parts, beginning with discussions of priorities, followed by consideration of aid responses to them. Formal presentations were limited to the four lead papers reproduced in this report, which their authors were invited to present rather than read. The rest of the time was for discussion in plenary, working groups, or informally.

Considerable prior thought and debate went into the agendas for the four working groups reproduced in this report. Some have since argued that they were too wide and detailed for the purpose for which they were designed. Were they not more suitable, someone asked, for a university course synopsis, rather than an agenda for discussion? In the event, the good sense of the working groups and Conference chairpersons ensured that they were used as reference points rather than rigid agendas. As resource documents they provide a valuable map of many of the issues which underlie this or any similar debate about priorities and the provision of aid.

One of the most useful sources of ideas was provided by participants themselves in the form of short 'think pieces' contributed before the Conference. Most of these were signed but a few, produced no doubt by civil servants, were anonymous. All were readable and valuable, and many extremely penetrating. These pieces have been used extensively in compiling this report and many are quoted in the text. A long extract from one, by the Minister of Higher and National Education for Senegal, has been included as an addendum to Chapter 1.

---

*Richard White, *Background Statistical Information on Educational Provision for Selected African Countries*, November 1984 (Conference document).

The Conference venue

The site chosen for the Conference, Cumberland Lodge in Windsor Great Park, was a former hunting lodge of the Royal Family, rebuilt and remodelled after a fire in the nineteenth century. At the end of World War II, it was given over to a trust with the express purpose of providing a tranquil venue for university students and staff to meet and discuss issues freely. It is used extensively by the University of London, and by many British and international groups of academics and professionals. It proved a perfect setting for the Conference: friendly, civilised and comfortable without being ostentatious. Ostentation would have sat uneasily with the issues we were discussing.

The Conference atmosphere

Thanks to the calibre of participation as well as to the venue, the atmosphere generated was particularly productive and friendly. Despite obvious calls on their time, busy statesmen, academics and executives stayed throughout all the sessions and contributed their experience. Informal meetings sometimes went on well into the night. There was no sense of division among the various groups within the Conference. A minister might chair a working group, or an aid executive, or a university professor. People spoke as individuals and their ranks and roles were temporarily set to one side. In such a friendly and relaxed atmosphere some of the hard things that always need to be said in such a gathering might have been left unsaid, out of fear of causing offence and breaking the existing accord. Fortunately, the participants did not succumb. Sensitive issues were raised, including the politics of aid and the current debate on UNESCO, and the ensuing frank talk did not break but enhanced the productive atmosphere. Characteristically, it was Dzingai Mutumbuka who both launched several of the most vigorous exchanges, and offered a warm, sincere and witty vote of thanks at the end of the Conference.

Reporting the proceedings

The proceedings were rich and stimulating, and this report, we fear, hardly does them justice, though we have tried to give some of the atmosphere of the plenaries and the quality of the 'think pieces' by including quotations from both.

The report reflects the two parts of our discussion, on priorities and on aid to education. Following a short chapter analysing the context, we have attempted in Chapters 2 and 3 to synthesise papers, responses, group reports and plenary into a coherent account, indicating areas of agreement. In a personal statement in Chapter 4, the ODA's Principal Education Adviser reflects on what he and his administration gained from the four days' work.

Two important limitations of this report must be acknowledged. First, as any well-informed reader will recognise, many of the important points that emerged at the Windsor Conference — particularly relating to past and present shortcomings in African education and to types of actions required to correct them — are not really new; they have been voiced repeatedly by various observers over a considerable time. What is perhaps new, however, is that they have rarely if ever been linked together in such a broad perspective or with such a compelling sense of urgency. A principal message of the Conference was that the time has come to translate the familiar rhetoric into concrete deeds, by taking much more serious and extensive actions to remedy these shortcomings, within the realistic framework of extreme budgetary constraints.

The second limitation is that the report, because of space limitations and because its focus is on the future rather than the past, gives little attention to the numerous instances where the actions of individual countries and external assistance agencies have anticipated the Conference's proposals. We salute all such efforts and hope they will inspire comparable action by others on a much broader scale.

Whatever the success or failure of the Conference in reaching consensus upon the hard priorities which face governments and aid agencies alike, no one can deny the immediacy of the issues to be faced. Nor, we believe, would it be prudent to ignore the many wise insights which have been provided by the Conference and recorded in these pages. Some clear priorities did emerge, but what distinguishes the Conference from others, in our view, is the record of concerned engagement not only with questions of educational policy, but with the mutual relationship — political, procedural and personal — of the African governments and their advisers on the one hand, and the variety of multilateral and bilateral aid agencies on the other.

We hope that our readers will include not only those who presently make decisions on educational priorities but also those now studying in universities and colleges who may follow in their footsteps. Finally, we trust that the style and format of the report make it interesting and challenging to both sets of readers, and any others who seek to understand and to serve the educational needs of the peoples of sub-Saharan Africa.

HUGH HAWES

Contents

Abbreviations

AfDB	African Development Bank
AUPELF	Association des Universités Partiellement ou Entièrement de Langue Française (Canada)
BREDA	Bureau Régional pour l'Education en Afrique (Regional Bureau for Education in Africa of UNESCO)
CDG	Carl Duisberg-Gesellschaft c.V (Carl Duisberg Company, Federal Republic of Germany)
CIDA	Canadian International Development Agency
DAAD	Deutscher Akademischer Austauschdienst (German Academic Exchange Service, Federal Republic of Germany)
DAC	Development Assistance Committee (of OECD)
DEO	District Education Officer
DSE	Deutscher Stiftung für Entwicklungsländer (German Foundation for International Development, Federal Republic of Germany)
ECA	Economic Commission for Africa
ECOSOC	Economic and Social Council of the United Nations
EDC	Department of Education in Developing Countries, University of London Institute of Education
EDF	European Development Fund (of the Commission of the European Communities)
EEC	European Economic Community
ELT	English Language Teaching
ESP	English for Special Purposes
GTZ	Gesellschaft für Technische Zusammenarbeit, GmbH (Agency for Technical Cooperation, Federal Republic of Germany)
IBRD	International Bank for Reconstruction and Development (The World Bank)
ICED	International Council for Educational Development
IDA	International Development Association (of the World Bank)
IWGE	International Working Group on Education (formerly the Bellagio Education Group)
IDRC	International Development Research Centre
IIEP	International Institute for Educational Planning (of UNESCO)
IMF	International Monetary Fund
KELT	Key English Language Teaching scheme (of the British Council)

1

NEIDA	Network of Educational Innovation for Development in Africa (of UNESCO)
NGO	Non-governmental organisation
OAU	Organisation of African Unity
ODA	Overseas Development Administration, United Kingdom
OECD	Organisation for Economic Co-operation and Development
SADCC	Southern African Development Coordination Conference
SAREC	Swedish Agency for Research Cooperation with Developing Countries
SIDA	Swedish International Development Authority
TETOC	Technical Education and Training Operations and Consultancies Group (of the British Council)
USAID	United States Agency for International Development
UNESCO	United Nations Educational Scientific and Cultural Organisation
UNICEF	United Nations Childrens Fund
UPE	Universal primary education

PART I COMMENTARY

Chapter 1
Context

This chapter examines

1 The wide diversities between African countries, common historical traditions and developmental challenges which unite them (p. 5)
2 The dimensions of population increase in sub-Saharan Africa, the implications for the environment, the economy and for education, and how education may contribute in the long term to reducing the rate of population increase (p. 10)
3 The problem of food production and natural resources management, and an educational package which would help African nations respond to the environmental and agricultural challenge (p. 12)
4 The squeeze on economic development and the deepening crisis of economic management, a proposed programme of action for economic recovery and some of the implications for educational change (p. 15)
5 Reflections on education in the broad sense and on finding reasons for hope and determination rather than despair (p. 21)

An addendum to this chapter examines

1 The context of educational needs in one West African country, Senegal, which may stand as a representative example for the experience of the region (p. 23)

Similarities and diversities

> . . . even though we are dealing with the same region the countries of the region are not necessarily the same and the educational priorities in one country may not necessarily apply to all the countries in the region. . . . This means that one is more competent to talk about one's [own] country, especially if one is a politician.
>
> *Kebby Musokotwane (Zambia)*

Citizens of 19 of the 41 countries in sub-Saharan Africa came to Windsor bringing with them very different national backgrounds and experiences. Their countries vary in size and population, in resources both human and natural, in economic wealth and in political systems and philosophies. They differ in their social fabric and historical traditions, in their cultural, religious and linguistic diversity, and in the nature of their response to the variety of colonial and post-colonial influences which have penetrated their societies from afar.

All of these elements have shaped the coverage, structure and pedagogical traditions of each national education system. Several of them,

---

This chapter has been written by Hugh Hawes and Trevor Coombe drawing extensively on material submitted prior to the Conference: statistics, aid agency data, and especially the 'think pieces' submitted by individual Conference members. It also includes material from lead papers on Theme I and from the plenary sessions in the first days of the Conference. As in all chapters in Part I, the editors have attempted to interpret and reflect upon the material.

especially the demographic and politico-economic factors, are often highly dynamic and volatile, and may alter a society's educational needs in ways which are profoundly far-reaching and problematic.

Consider just four of the countries of the subcontinent.

Botswana   Great in size and tiny in population; stable politically and achieving a steady economic growth rate; but at risk both ecologically and politically from its two uncomfortable neighbours — the Kalahari Desert and the Republic of South Africa.

Benin   One-fifth the area and four times the population of Botswana, and with one-third the per capita income; a government committed to equitable sharing of resources in a country where variations in culture, wealth, religions and traditions, as well as educational enrolments between regions and between sexes, are still strongly apparent.

Zimbabwe   Three times the size and twice the population of Benin; rich in resources, both human and natural, but only recently emerged from an armed struggle, with wounds to heal, differences to reconcile and a new nation to build.

Nigeria   Over ten times the population of Zimbabwe, with each of its 20 states more populous than Botswana: rich and poor, Islamic and Christian, with 250 recorded languages and a

---

The countries of sub-Saharan Africa

The World Bank classifies the 39 countries of sub-Saharan Africa (excluding South Africa and Namibia) into low-income economies (semiarid and other) and middle-income economies (oil-importers and oil-exporters).

Low income economies (those with 1982 per capita gross national product [GNP] of less than $410): (a) semiarid economies include Chad, Mali, Burkina Faso, Somalia, Niger and The Gambia; (b) other economies include Ethiopia, Guinea-Bissau, Zaire, Malawi, Uganda, Rwanda, Burundi, Tanzania, Benin, Central African Republic, Guinea, Madagascar, Togo, Ghana, Kenya, Sierra Leone and Mozambique.

Middle income economies (those with 1982 per capita GNP of $410 or more): (a) oil importers include Sudan, Mauritania, Liberia, Senegal, Lesotho, Zambia, Zimbabwe, Botswana, Swaziland, Ivory Coast and Mauritius; (b) oil exporters include Nigeria, Cameroon, Congo, Gabon and Angola.

The 1982 per capita gross national product ranged from US$80 (Chad) to $4000 (Gabon). Twelve countries had a per capita GNP of less than $300, 26 less than $500, and 31 less than $900.

Source: *Toward Sustained Development in Sub-Saharan Africa: A Joint Programme of Action* (Washington, D.C.: The World Bank, 1984), p. viii.

cultural tradition boasting great ancient cities of the north and the artistic masterpieces of Ife and Benin; politically and economically so volatile, yet possessing perhaps the greatest pool of trained human resources on the subcontinent.

With such diversity it could be argued that generalisations are neither profitable nor possible, and that we should be wary in seeking common experiences and approaches. Yet countries in the region also share many characteristics that shone through in the discussions at Windsor:

1 They have common political and economic links both with their neighbours and through Africa-wide organisations such as the OAU and the ECA.
2 With few exceptions they share a colonial past with its ambiguous political, social and educational legacies.
3 Their state boundaries were fixed by the colonial powers and were often arbitrarily drawn. Almost all states in the region therefore enclose disparate varieties of people, and political leaders face the critical task of welding them together as a nation.
4 They are all styled 'less developed countries' within the economic classifications used by the United Nations, and include a large proportion of the world's 'least developed countries'.
5 They are all largely agrarian and share the problem of unequal development between rural and urban areas.
6 They are all undergoing rapid population growth and urbanisation.
7 Because of their past histories, their relative poverty and the problems of development that confront them, their governments are particularly vulnerable to the effects of international economic recession and fluctuations in international commodity markets, and natural setbacks such as drought, floods or plant disease.
8 Finally, they are all part of our one world, increasingly linked by technology and trade, and by the imperatives of the survival of mankind as a species through the twenty-first century and beyond, since in Franklin's words 'we must, indeed, all hang together, or most assuredly, we shall all hang separately'.

Strong as are the differences between African nations, it was the broad similarities in their ecological, social, economic and educational conditions, which tended to shape the discussions at Windsor on educational needs and priorities.

Historical traditions are often common, for nations in sub-Saharan Africa share, with only two exceptions, the experience of colonialism. Its educational legacies are to be seen in structures, curricula, patterns of assessment and languages of instruction.

The nature and effects of this legacy on one nation and region have been analysed with clarity and insight by the Minister of Higher and National Education, Senegal, in his personal statement appended to this chapter. Some of the effects he notes will be common to most countries, some very different, but in every case history presents a balance sheet with credits as well as debits.

One element deriving in part, but only in part, from these historical

Table 1. Sub-Saharan Africa: population growth and projections

	Average annual growth of population (percent)			Population (millions)		
	1960–70	1970–82	1980–2000	1982	1990	2000
Low-income economies	**2.4w**	**2.8w**	**3.3w**	**217t**	**278t**	**386t**
Low-income semiarid	*2.5w*	*2.6w*	*2.7w*	*31t*	*37t*	*48t*
1 Chad	1.9	2.0	2.5	5	6	7
2 Mali	2.5	2.7	2.8	7	9	12
3 Burkina Faso	2.0	2.0	2.4	7	8	10
4 Somalia	2.8	2.8	2.4	5	5	7
5 Niger	3.4	3.3	3.3	6	8	11
6 Gambia, The	2.2	3.2	2.3	1	1	1
Low-income other	*2.4w*	*2.9w*	*3.4w*	*186t*	*241t*	*338t*
7 Ethiopia	2.4	2.0	3.1	33	42	57
8 Guinea-Bissau	..	..	2.3	1	1	1
9 Zaire	2.0	3.0	3.3	31	40	55
10 Malawi	2.8	3.0	3.4	7	8	12
11 Uganda	3.0	2.7	3.4	14	17	25
12 Rwanda	2.6	3.4	3.6	6	7	11
13 Burundi	1.4	2.2	3.0	4	5	7
14 Tanzania	2.7	3.4	3.5	20	26	36
15 Benin	2.6	2.7	3.3	4	5	7
16 Central African Rep.	1.6	2.1	2.8	2	3	4
17 Guinea	1.5	2.0	2.4	6	7	9
18 Madagascar	2.2	2.6	3.2	9	12	16
19 Togo	3.0	2.6	3.3	3	4	5
20 Ghana	2.3	3.0	3.9	12	17	24
21 Kenya	3.2	4.0	4.4	18	26	40
22 Sierra Leone	1.7	2.0	2.4	3	4	5
23 Mozambique	2.1	4.3	3.4	13	17	24
Middle-income oil importers	**2.7w**	**3.3w**	**3.3w**	**57t**	**74t**	**101t**
24 Sudan	2.2	3.2	2.9	20	25	34
25 Mauritania	2.3	2.3	2.6	2	2	3
26 Liberia	3.2	3.5	3.5	2	3	4
27 Senegal	2.3	2.7	3.1	6	8	10
28 Lesotho	2.0	2.4	2.8	1	2	2
29 Zambia	2.6	3.1	3.6	6	8	11
30 Zimbabwe	3.6	3.2	4.4	8	11	16
31 Botswana	2.6	4.3	3.6	1	1	2
32 Swaziland	2.7	3.2	3.9	1	1	1
33 Ivory Coast	3.7	4.9	3.7	9	12	17
34 Mauritius	2.2	1.4	1.6	1	1	1
Middle-income oil exporters	**2.4w**	**2.6w**	**3.4w**	**111t**	**144t**	**203t**
35 Nigeria	2.5	2.6	3.5	91	119	169
36 Cameroon	2.0	3.0	3.5	9	12	17
37 Congo, People's Rep.	2.4	3.0	3.8	2	2	3
38 Gabon	0.4	1.4	2.6	1	1	1
39 Angola	2.1	2.5	2.8	8	10	13

	Average annual growth of population (percent)			Population (millions)		
	1960–70	1970–82	1980–2000	1982	1990	2000
Sub-Saharan Africa	**2.4w**	**2.8w**	**3.3w**	**385t**	**496t**	**690t**
All low-income countries	2.3w	1.9w	1.7w	2,269t	2,621t	3,097t
All lower middle-income countries	2.5w	2.5w	2.4w	673t	816t	1,023t
All upper middle-income countries	2.6w	2.3w	2.1w	490t	588t	718t
Industrial market economies	1.1w	0.7w	0.4w	723t	749t	780t

Source: Adapted from World Bank, *Toward Sustained Development in Sub-Saharan Africa*, p. 82.
Note: Readers are advised that the projections in this table, while based on internationally available data, depend on assumptions about future mortality and fertility rates which are unavoidably speculative. The projections are not presented as predictions. Further details may be consulted in the source document, pp. 96–97.
w = Weighted averages
t = Totals

influences was recognised by the conference as both pervasive and disturbing. That is the attitude of passivity and dependency still, to a considerable degree, engendered by education systems and reinforced sometimes by curricula, often by methodology and very frequently by patterns of selection and certification. A graduate of a primary or secondary school or of a university still looks first towards a job in the public sector for which he has 'passed' or 'qualified'. He seeks preferably to become an 'officer' rather than a producer or entrepreneur. These roles he is content to leave to those with less formal qualifications. In school, pupils seek to satisfy the examiners rather than their own curiosity, and though curricula make some attempt to encourage problem solving and to produce 'job makers' rather than 'job seekers' they are often frustrated by other influences, economic as well as social. For public opinion reinforces these attitudes as it reinforces the demand for certification. 'If you want to get a cleaner in the office,' notes Denis Okoro (Nigeria), 'they will be asked to come for interview and the first question is "Have you Primary 6?"'

The extent to which such passivity and dependency are derived from colonialism is a matter for debate. The need to overcome them is not. Thus the demand for education to broaden outlooks, promote autonomy in learners and develop their ability to recognise and solve problems was a major theme underlying conference discussions, though nobody under-estimated the difficulty of achieving such an aim against a background of manpower shortages, financial constraints and rapid numerical expansion.

In addition to common historical traditions formidable developmental challenges confront all the countries of the region. Three are singled out here for special mention because they attracted repeated attention in the Conference, both in their own right and because of their implications for educational action:

1 The rapidity of population growth

2 The conservation and development of Africa's natural resources and food supply

9

3 The management of national economies in the face of world economic pressures.

Though each will be discussed separately, the inter-relationships between them will not be disguised.

Population

In the 24 countries most seriously affected by the recent drought, the food production [per capita] has been going down for the past 15 years at a rate of 2 per cent a year, whereas the population growth rate has accelerated from 2.3 per cent in 1960 to 3.1 per cent today — the highest rate among all developing regions in the world. The ecological balance has been shattered by the rising demand for fuel and food by an ever-growing population. Soil erosion, deforestation and water shortages are inevitable consequences, the effects of which have been aggravated by the periodic droughts that visit sub-Saharan Africa every few years. The dry sands of the Sahara inexorably advance on the Sahel as 1 per cent of the natural vegetation cover is lost every year in that part of Africa.

Manzoor Ahmed (UNICEF)

The irreducible cause of drought is the absence of rain, not the presence of many people. But the African famines which have grieved the world in recent years have focused attention on the problems of survival and development in a region which not only has some of the world's most vulnerable climatic and ecological conditions, but also experiences extremely rapid rates of population growth. Africa is now the only major region in the world where the rising curve of birth rates has not yet peaked out and begun to decline. As a result, there is a built-in momentum in African populations which guarantees massive overall numerical growth into the next century, as the projections in Table 1 indicate (p. 9).

From these raw figures of population increase, we can extract some disturbing implications, such as: imbalances between national growth rates, with some of the highest rates evident in countries least able to sustain them; growth of urban populations outstripping the abilities of towns to house, feed and employ those who live in them; and, most disturbing of all, the broadening base of the age pyramid. Already nearly half the population in Africa is under 15 years old. In two countries — Kenya and Botswana — the 1981 figures indicate that slightly *more* than half the population are infants or children under 15.

The economic and educational implications of such figures are inescapable. In the first place, the very high dependency ratio increases the burden on working adults. Projections indicate that

In the year 2000 in developed countries, the ratio of people aged over 19 to those aged under 19 will be 71:29. In Africa, it will be 45:55. So in developed countries every 100 adults will have 41 'minors' dependent on them, compared with 122, three times as many, in Africa. (Peter Williams, p. 93 below)

In the second place, these growing populations must be fed. The alarming evidence of long-term decline in per capita food production and the implications for education policy are discussed in the next section.

10

Thirdly, the population growth rates carry a disturbing message for those who are struggling to eliminate illiteracy and extend primary education (let alone secondary) to all children. In most countries, it will be a very long time before there is any slackening in the upward curve of the child population requiring schooling or in the number of illiterate adults.

The immediate past gives a clue to the size of the task that lies ahead of African governments. Between 1960 and 1980, Africa's secondary and tertiary enrolments increased more than fourfold (from very low initial figures) while gross enrolment rates at the first level of schooling almost doubled. At the primary level the significance of this impressive growth is put into perspective by Philip Coombs' observation that one half of the enrolment increase in this period had been 'offset' by rapid population growth.

> To put it bluntly, the schools of Africa have been forced to run fast just to stand still in relation to their existing enrolment ratios, and even faster to boost those ratios.
>
> *Philip Coombs (ICED)*

A rough idea of the present educational coverage is obtained from the World Bank's 1981 figures for gross enrolment ratios (the ratio of enrolment to estimated school age population). The ratio for all children in primary school in sub-Saharan Africa is reported as 78 per cent. For girls in primary school it is 64 per cent, ranging from apparent 'surplus' of school places in relation to age group in some countries, to rates of 15, 20 or 33 per cent in others. The overall ratio at secondary school is reported as 15 per cent, and at this level the balance is tipped even more heavily in favour of boys.*

Such figures, however crude, indicate two conclusions of great significance. The first has already been referred to: the arithmetic of the numbers explosion makes it increasingly difficult for many African countries to achieve universal schooling in the foreseeable future, or to sustain it once achieved. The second is less obvious. The deficit in overall educational provision, and especially the large backlog in girls' schooling, increase the probability that women's fertility rates will remain high and so will the rates of population increase in sub-Saharan Africa. This is because (as recent demographic research in developing countries has indicated) the mass education of women appears to be an essential factor in slowing down population growth rates.

This does not happen automatically, or quickly. In fact, in poorer countries, women with a few years of primary schooling may be slightly more fertile than unschooled women. But the trend changes as more and more women complete primary education, and fertility declines sharply as the proportion of mothers with post-primary education increases. In such a complex field of social and personal behaviour many of the reasons for this association between more education and less fertility are necessarily

---

Toward Sustained Development in Sub-Saharan Africa, p. 87. Gross enrolment ratios invariably overstate actual provision because they are not adjusted for enrolment of children outside the nominal school age group. Also the estimates of school age population are seldom reliable.

conjectural. It is especially important to note that sustained educational advance seldom occurs in the absence of other favourable socio-economic conditions, and the best outlook for fertility decline is to be found in countries which are experiencing rapid economic growth, increased life expectancy, a vigorous national family-planning programme — and high educational participation by women.*

Such conditions in combination occur in few African countries, so a rapid overall decline in fertility cannot yet be anticipated.

> Meanwhile, sub-Saharan Africa's current population of 385 million seems set to double by the year 2005. That much is almost inevitable. The real question is whether populations will merely triple in size in the next half-century or increase even more rapidly, to five or six times their current size. (*World Development Report 1984*, p. 163).

So the sheer pressure of demand for schooling is likely to continue as long as anyone can foresee, and in the immediate future the governments and peoples of sub-Saharan Africa are required to respond at a time of prolonged economic stagnation and distress. To the difficulty of maintaining quantitative growth must be added the even more intractable problem of ensuring or restoring acceptable levels of educational quality. As the Conference acknowledged, this will have to be done in the perspective of better management of resources, alternative patterns of schooling, new curricular initiatives, or a combination of all three.

Moreover, in these conditions, there is an increasingly important role for every variety of non-formal education which may help improve the capacities of African peoples to cope with their circumstances and change them for the better. In primary health care and nutrition, family planning, early childhood education, agriculture, fisheries, small industries, development-related literacy, and community development (to name only some of the most obvious), there are ever-mounting educational challenges begging for greater attention by both governmental and voluntary agencies, and the Conference gave them appropriate recognition.

The population issue was never far from the minds of Conference participants and several times it was brought to the centre of discussion. Even though no sustained analysis was made of the educational implications, it is important to recognise that education need not just be a victim of population pressure. In fact, educational interventions, both direct and indirect, formal and non-formal, especially among women, can be an exceptionally important, perhaps indispensable, long-range means of controlling the African population explosion, quite apart from their other benefits.

Natural resources and food

Population issues are linked inescapably with others, particularly natural resources and food, as the remarks of Manzoor Ahmed on p. 10 above make clear. Though he referred particularly to the Sahel, the situation is

---

* A major recent analysis of population change and development, with much data on sub-Saharan Africa, is contained in World Bank, *World Development Report 1984* (New York: Oxford University Press, 1984), Part II. See also *Toward Sustained Development in Sub-Saharan Africa*, pp. 26 – 29.

grave in many parts of Africa where the ecological balance has been upset by overcropping, overgrazing, and reduction of natural forest for fuelwood or additional cultivation. Population pressure in many rural and pastoral regions, and the fuel and food requirements of rapidly growing urban communities are the immediate causes, but behind them lie the complexities of individual country situations, including geographic and climatic conditions, ethnic tensions, the clash of differing local cultures and social systems, land holding and land-use patterns and the worsening terms of trade between peasant rural and urban economies. Meanwhile, as World Bank specialists report,

> In many countries, forest cover is being irretrievably damaged, with appalling consequences for household fuel supplies, soil fertility and water supply. . . . Fuelwood consumption alone now exceeds the growth of new trees by a factor of ten in Mauritania and Rwanda, by five in Kenya, and by about two and a half in Ethiopia, Nigeria and Tanzania. (*Toward Sustained Development in Sub-Saharan Africa*, p. 32)

Such conditions are all the more alarming when the food needs of Africa's inexorably growing populations are considered, because the subcontinent's farmers have not been producing more food per person but less. Figure 1 shows statistics of grain production in countries affected by drought and indicates a steady decline rather than a short-term crisis. These no doubt represent the most serious cases, but Figure 2 shows that per capita food production in sub-Saharan Africa as a whole declined significantly between 1969 and 1983, in contrast to Latin America and Asia where the trends have been generally positive. There are some happy exceptions, like Ivory Coast and Swaziland, but no fewer than 32 countries in the region recorded negative average annual growth rates per capita in food production and 30 countries had negative growth rates per capita in total agricultural production between 1970 and 1982. Not surprisingly, agricultural imports soared, to a total annual value of US$6.8 billion by 1982.*

It would be foolish to make exaggerated claims for the power of education to solve such profound problems of ecological imbalance and agricultural failure in the subcontinent. Major questions of international trade and financial policies as well as national fiscal, pricing and investment policies are at issue, quite apart from the familiar natural constraints of climate and soil, or the deep-seated social factors referred to earlier. But it is important to recognise, as the Conference did, the urgency of human resource development for the management and wise exploitation of Africa's natural resources, and the achievement of food self-sufficiency. Education is not synonymous with human resource development, but education, training, research, communication and awareness-raising are vital ingredients of it. It is not fanciful to think of an inter-related package of educational measures, in the broadest sense of the term, which would enhance the capacities of African nations to respond to the environmental and agricultural challenge. These would include, among others:

1 Well-directed training of African research personnel in agriculture, fisheries, food conservation, hydrology, forestry and fuel technology, in

---

* *Toward Sustained Development in Sub-Saharan Africa*, pp. 77, 79.

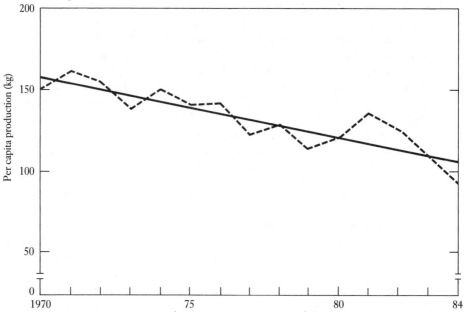

Figure 1. Per Capita Grain Production in 24 African Countries Affected by Drought, 1970–84

Source: World Bank, *Toward Sustained Development in Sub-Saharan Africa,* p. 14. Based on Food and Agriculture Organization (FAO) data, except that the 1984 figure is a projection using data from FAO, the US Agency for International Development, and the US Department of Agriculture.

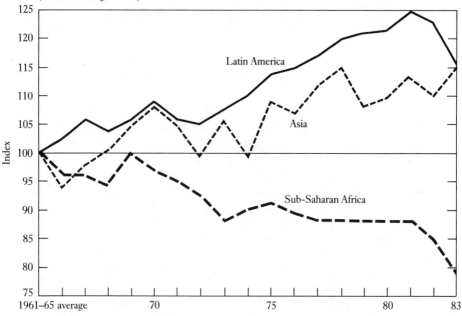

Figure 2. Index of Per Capita Food Production, 1961–65 to 1983

(1961–65 average = 100)

Source: World Bank, *Toward Sustained Development in Sub-Saharan Africa,* p. 15. Based on data provided by the US Department of Agriculture.

14

most of which fields the subcontinent remains grossly under-provided or dependent upon expatriate specialists.

2 Equally well-directed training of high- and middle-level extension specialists who would improve the linkage between research and the farmers, fishermen or other field producers.

3 Improved and better co-ordinated public information and outreach programmes for men and women in basic survival and developmental skills and awareness, related to community and family health, nutrition, food production and conservation, forest and soil conservation, and literacy.

4 Engagement of the school curriculum with the problems of natural resources and food, not only through strengthening the knowledge base, but by striving to encourage the achievement of skills of observation, enquiry and problem-solving, and attitudes of responsibility toward the environment in relation to community and family needs.

Such items so obviously belong together in one co-ordinated programme that it is difficult to credit that in practice the links between them are often tenuous and many of the items themselves may be poorly supported by government agencies and NGOs. This is partly a question of resources, partly an organisational problem. In the schools, such approaches are difficult to adopt and sustain in an overloaded system, with embattled teachers and a lack of educational materials. But as much as anything else, what is needed, both nationally and among aid agencies, is a clear sense of priority and urgency. So the familiar dilemma reasserts itself: rethink, reform or regress. The Conference was greatly preoccupied with this question throughout the four days at Windsor.

National economic management

In 1981, Africa's political leaders assessed the economic situation of the continent and concluded that 'Africa is unable to point to any significant growth rate, or satisfactory index of general well-being, in the past 20 years.'* This bleak statement is unusual in a political document, since it errs somewhat on the pessimistic side. In fact, many African countries achieved impressive rates of economic growth during the 1960s, and some maintained a steady economic performance during the 1970s. Nor should the wider discrepancies between countries be forgotten, with the more prosperous middle-income countries having four times the per capita GNP of the poorest low-income countries. (See Table 2.)

But the OAU leaders were making a global statement and the evidence supports a grimly serious conclusion. In many African countries the earlier economic success unravelled as booms in commodity prices collapsed in the world recession, and high investments in projects and services have proved difficult or impossible to sustain. The average annual per capita GDP, which barely increased in the subcontinent during the 1970s, has sharply decreased during the 1980s. Food and agricultural production per capita have continued a 15-year decline, as has already been observed, and protectionist measures in developed countries have raised new barriers

*Organisation of African Unity, *Lagos Plan of Action for the Economic Development of Africa, 1980–2000*. 2nd rev. ed. (Geneva: International Institute of Labour Studies, 1982), p. 1.

15

Table 2. Sub-Saharan Africa: selected economic indicators

	Average annual growth rate of GDP (percent)		External public and publicly guaranteed debt outstanding and disbursed (US$ millions)				Average annual growth rate of terms of trade (percent)
			Total		Debt service		
	1960–70[a]	1970–82[b]	1970	1982	1970	1982	1970–82
Low-income economies	**4.0w**	**1.8w**	**2,777.9t**	**20,172.0t**	**188.4t**	**1,475.0t**	
Low-income semiarid	*2.4w*	*2.6w*	*404.1t*	*3,026.8t*	*8.6t*	*165.3t*	
1 Chad	0.5	−2.6	32.1	189.3	2.7	0.2	1.5
2 Mali	3.3	4.3	237.6	822.0	0.7	8.1	−1.5
3 Burkina Faso	3.0	3.4	20.5	334.8	1.9	20.0	−2.5
4 Somalia	1.0	3.8	77.1	944.0	0.9	19.8	−3.4
5 Niger	2.9	3.4	31.7	602.6	2.3	110.2	−5.1
6 Gambia, The	6.2	4.5	5.1	134.0	0.1	7.0	−2.4
Low-income other	*4.2w*	*1.7w*	*2,373.7t*	*17,145.2t*	*179.8t*	*1,309.6t*	
7 Ethiopia	4.4	2.2	168.9	874.6	21.1	54.8	−4.9
8 Guinea-Bissau	..	3.1	..	125.8	..	2.5	..
9 Zaire	3.4	−0.2	311.1	4,040.3	36.8	81.2	−5.9
10 Malawi	4.9	5.1	122.4	691.8	5.9	64.3	−2.7
11 Uganda	5.6	−1.5	137.5	593.8	7.9	132.1	0.5
12 Rwanda	2.7	5.3	1.9	189.3	0.3	5.2	0.8
13 Burundi	4.4	3.5	7.3	200.9	0.6	5.2	..
14 Tanzania	6.0	4.0	248.5	1,631.6	15.7	112.6	−1.3
15 Benin	2.6	3.3	40.5	556.4	1.7	46.4	−6.3
16 Central African Rep.	1.9	1.4	23.9	222.0	2.9	4.5	−0.6
17 Guinea	3.5	3.8	314.1	1,229.9	14.5	78.5	..
18 Madagascar	2.9	0.2	92.6	1,564.8	6.9	112.2	−2.3
19 Togo	8.8	3.0	39.8	819.0	2.3	33.7	3.7
20 Ghana	2.2	−0.5	489.4	1,115.6	23.7	65.1	0.2
21 Kenya	5.9	5.5	316.3	2,401.6	27.4	376.2	−0.4
22 Sierra Leone	4.3	2.0	59.4	302.9	12.0	40.6	−3.3
23 Mozambique	..	..	..	585.0	..	94.4	−2.0
Middle-income oil importers	**4.2w**	**3.7w**	**1,804.8t**	**17,095.4t**	**176.3t**	**1,683.3t**	
24 Sudan	0.7	6.3	318.7	5,093.5	34.6	79.3	−0.6
25 Mauritania	6.7	2.0	27.3	1,000.7	3.3	39.7	−5.1
26 Liberia	5.1	0.9	157.9	641.2	17.6	33.2	−6.0
27 Senegal	2.5	2.9	98.0	1,328.5	6.7	101.9	−0.3
28 Lesotho	5.2	6.6	8.1	138.6	0.5	8.0	..
29 Zambia	5.0	0.9	622.5	2,380.6	59.0	184.3	−9.0
30 Zimbabwe	4.5	2.2	232.7	1,220.8	9.4	145.8	..
31 Botswana	5.7	12.6	14.7	209.0	0.6	13.4	..
32 Swaziland	7.7	4.4	37.0	177.7	3.3	17.7	..
33 Ivory Coast	8.0	5.7	256.1	4,537.3	38.5	996.7	0.6
34 Mauritius	1.7	5.8	31.7	367.4	2.9	63.1	−2.1
Middle-income oil exporters	**3.5w**	**4.1w**	**836.2t**	**10,796.0t**	**84.5t**	**2,305.7t**	
35 Nigeria	3.1	3.8	479.6	6,084.7	55.7	1,339.5	15.7
36 Cameroon	3.7	7.0	131.2	1,911.9	8.6	264.2	0.3
37 Congo, People's Rep.	3.5	6.8	134.6	1,369.9	8.8	272.9	17.4
38 Gabon	4.4	2.0	90.8	871.4	11.3	288.1	17.6
39 Angola	..	..	..	558.0	..	141.0	14.2

	Average annual growth rate of GDP (percent)		External public and publicly guaranteed debt outstanding and disbursed (US$ millions)				Average annual growth rate of terms of trade (percent)
			Total		Debt service		
	1960–70[a]	1970–82[b]	1970	1982	1970	1982	1970–82
Sub-Saharan Africa	3.8w	3.0w	5,418.8t	48,063.4t	449.1t	5,464.0t	
All low-income countries	4.5w	4.5w					
All lower middle-income countrie	4.9w	5.3w					
All upper middle-income countrie	6.4w	5.4w					
Industrial market economies	5.1w	2.8w					

Source: Adapted from World Bank, *Toward Sustained Development in Sub-Saharan Africa*, pp. 58, 67, 70.

Notes:
1 Gross Domestic Product (GDP) measures the total final output of goods and services produced by an economy.
2 Public debt figures *exclude* data for (a) IMF transactions except Trust Fund Loans, (b) debts repayable in local currency, (c) direct investments, and (d) short-term debt (maturity of one year or less).
3 The terms of trade indicator shows the change over time in the level of export prices as a percentage of import prices.
a Figure for Ethiopia is for 1961–70.
b Figures for Chad, Burkina Faso, Guinea-Bissau, Zaire, Botswana are for 1970–81.
w Weighted averages.
t Totals.

against some of Africa's exports at a time of slow growth in external demand and deteriorating external terms of trade. Africa's external borrowings for investment in development in the past are causing acute debt servicing problems at a time of reduced capacity to pay, and most countries are on a treadmill of arrears, re-scheduled debts and additional borrowing to finance debt servicing. Add to these woes the specific calamity of drought in many countries, and the frustration of individuals and governments boxed in by insurmountable odds is fully understandable:

> For years and years we have had to live with the persistent drought, [as a result of] which despite government input, despite farmers having to work very hard, you get diminishing returns. In other words, you work hard, you produce, you see the whole thing grow up and right in front of you, you see it all dry away. Your input, your efforts, your money, your labour … everything goes. … Because you produce less, it automatically follows that you have less to export. If your export earnings are low, then so follows your foreign exchange reserve. If you have limited foreign exchange to service all of the sectors of the economy then you are in trouble.
>
> *A A N'Jai (The Gambia)*

The authors of the World Bank's report *Toward Sustained Development in Sub-Saharan Africa* (1984), on which we have relied heavily for data, drive home the consequences of 'the deepening crisis': 'No list of economic or financial statistics can convey the human misery spreading in sub-Saharan Africa' (p. 9) — and they offer a sampling of other evidence to confirm the point:

17

1 Child mortality in the region is now double the average for developing countries

2 More than one-quarter of Africa's people are estimated to suffer severe hunger or malnutrition

3 Political instability has created 2.5 million refugees: one out of every 200 Africans is a refugee

4 In many countries certain public services have disappeared as governments concentrate on survival.

The list is bad enough, but it would not be difficult to expand. Taken altogether, the evidence spells out the prospect of an unfolding cumulative catastrophe for many of Africa's peoples, of whom the drought-stricken victims in Ethiopia, Sudan, Mozambique and elsewhere are perhaps the most recent but certainly not the last.

How much suffering could have been avoided is now a less important question than whether the decline can be halted and reversed. There are bound to be strong differences of view about the mechanics of a rescue operation and resuscitation procedures. The World Bank study claims that rescue is possible because there is now a high level of agreement among governments in Africa and the major international financial and aid agencies about what must be done.*

For instance, the African Development Bank and the Economic Commission for Africa have agreed that a range of policy measures are necessary to correct the region's structural problems. They include health and other programmes to reduce the rate of population growth; changes in the structure of education and training to ensure greater relevance to the needs of African economies; and a number of financial and other measures to improve the internal terms of trade for agriculture, to favour smallholders, improve the efficiency of investment projects, stimulate foreign exchange earning and saving, and stimulate employment outside the public sector.

For their part, the authors of the latest World Bank study propose a six-point programme of action which can be briefly summarised as follows:

1 *National economic management.* Urgent and wide-ranging programmes of national rehabilitation and development must be formulated by national governments, adopting strategic, flexible planning models with firm spending priorities to be observed by government agencies and donors.

2 *Donor programmes and aid co-ordination.* Increased consultation is necessary among donors and between donors and recipients to ensure that donors are working within a well-articulated government programme. Priority, efficiency and relevance should outweigh strategic and commercial considerations in determining donor assistance decisions.

---

* The OAU's significant *Lagos Plan of Action* has been followed by three World Bank reports, the latest being *Toward Sustained Development*, and studies by the African Development Bank (AfDB) and the ECA: *Economic Report on Africa 1984, A Report of the Staffs of the African Development Bank, Abidjan, and the Economic Commission for Africa, Addis Ababa* (1984). The European Communities (EC) have made their own study of the problem. In mid-1985 another OAU summit on the economic situation in Africa reaffirmed the Lagos Plan of Action but approved a new priority programme for the next five years, including special action to improve the food situation and to alleviate the debt burden.

3 *External support for reform programmes.* Flexible, adequate and sustained external support is needed to buy the wide range of agricultural inputs, industrial materials, spare parts, fuel and vehicles required to evoke increased output of the directly productive sectors, especially agriculture.

4 *Infrastructure.* Rehabilitation and maintenance of existing infrastructure must be emphasised in public expenditure and donor assistance, rather than new capacity, as essential components of reform programmes.

5 *Basic constraints on development.* The immediate priority is to make better use of existing schools, clinics, and environmental programmes which have been neglected in recent years of crisis management, so rehabilitation, maintenance and operational funds (especially foreign exchange) are required from donors in support of government expenditure. Increased investment and continuous and reliable donor support to these basic development areas are needed in the medium to long run, within agreed sectoral policies. Initial priorities: health and population, forestry, adaptive agricultural research, education and training.

6 *External finance.* Economic crisis requires that the sole goal of donor assistance must be to support African development needs, especially in countries implementing major reforms. Large capital inflows are necessary to improve import capacity and external debt management. Rescheduling of amortisation and increased gross disbursements are required.*

While the elements of this 'joint programme of action' may not be novel, the programme is bound to be regarded as an important World Bank pronouncement by governments and the donor community alike, and it is likely to influence the terms of the debate on the African crisis for some time to come. It has several implications for education in Africa (as well as aid policy), both explicit and implicit, of which three will be referred to.

The first concerns the level of financial support to formal education. The current position, broadly speaking, is as follows. Educational policies made in the sixties and seventies largely determine the current level of provision. Increased enrolments at the base of the education system made possible by increased revenues and high expectations in past years left governments with the dilemma of maintaining participation rates in the face of rising populations, and of seeking to provide further educational opportunities demanded by an increasing number of jobless school leavers. As Sam Aleyideino of Nigeria put it, doubtless with his country's recent experience in mind:

What we are witnessing today is clearly the result of previous over-optimistic educational planning. The educational blueprint was fashioned at a time of brightening economic fortune, but unfortunately its implementation has coincided with a period of global economic recession. This suggests that educational planners did not anticipate these kinds of problems, otherwise they could have considered other, less ambitious, alternatives.

---

*Toward Sustained Development in Sub-Saharan Africa, pp. 1–8.

Hence there is, simply, greater educational demand at all levels to be met by an education budget which cannot, in current conditions, be expected to expand.

Since it is impossible to close off demand for education, and virtually impossible on political or ethical grounds to reduce a level of educational provision once it has been established, three results will follow. First, cuts will be made in government allocations to schools, employment of trained teachers, textbooks and equipment, in-service education and support services. Second, there will be a deterioration of educational quality and effectiveness as limited resources are spread thinner over more and more students. Third, the proportion of financial support expected from state or local authorities, communities and individual parents, will rise. It is fair to say that scarcely an education system on the subcontinent has escaped all three consequences.

The third result of the financial squeeze, namely increased local or private funding, may not have been favoured previously by governments which sought central control to reinforce national unity or conformity, or to promote equity. Hence, to invite greater local participation and local funding of education may mean something considerably more fundamental than mere sharing of financial burdens. It may represent a shift of responsibility for educational provision and decision-making to people who have hitherto not been entrusted with it. On the other hand, parents, communities and local authorities have different economic capacities, and a policy of devolution of financial responsibility for education without counterbalancing measures would make a bleak situation even more inequitable.

In the World Bank's proposed joint programme of action, as noted in point 5 above, the need to rehabilitate the run down schools of Africa is given priority along with other basic aspects of development, and both donors and governments are reminded to pay specific attention to past underfunding of critical components of recurrent spending. Some donors already follow this line. It is possible that more may now be encouraged to do so. A strategic approach is clearly desirable as under no conceivable circumstances could total external assistance in this area account for more than a fraction of the cost of running the formal school system. In any case, the Bank is not recommending *carte blanche* expenditure on education of any description. But carefully programmed assistance could infuse new life into schools and training institutions which are struggling to survive, especially if it helps the teachers gain and apply more skill, confidence and professional autonomy. This was also the view of the Conference.

Finally, on this point, it is important to note that, in terms of immediate priorities, the Bank seeks to discourage further investment in additional educational and training facilities until such time as existing capacity has been renovated and brought to full and efficient use and is being sustained by re-invigorated national economies. Thereafter, in the medium and longer term, the Bank envisages substantially increased investment in new and reformed programmes, both national and regional, with sustained donor support.

The second important implication of the Bank's proposals for education in Africa, already discussed extensively in this chapter, is that the non-formal educational requirements of the basic developmental sectors receive strong support.

Thirdly, there are important implications for management development throughout the joint programme of action, and none is more important than the need for more efficient, well-informed, technically competent, flexible, analytical public servants and parastatal officers in control of the main levers of development policy in every sector. It is perhaps a typical irony of the development process that the capacities that are most needed to set and adjust the controls of national policy are those which are least abundant. The prerequisite of national and regional recovery (according to the joint programme of action) is the design of programmes on the basis of flexible long-range planning models, with clear public spending priorities and the authority to enforce them throughout government and in the donor community. But weak administrative systems cannot be effectively co-ordinated. They will not adjust rapidly to changed conditions, assess new data, and carry through mid-course corrections with requisite speed. The result is rigid adherence to obsolete positions, missed opportunities, an inadequate data base and management information system, poor linkage with related development activities, and low levels of efficiency.*

The education sector (not restricted to the ministry of education) is clearly challenged both to analyse and attend to its own management development needs, and to help achieve the appropriate management training capacity for other branches of the public service and the economy. The contribution of aid agencies to these activities is likely to be essential, and the Conference analysed it at some length.

Educational priorities and aid responses

Such is the background (or some conspicuous parts of the background) against which the Conference examined current educational priorities in Africa, requirements for aid and the ways in which aid should be transacted. In the Addendum to this chapter, Professor Iba Der Thiam makes an eloquent analysis of the context against which the educational needs of his country can be assessed. Ian Clifton-Everest's paper in Part II documents the context of aid agency policy, at least for seven agencies, and the operating procedures they have adopted.

It remains for us to offer one or two closing reflections. Firstly, a comment on what the Conference called education 'in the broad sense', as distinct from just schooling. Education in the broad sense is sometimes called human resource development, which is often taken to mean enabling people to become more healthy, more able to cope with their circumstances and to change them for the better, more productive in their line of work. We should like to think that education in the broad sense also means education in the great humane values which true education neglects at its peril. Human resource development means changing attitudes as well as developing knowledge and skill. In short, it means 'people-changing' and there are those who doubt the capacity of education to achieve it. Certainly

---

* See *Toward Sustained Development in Sub-Saharan Africa*, pp. 38–39; also (for an illustration of implicit management development requirements in the natural resources sector) *Lagos Plan of Action*, p. 27.

people-changing is no easy task and many current approaches to education are ill-suited to accomplish it. But short of spontaneous enlightenment, there are no alternatives to education (in the broad sense) as a means of people-changing, and no question that what Peter Williams calls the 'sit-out option', which involves waiting for things to get better, is a recipe for disaster.

Secondly, it will not help to feel overwhelmed by the challenges to be faced. The people of sub-Saharan Africa have endured and persevered in the face of unimaginable suffering not only now but in the past. Their suffering must be relieved, and those who work in the field of education should do so in hope and determination.

> I am worried that there is far too much emphasis on the negative aspects and not enough emphasis on what has been achieved. The truth of the matter is that since the decolonisation of Africa started, major achievements have taken place in Africa and most of this is due to educational improvements. . . . If we go into battle so demoralised — 'Ah, the situation is bad, everything is collapsing, we are under siege' — perhaps we might not be able to see our way out of the siege. It is very crucial that we appreciate that there has been a lot of achievement in Africa. To quote Mao Tse-Tung: 'Only those people who do not do anything do not make mistakes'.
>
> *Dzingai Mutumbuka (Zimbabwe)*

Clearly there is a need to derive a sense of encouragement from the substantial progress already made, while having no illusions about the magnitude of the problems ahead.

Suggestions for further reading

Interested readers may wish to go deeper into the main themes of this chapter, so the following list of recent titles is provided as an introduction to the relevant literature.

Allison, C. and R. Green (eds.). Sub-Saharan Africa: Getting the Facts Straight. *IDS Bulletin* 16.3, July 1985.

Carlsson, J. (ed.). *Recession in Africa.* Background Papers to the Seminar, Africa — Which Way out of the Recession? Uppsala, September 1982. Uppsala: Scandinavian Institute of African Studies, 1983.

Christensen, C. *et al. Food Problems and Prospects in Sub-Saharan Africa: The Decade of the 1980s.* Washington DC: United States Department of Agriculture, Economic Research Service, 1981.

Cleland, J. and J. Hobcraft with B. Dinezen (eds.). *Reproductive Change in Developing Countries: Insights from the World Fertility Survey.* Oxford: Oxford University Press, 1985.

Coombs, P.H. *The World Crisis in Education: the View from the Eighties.* New York; Oxford: Oxford University Press, 1985.

ECA and Africa's Development 1983–2008: A Preliminary Study. Addis Ababa: United Nations Economic Commission for Africa, 1983.

Eicher, C.K. and D.C. Baker. *Research on Agricultural Development in Sub-Saharan Africa: A Critical Survey.* MSU International Development Paper

No.1. East Lansing, Michigan: Michigan State University Department of Agricultural Economics, 1982.

Ghosh, P.K. (ed.). *Population, Environment and Resources, and Third World Development.* Westport, Connecticut; London: Greenwood Press, 1984.

Green, R.H. (ed.). Sub-Saharan Africa: Towards Oblivion or Reconstruction? *Journal of Development Planning* 15. New York: United Nations, 1985.

Jolly, R. and G.A. Cornia (eds.). *The Impact of World Recession on Children: A Study Prepared for UNICEF.* Oxford: Pergamon Press, 1984.

Ndegwa, P., L.P. Mureithi and R. Green (eds.). *Development Options for Africa in the 1980s and Beyond.* Nairobi: Society for International Development, 1984.

Rose, T. (ed.). *Crisis and Recovery in Sub-Saharan Africa: Realities and Complexities.* Paris: OECD Development Centre, 1985.

Some Fertility Indicators and their Implications for Africa. African Population Studies Series, No.3. Addis Ababa: United Nations Economic Commission for Africa, 1979.

UNICEF. *Within Human Reach: A Future for Africa's Children.* New York: UNICEF, 1985.

Addendum to Chapter 1
The context of change: perspectives from one country

Iba Der Thiam

The broad aims of education in sub-Saharan Africa are more or less the same as anywhere else: schools need to turn the children entrusted to them into citizens able to make sound judgements on questions of national concern, capable of consciously exercising their rights and respecting their duties. They must also be educated to be useful and capable of fitting smoothly into the different levels of the economy of the country and participating as efficiently as possible in its development. The aim is to turn out men and women who can wholly fulfil their physical, intellectual, artistic, moral and spiritual potential.

Senegalese law, which lays down broad guidelines for national education, stipulates

> National education ... aims (1) to raise the cultural level of the population and (2) to train free men and women capable of creating conditions for their self-

This is a long extract from a statement prepared for the Conference by the Minister of Higher and National Education of Senegal, Professor Iba Der Thiam. It is a lucid analysis by a statesman of great experience of the context underlying change in one African nation. The issues affecting Senegal are shared in differing degrees by all the countries of sub-Saharan Africa. Iba Der Thiam's paper is in two equal parts, the first analysing the context of change, the second the policies necessary in Senegal. The first part only is reproduced here, translated from the French by Colette Hawes.

fulfilment at all levels, of contributing to the development of science and technology and of providing effective solutions to problems of national development.

These aims are appropriate to any educational system even if it might wish to express them in different terms.

But these aims have to be implemented in a context. Hence, the particular form that schools now assume and the difficulties that educational undertakings currently meet in sub-Saharan Africa can be explained by this context.

Nearly all the countries in the area which concerns us had, for many years, been subjected to foreign rule. Once they had regained their independence, our nations discovered that they had inherited political, economic and social inhibitions which hampered their development. There is no need, here, to recall all the malfunctions which can be attributed to the after-effects of colonialism: dependency and unrestricted economic practices; over-expansion of the imported culture at the expense of the local; paucity of processing industries; weak and cumbersome administrative systems — many factors all too familiar now and often described.

Having gained independence, each individual government immediately set to work to overcome the handicaps accumulated in the past. In each case they looked to education to achieve this since it has always been considered one of the essential factors in development and a major priority: on average a quarter of the national budget goes to education. It has to be admitted, however, that the fruits of efforts and sacrifices so willingly made have fallen far short of expectations. No one can be sure that pupils who have been given education at school in the hope of making them into agents of national development have indeed fulfilled this role.

It would have been surprising if they had. Today's schools are usually the direct descendants of colonial schools and if the latter adequately fulfilled the role assigned to them by the colonisers, they would have been ill-suited to be equally successful in carrying out the functions demanded of them once the countries had become independent. Besides its mission to 'civilise' and spread ideology, it was the task of the colonial school to train junior administrative staff mainly entrusted with carrying out tasks which could be done with minimal instruction and requiring first and foremost the knowledge and use of the coloniser's language. By a quirk of fate which often occurs in history, the colonial school was the very place which bred the first African élites. These, believing the coloniser to be speaking the truth, hoisting him indeed by his own petard, appropriated foreign education so thoroughly that they used all its resources to gain recognition and demand freedom from colonialism. It follows that these élites, having inherited political power and being responsible to shape the destiny of the newly independent states, considered it natural that their compatriots would best benefit from the type of education which had made them what they were. Let us add that it is always easier to expand an existing system than to build a new one from scratch. The existing system seemed to have proved successful. The need to change was not therefore immediately apparent. When, finally, our nations evolved and new needs became evident, the status quo was maintained by the over-riding need, in the first years of independence, for technical assistance from the former metropolis.

In short, methods, syllabuses and curricula remained unquestioned, while schooling spread and developed. As the number of children attending school grew, so did the imbalance between, on the one hand, the reality of the way schools operated, and, on the other, popular aspirations and the goals required for development.

The colonial school system was above all quantitatively inadequate. It was reserved for a minority within which even fewer students could reach secondary and university levels. Today, although the intake is wider at the base of the pyramid, education is still élitist in character, the summit remains very pointed. Thus, in Senegal for instance, it is estimated that 804 out of 1000 children who enter school reach the end of the primary cycle. In fact, allowing for repeaters, only 416 pupils complete the full cycle in six years; and compared to other systems our schools have a high retention rate. Only 241 students enter the first class of secondary school, 181 the fourth, 85 the fifth, and finally only 41 manage to get into the top class. In other words, only 4 per cent of all pupils who enter the system will have the opportunity of sitting their *baccalaureat*. Thus, not only are today's schools a long way from taking all those children who could go to school, they also eliminate a large proportion of pupils before they have completed a full cycle and make passing from one cycle to another highly selective. These overall statistics must also be interpreted bearing in mind the part of the country the pupils come from and their sex: more boys go to and stay longer at school than girls; many more urban children go to school than ones in rural areas — numbers are double, treble and sometimes four times greater in towns than in the country.

In addition to this quantitative élitism there exists an even more serious qualitative inadequacy. As the descendants of a colonial system, schools stress general education to the detriment of technical education, theoretical training to the detriment of the practical, terminal initial education to the detriment of continuous learning when our countries require exactly the opposite. No effort is being spared to give more space to the applied sciences and technology: for instance, the policy of the inclusion of special scientific units in school programmes. But one must ask whether the changes brought in are radical enough or whether they are merely cosmetic measures in programmes still remaining captive to a wholly European-centred concept.

Indeed, the main difficulty, over and above that of subject content, which faces our educational system, is that the very spirit of our teaching remains alien to the essential reality of our life. In an Africa where community values of solidarity and sharing are still very much alive despite the upheavals caused by poorly controlled urbanisation, schools promote among all a competitive spirit and through their methods of evaluation overstimulate individualism.

In an Africa where the elders are repositories of wisdom and knowledge, schools are too closed either to accept any teaching other than that found in books or to listen to the words which spring from our most venerated traditions. In an Africa where even everyday actions must keep step with sacred rites, where the life and actions of the large majority are guided by religious values, the secularised schools exclude any ideas of a religious nature. Hence, they run the risk of being considered by the parents as hostile to the values they hold most deeply sacred.

Finally, and perhaps this might have been put first, the very language in which the teaching is done is a legacy of colonialism. There are undoubtedly some advantages in using French, English or Portuguese but these are not enough to counterbalance the shock caused to the young pupil who must suffer his first educational experience in a language which is not his own. Nor must we forget that schools which use a borrowed tool for their expression leave out entire sections of national cultures. Even when a language is not confined to mere words and when different aspects of it receive different emphasis, it remains a way of being to the exclusion of all others. That part of the language which cannot be translated is not so much a jealously-guarded mystery as the ground on which to find a foothold or a landmark from which bearings can be taken.

There is a very good reason why in Senegal and in other francophone countries the term 'French' school is commonly used to signify the formal system of education for which the National Ministry of Education is responsible! The school seems to be artificially grafted on to a social body which can find within it neither the values it holds dear nor the fundamental aspirations it desires.

But if school is considered an alien body it is nevertheless accepted as a necessary evil. It is in fact the only way up the social ladder. It is difficult to be anybody in the political or the economic world without having been through the school. It is the only way to follow if modern standards and life-styles are to be attained.

Hence schools give rise to ambivalent feelings of fear and desire. An illiterate father knows full well that when he entrusts a teacher with his son he runs the risk of soon losing sight of him, of no longer being able to exercise authority over one who is more learned than he, of being gradually left behind. At the same time, the child who attends school is a source of hope for his family: sooner or later that child expects to benefit from the position he believes he cannot fail to occupy since it will be guaranteed by the diploma he is expected to receive. The demand for education is very high and frustration is proportionately great when schools do not satisfy these hopes, schools which cannot accept all those who apply for entry nor even take all those who deserve as far as they might hope to go.

It is in this context that we must consider profound change.

Chapter 2
Priorities

This chapter examines

1 The reasons why educational priorities were not ranked and ordered by the Conference, the inescapable connection between priorities and resources, and the areas of educational action to which the participants gave special attention (p. 27)

2 The priority attaching to education itself in the current crisis of development (p. 30)

3 The varied meanings of the term 'educational priority' from the point of view of African governments and aid agencies, and the question of who decides what is and what isn't a priority (p. 32)

4 Proposals for the extension of multi-faceted, development-oriented basic education for children and adults, and the required resources, organisation, content and clientele (p. 34)

5 How the effectiveness and quality of primary schooling could be improved, as an important component of basic education (p. 40)

6 The extension of appropriate formal and non-formal occupational training and the social context in which it must occur (p. 45)

7 The qualitative development and re-definition of the national role of African universities as centres of excellence, resources of applied expertise, and catalysts for policy review (p. 47)

8 The improvement of management systems in education, and in particular the enhancement of information and planning capacity (p. 48)

Introduction: hard choices?

By comparison with the theme of Aid, the discussions on Priorities were mainly low-key and widely focused. It would be a mistake to infer from this that the topic itself lacked interest or importance. If anything, the reverse is the case. The question of what forms, sectors and levels of education should take priority over others is the daily stuff of life for African decision-makers and their advisers. It is not an issue which could be knocked off in a day or two's discussion at Windsor.

No serious effort was made, therefore, to attempt the impossible. No lists were compiled, assigning a rank order to each part of the educational enterprise. The discussions were open and informal. Working group reports were summarised and discussed in plenaries, but the Conference made no attempt to reach systematic conclusions, and indeed resisted the efforts of the organisers to formulate consensus.

This chapter was written by Trevor Coombe with research assistance by Carol Coombe, drawing on all Conference documents, particularly those relating to Theme I, as well as working group reports and verbatim records of plenary discussions. As in other chapters, there are passages where the writer has gone beyond the Conference record in order to set it in context and to interpret it.

There may be deeper reasons why the Conference made no priority list. One concerns the problem of making generalisations about the needs of an entire subcontinent. However much the African countries have in common, each has its own historical legacy and current conditions. However necessary it is to learn from the experience of other states (and this was strongly urged), in the end each country's authorities have to make decisions according to their own circumstances. This suggests another reason, namely that priority-setting is an outcome of a political process, not a technical exercise which may be undertaken *a priori* at an international meeting. Nor does the implementation of educational priorities move effortlessly from plan to action. It is an untidy business, and often a frustrating one.

Dorothy Njeuma (Cameroon) illustrated the last point well when she listed the allocations of capital investment in her country's educational sector, but added at once: 'These percentages, of course, do not reflect the priority that government places on the various levels of education but are mostly a reflection of internal pressures on the educational system'. So there is a frequent tension between what governments want to do and what they consider politically feasible or advantageous. Moreover, what comes out of the decision-making process is not the outcome of a debate on educational issues only but of the perennial jostling for attention between education and other sectors. In this respect, as in several others noted by Kenneth King (Edinburgh University) in his lead paper, donors and recipients resemble each other and need to understand each other.

Ian Buist of ODA, for instance, described the challenge of trying to reconcile conflicting sectoral claims in country programmes of assistance. Because funds are limited, the developmental merits of an education project or programme may have to be weighed against others in health, rural development, or natural resources. In present economic circumstances in most of Africa, what is often most important is a substantial likelihood of early pay-off. If the education proposal does not have the highest priority, then the money will go elsewhere: to another ministry and another programme.

The question of resources suggests a third reason why the Conference may have been content to discuss educational priorities without formulating them very rigorously. The ten-year-long recession was the dark backdrop against which the Conference was convened. The sponsors were convinced that the shrinkage of real resources available for education laid an obligation on African governments and donors alike to think again about what they were trying to do. 'Hard choices' needed to be made. Joseph Kotsokoane (Lesotho) threw an interesting light on this proposition when he reported on behalf of the working group he chaired:

> We felt one should know what the problems are before you can think in terms of how you are going to finance them. ... The best thing is to have your priorities and then try to find the money to finance the priorities. Key issues were: How is education financed? Given the resource crisis, how might it be financed? What were government policies? Could they afford to pay for them? If they could not, what roles might donors play?

These remarks illustrate well the inescapably close connection between

28

education policies and finance. It is a truism that official priorities may not be affordable. It follows that they will be adjusted in practice according to the availability of resources to implement them and will be influenced by the very process by which governments are compelled to raise the funds or technical assistance they seek. For many African participants, therefore, the question of educational priorities boiled down to the search for resources, and thus involved matters to be negotiated with the aid donors or lenders.

In short, the priorities of educational development, however critical and absorbing they may be in national affairs, were not in themselves a *Conference* priority for the African side, whatever the organisers might have hoped. For African participants, especially, the central business to be transacted concerned the level, focus, process and conditions of aid flows to education.

Even if educational priorities were not defined in so many words, some strong preferences were expressed, in the sense that the Conference gave marked attention to some issues and little if any attention to others. It would be wise to take the preferences seriously, but unwise to conclude that topics which were barely noticed in the discussion are unimportant to Africans or African governments. The discussions were simply not that systematic, and the time was short.

The general mood of the Conference in discussing educational priorities was sombre, reflecting the context of discussions analysed in our first chapter. While no one contradicted Dzingai Mutumbuka (Zimbabwe) when he pointed out the qualitative transformation that education had brought about in African societies in the past 25 years, the general accounting of the condition of African education and its social contribution was grimly realistic and unsentimental. The massive gains in enrolment at all levels were weighed in the balance against high rates of population growth and urbanisation, heavy rates of drop-out and repetition, falling levels of scholastic performance, low teacher morale, decrepit and ill-equipped schools and shrinking per pupil expenditures. There was an almost universal view that Africa's formal education systems operate as vast, inefficient engines of competition to propel a small fraction of the population into wage employment, and are no more related today than they have ever been to the real-life needs and circumstances of the rest. Most participants were therefore not unduly impressed by the virtues of educational expansion as such. No one made claims for the contribution of education to economic growth and national development without at once insisting that education will not do this job properly unless it is better managed, with accompanying changes in balance, orientation and quality.

Moreover, the Conference accepted without question that the concept of education itself, as a responsibility of national governments and the international aid community, must embrace both formal and non-formal provision, involving many government and non-government agencies, at all levels from the community upward, in the grave and urgent tasks of human resource development. No one seemed to think that solutions would be possible except by long, hard collaborative effort.

Within this broad field of action, the Conference gave special attention to the need to support:

29

1 The steady expansion of basic educational provision for children, youth and adults, especially in connection with a long-range strategy for enhancing food production and human survival in the subcontinent; coupled with
2 The improvement of the quality and relevance of basic education, embracing continued work in curriculum, examinations, teacher education (both pre-service and in-service), production of teaching materials and resources, school management, inspection and supervision
3 The expansion of technical education and vocational training suitable to actual work requirements and community needs, with stress on productive and entrepreneurial skills
4 The maintenance of the quality of university provision, including an ever closer commitment of research and teaching to ameliorating the needs of African societies, and enhancing the role of universities in appraising and improving national policies
5 The improvement of management systems in education, especially data collection and analysis, research, information sharing, planning, administration, industrial (personnel) relations, and staff development.

These issues are now considered in more detail, starting with the underlying question of what priority education deserves in relation to the social and economic conditions of the continent.

Education as a priority

The catastrophic African drought focused the mind of the Conference on the question whether education could any longer make plausible claims on the national exchequers for priority treatment. Some participants argued that formal education had received too large a slice of the national cake in the past. This had occurred at first in the expectation that educational provision would promote rapid economic growth, and latterly (as rates of growth have stalled or reversed) it has continued mainly in response to public demand. It was recognised that people would clamour to open up ever higher levels of education in an attempt to secure for their children access to wage or salaried employment.

Some participants saw this familiar syndrome as an inevitable con-sequence of the unbalanced social system and social relations of production in most African countries, and considered that the first order of business was to address the exploitative class relations of production in Africa and the unequal system of investment, trade and aid governing relations between Africa and the industrialised north. Such views were not contradicted but they were not pursued at length.

Many participants considered that the high rates of population growth (as distinct from the sizes of African populations) were making a dangerous contribution both to starvation and mass poverty on the one hand, and the decline in standards of educational provision on the other. It was not that rapid population increase was a unique cause of both phenomena, but that population pressure was seen to bear down heavily on land and food resources, on the provision of social services, particularly schooling, and on the capacity of poor countries to generate employment commensurate with the growth of the labour force. Appeals were made to place the issue of

We realise that education responds to the existing social structure unless it is deliberately meant to challenge it. Therefore, the nature of the social structure reproduces itself through education. Parents send their children to school so that they can achieve the same social status as those who have achieved it through education. Children too will go to school with the same objectives in mind. They will aim at driving the big cars that we ride. They will aspire to live in the plush comfortable houses that we live in.They will aspire for the same kind of life which we have because we went to school. The problem becoming clear to us all is that the socio-economic base which provides this comfort is increasingly being eroded by the same production structure which we maintain. The conflict between forces of production and consumption patterns becomes quite clear here.

As these contradictions have become more clear we have evaded the real issues, conveniently terming the manifested problems as: a problem of the overeducated; the unemployed educated; the diploma disease; brain-drain, and so forth. We have never run short of impressive catch-words. This does not help us much. We need instead to address ourselves to the real fundamental issues in social development in order to locate answers for education.

Joseph Rugumyamheto (Tanzania)

population policy at the head of national development agendas, but it must be noted that such appeals were made mainly by non-African participants, and although they were not disputed, the issue was not taken up in these terms by the Conference as a whole.

In considering the priorities attached to education in the face of the 'crisis of development', the Conference seemed to make two complementary responses. One asserts that education cannot claim a greater share of national budgets than it already gets.

In the face of increased drought and famine, as well as the need to develop other vital sectors of the economy such as agriculture, road infrastructure, health, water, electricity, etc., the portion of national budgets allocated to education cannot be increased further without jeopardising overall development
Dorothy Njeuma

The parallel view recognises that the very sectors listed by Dr Njeuma cannot be expected to function effectively without skilled manpower to instal, operate and maintain them, and a knowledgeable and receptive public to put them to good use.

Africa's most valuable asset is its people. The human person is the beginning and the end of all economic developments. Africa needs literate manpower to help develop her tremendous natural resources and maintain and sustain her development. However excellent our programmes may be in agriculture, health, housing to mention a few areas, they will come to naught if the people are not trained to use the facilities properly. . . . Education of course goes beyond manpower development and judicious use of facilities. As Thomas Jefferson rightly observed: 'If a nation expects to be ignorant and free it expects what never was and never will be.'
Yahaya Hamza (Nigeria)

31

The implication is that education, both broad and deep, remains a prerequisite of successful development efforts in other spheres, and a necessary condition (though not a guarantee) that the fruits of development will be secured by the people of Africa for themselves and their posterity. It is a continuous and many-sided process, and the school or the formal education system is only one of its agents. This is where the Conference found the essential reconciliation between the austere budgetary diagnosis and the conviction that education remains indispensable in the service of Africa's immediate and long-range needs. The Conference viewed education as a social, cultural and economic function which is not monopolised by the institutions falling under ministries of education, but cuts right across most spheres of human need and human endeavour.

This comprehensive view is especially relevant to Africa's present crisis. The educational needs of maternal health and child care, family health and shelter, food production and security, environmental conservation and energy use, occupational and entrepreneurial competence, and the range of associated personal and social values, must be addressed more urgently, coherently and effectively than before, using both formal and non- formal technologies. The priority which must be assigned to education in this global sense should call up additional resources from within the economy, from communities and private sources, and from other government departments, even if the schools budget maintains its present level.

This was the outlook of the Conference, insofar as it can be fairly summarised. It was not a romantic view. Speaker after speaker emphasised the dimensions of the task and the need for each government to assess its own situation and devise its own strategy, learning where possible from the experience of other nations, as well as from its own mistakes. Arthur Porter (Sierra Leone) expressed the hope that governments could be persuaded to invest more commitment in the educational enterprise, properly conceived, even if they could invest no more funds. Philip Coombs (ICED) sketched a grim account of the African predicament, not in a despairing vein, but as an encouragement to policy-makers and others

> to come to grips with these hard realities and seek out workable solutions. Clearly there are no simple, overnight panaceas. It will take a combination of efforts by many different individuals and organisations — public and private, local, national and international — pursued over many years.

Faced with massive educational needs in all sectors of national life, and grossly inadequate means to satisfy them, African governments (and aid agencies) are bound to confront questions of choice and priority at every turn.

Formulating priorities within education

Formulation of educational priorities is not an easy matter. There is first the question of definition. What did the Conference understand by the term?

In one sense, it meant 'needs'. But the needs expressed in the form of public demands for educational services may be very different from the needs identified by national policy-makers, with their global vision of a country's problems and development potential, and the different time-scale by which they judge the relative urgency of one educational programme over another. On the other hand, national policy-makers are not immune to popular pressure and, as we have noted above, are often compelled to bow to public demand against their better judgement. So policies-as-implemented may differ from planned priorities by reflecting an amalgam of what governments think their people *should have*, and what they think they *want*. In this respect Africa is not much different from anywhere else, except that the needs are so much greater than governments' capacity to respond.

In another sense, the term 'priorities' was taken to mean inescapable choices. As Roger Iredale (ODA) notes later in the book, 'the Conference was intended to dwell on the hard choices facing African educationists'. The assumption appears to have been that governments were in a position not only to identify alternatives but also to choose between them. But Peter Williams (Commonwealth Secretariat) pointed out in his lead paper that most African governments whose educational systems are under siege have been unwilling or unable to make such choices and instead have made 'responsive adjustment . . . to successive pressures afflicting the system'. Perhaps most governments anywhere would prefer the path of drift, or 'subtle adjustment and dilution', rather than risking public wrath by cutting ongoing programmes outright.

The intractable problem is that qualitative decline has been precipitated by quantitative expansion while simultaneously the public is demanding more education at higher levels and governments have fewer resources per capita at their disposal. It is true that many governments have been compelled to defer some new projects and prolong others. But as both Peter Williams and Kenneth King have remarked, African governments have also repeatedly confounded observers and critics by embarking on educational initiatives and sustaining them with no visible additional means to support them. The political instinct to satisfy demand by expansionist policies often runs counter to the professional instinct to consolidate quantitative gains by qualitative reinforcement. The problem, wrote Aklilu Habte (World Bank), is that 'Africa faces a dilemma in supporting all levels of education without differentiated priority emphasis'.

There is a third sense in which 'priority' is used: the choice of programmes or projects for external assistance. This meaning was also in the minds of the Conference organisers: 'the need to achieve a better sense of needs and priorities, particularly in relation to the urgent and conflicting demands for educational assistance to Africa'. As Charles Bassett (CIDA) put it:

> Within the overall priority on education how do you make the best advantage of the money you have got available? You cannot do everything at the same time. We have to make some hard decisions.

The interchangeable pronouns in this passage indicate that the hard choice of aid priorities was considered to be a joint task of donor and recipient. Probably all the donor agencies represented at the Conference saw the process in that light. Ralph Romain (World Bank) took for granted that the Conference was 'not so much concerned with education priorities as priorities for educational aid and — more specifically — aid co-ordination'. But Abdul Menan Ahmed (Ethiopia) considered this distinction between educational priorities and educational *aid* priorities to be artificial:

> We are invited [to the Conference] to discuss priorities for development and then the modalities of aid. In fact . . . one is impossible without the other. It is a fact of life that most forms of development action in developing countries could not take place without some element of aid. Our own resources are stretched to the utmost in running the infrastructure we have managed to develop and in securing budgetary increases for new infrastructure. The development discussion and its internal priorities is therefore inevitably the aid discussion.

Abdul Menan Ahmed went on to make clear that settling policy is the government's business, in the light of the country's history and social conditions, and that 'in most circumstances it is more appropriate to talk about *adjustments* to priorities and strategies' (our emphasis) to meet changing developmental requirements. In order to participate equally with the aid donor in the 'process of systematic review and evaluation', the Ethiopian Ministry of Education had therefore improved its general planning capacity (with aid assistance) and established a Project Preparation Office and a Project Management Office. Apart from their obvious functions, these offices participate in appraisal and negotiation. As a result, donor–recipient relationships have been facilitated 'at all stages from initial interest in aid to final review of outcomes'.

In these repects Ethiopia seems to have constructed unusually favourable conditions for the transaction of business with aid agencies. By contrast, there are many cases where the donor community could claim, with more or less justification, that diagnosis of needs was unclear and that priorities were hazy or undefined. This is fertile ground for the ascendancy of what Kenneth King calls the external aid agenda over the internal agenda, with the likelihood in these circumstances that the 'hard choices' would be determined rather more forcibly by the donor than the recipient.

Improving the coverage and relevance of basic education

No dissenting voice was raised to the proposition that the greatest task of African education was to extend basic education more widely and make it more effective. The term 'basic education' was used at the Conference both in its narrower sense, as primary education, and in its wider sense. The wider interpretation was of particular interest to participants. There was a large measure of agreement that basic education did not mean primary education alone, nor literacy alone. It included both these systems of learning and more, both formal and non-formal, government sponsored and non-government sponsored. It was 'basic' in the sense of attending to the fundamental learning needs of young and adult members of particular societies.

Manzoor Ahmed (UNICEF) reported on behalf of his working group that they had reaffirmed 'the main element and concept of basic education' as

> a kind of nationwide learning opportunity for children [and] adults, including of course women, which would help people to function more effectively in their own environment. . . .

It did not necessarily mean introducing an entirely new programme, since many elements of basic education were already in place in all countries. Some would need strengthening or expanding, while new elements might be needed depending upon an assessment of what was there in relation to the society's developmental objectives.

Agreement in the Conference about the priority and the meaning of basic education is one thing, but it is quite another to translate these ideas into functional programmes within individual countries. It was recognised realistically that the components or topography of each country's basic education system would differ according to its needs, wealth and internal developmental policies. But discussions focused on several issues of common concern, especially questions of resources, organisation, content, clientele and effectiveness.

1 Resources for basic education

The Conference understandably had rather more to say in relation to external resources, which are discussed in the next chapter, than internal ones. Nevertheless, the relentless pressure on government budgets was a common topic of discussion. More than one speaker suggested that formal education could not and should not expect to receive a higher proportion of budgeted funds. If primary education (as a major component of the basic education network) were to receive more from the public purse in future it would have to be at the expense of other sectors of the formal education system. Given the political muscle of the upwardly mobile classes in virtually all African societies, this was unlikely to occur without a fight. Dzingai Mutumbuka suggested harshly that the policy-makers all over sub-Saharan Africa were evolving 'a unique class of their own'.

> It is a class problem because they themselves want to ensure that their kids will get the secondary schooling, will get the university education, and therefore you cannot tamper with that level. What about basic education where every child should have the right? They are not interested.

One working group observed that even if governments made changes in spending priorities, the savings in one area could be pre-empted by the treasury rather than being deployed elsewhere, though they noted that in some countries redistributions *have* taken place in favour of basic education.

An alternative, or additional, solution would be to make the budget go further in primary education (along lines suggested by Peter Williams in his lead paper) by driving down unit costs or throwing more of the burden of raising revenue on local communities. It must be recognised, though, that at a certain point, already reached by some countries, such measures would make unacceptable inroads on educational quality or impose unacceptable burdens on the poorest sections of society.

A more obvious saving in capital costs would accrue from putting as many appropriate formal education facilities as possible at the disposal of non-formal basic education agencies, in afternoons and evenings, weekends and vacations. Apart from capital cost reduction this would help forge practical links betweeen the formal and non-formal sectors.

Abdul Menan Ahmed reminded the Conference, however, that non-formal education was likely to be very expensive the more successful it became, not only in terms of structures, course development and instructor training, but in 'meeting the astronomical increase in the demand for paper which will be generated by widespread cultural change'.

2 The organisation of basic education

The second issue concerned the organisation of basic education. There was plenty of discussion about management (reported later) but surprisingly little about organisation. Philip Coombs from the chair reminded the Conference that basic education involved not only the ministry of education's mandate, but reached well beyond the schools 'into such matters as health, agriculture, small industry, family planning and the like'. This suggested the importance of collaboration between the ministry of education and the other ministries — 'one of the hardest things in the world to achieve'.

Participants were invited to see the basic education system whole, both the formal and non-formal elements, to describe and clarify them and recognise the linkages between them — but the Conference did not go further. This reticence may simply reflect the fact that no single international formula exists that would apply equally to Botswana and Senegal, Ethiopia and Mali. However, it must be admitted that, some brilliant exceptions apart, the Conference was short on first-hand expertise from the non-formal education sector in Africa. As a result, much of the organisational challenge and promise went by default. However, if basic education *is* to become an articulated system which is more than the sum of its parts, directed to meeting defined learning needs, then African countries will have to find ways to bridge the gulf between all their principal education and training agencies at this level, both within and outside of government.

One profitable policy alternative might be to recognise the priorities accorded by governments and parents alike to formal primary schooling, yet to seek progressively to deformalise this sector in order to serve the needs of a wider variety of citizens.

> Probably basic education will be conceived as primary first-level education, but this may well be interpreted in a non-formal style, for example
>
> a Much more flexible and problem-centred curricula
>
> b More flexible use of classroom space
>
> c New approaches to pedagogy to serve the needs of large groups or groups of mixed ages and backgrounds
>
> d Use of local human resources for teaching (including parents).

Working Group 3, Report on Theme I
Chairman: Yaya Mede Moussa (Benin)

3 The content of basic education

Organisational changes are therefore implied in the third issue, namely the content of basic education. The Conference as a whole argued resoundingly for a system of basic education which addressed the overriding necessities of African societies and their environments. The first and foremost issue was sheer survival. This theme was sounded particularly by the participants from the Sahelian region, and the donor representatives with the closest experience of the drought.

> These are above all countries that are agricultural and pastoral, and industrialisation is rather a marginal activity. They are also countries that are very threatened by certain problems that come from the international economic situation. They are threatened by the advance of the desert, the continual drought, the continuing degradation of the soil, the ecosystem, and the agriculture which is the basis is no longer able to fulfil its role. So we have the phenomenon of famine which is aggravated by the population increase which is particularly strong in Africa. So they are countries that have very fragile economies and are threatened in their very survival. If you take all these things into account we should be able to identify the priorities. Education is not a neutral activity. It must play its role in solving the problem and so education must concentrate on adapting itself to these problems of development.
>
> *Iba Der Thiam (Senegal)*

The obvious need was for a reorientation of education away from formalism and paper competence.

> If education is the most important instrument for our survival in terms of national mobilisation for the production of food, provision of decent shelter and health care delivery, protection of life and property and as an instrument of manpower development, we must eke out a curriculum that is functional and result oriented.
>
> *Yahaya Hamza*

Manzoor Ahmed spelled out the contours of such a curriculum as follows:

a The learner should be able to acquire a functional level of proficiency in basic communication skills or the three Rs

b The educational programme should address the question where the learner fits in society after completing primary education or other forms of basic education, especially if he or she does not continue in formal secondary education

c The educational programme should be meaningful to the life and circumstances of the learner and contribute towards the solution of such urgent problems as ill health, poor nutrition, food production, polluted water and preventable death of infants and children, and

d The educational programme should be affordable on a mass scale for the society it serves with resources that are available.

The question arises whether the primary school or community-based educational programmes are suitable vehicles for this kind of learning. Cynthia Perry, of USAID, speaking in the context of her agency's priority of aid to food production and food security, admitted that there was some question in their minds as to the role of basic education in these processes. It seemed at best a long-term investment. Could food self-sufficiency be achieved 'quicker than going through basic education'? The question is entirely legitimate and merits an empirical not a rhetorical response. For the time being, though, the Conference had to satisfy itself with formulating what basic education ought to be about, rather than documenting verified achievements at the grassroots.

Implicit in this view of the content of basic education is the belief that such content should be locally relevant and to some extent locally determined. Hence national prescriptions for content would be inappropriate.

> There was consensus about the need for far-reaching reform of basic education, with a curriculum based on skills and competences to be realised, and local problems that need solving, rather than on traditional subject areas.
>
> A unified monolithic curriculum for basic education is not workable, because it will be of necessity involved with community priorities, which will differ from area to area. It may well need to incorporate, and adjust to traditional systems of education (e.g., Mauritania, Senegal), where enrolment in such alternative systems may well be preferred to the formal system at local level.
>
> The dichotomy between the home and the school in some countries draws attention to the need to involve the community in decisions about curriculum content — especially if this is to become more relevant. . . .
>
> *Working Group 3, Report on Theme I*
> *Chairman: Yaya Mede Moussa*

It may be noted that the ambition to achieve such locally relevant content is not new in Africa. No theme of educational theory on the subcontinent has had a more enduring life, spanning at least 60 years, than the theme that education at the base should be made relevant to the actual conditions of production and social organisation of Africa's rural communities. It has been honoured more in the breach than in the observance. It has died and been reborn again and again under new slogans and on the lips of new educational apostles, since the travels of the Phelps-Stokes Commissions in the 1920s, and their message of rural self-reliance and formal/non-formal educational integration on the Tuskegee model. It is reasonable to ask what conditions now make it likely that the reorientation of basic education will be achieved and have the desired effect.

Two conditions appear to be novel in the present situation. One is the gravity of the crisis of African population, ecology, food and survival. The other is the impressive weight of opinion of African educators. What remains to be tested, again and again in different countries, is the willingness of the clientele to accept a new orientation, and the capacity of formal and non-formal educational programmes to engage effectively with the systems of production, community health and nutrition, which are embedded in the social, political, economic and ecological conditions in each community.

Other forms of linkage received less attention from the Conference but are likely to continue to be important. One is the need to relate the task of basic education to the specific requirements of people living in cities and towns. A second concerns the fact that basic education is intended to prepare people for life at the base, and yet it is expected to help a minority to leave the basic community for life and work in a wider sphere. How can both functions be accommodated in one and the same system?

These two problems, spanning mobility in space and social mobility, are thrown into relief by a comment by Kebby Musokotwane (Zambia), whose country has (proportionately) one of the largest industrial sectors and one of the highest urbanisation rates on the continent. He made a plea for African education at all levels to give priority to science and technology.

> Industrialisation cannot take place without technological development and our dependence on imported, manufactured goods will continue unabated, and the depletion of our foreign exchange reserves through the importation of these foreign manufactured goods will continue, until and unless, our scientific and technological base has been developed. The concern for scientific and technological development is not only with regard to manufacturing in urban areas. Improved agricultural development is itself dependent upon science and technology. There is need for research in agriculture and animal husbandry. Extension workers with technical and scientific know-how, in such areas as pest control, will play an important role in helping not only the commercial farmer, but also the peasant farmer in improving his output. The centrality of science and technology is also seen in such areas as medicine and mining.

This reminds us that in a developmental perspective, the concerns of basic education and advanced education are mutually dependent.

Another, more general, caution about the high responsibility of educators at all levels, was expressed by Hugh Hawes.

> Quality of thought in education remains exceptionally important. Whatever else we do, we must continue to reaffirm that an education that doesn't teach learners to think independently and to value that independence, is a tool for domination and not development.

There is, of course, no conflict in principle between the development of appropriate forms of basic education and the cultivation of a scientific and technological approach or an independent and critical mind. A very strong argument could be put up for regarding the latter as a prerequisite for the success of the former. It is perhaps salutary to be reminded that basic education requires analysis, curriculum planning and teaching of a very high order if such objectives are to be realised.

4 The clientele for basic education

Both written and spoken contributions to the Conference implied that the potential clientele for basic education was virtually unlimited. For example, it included all children as candidates for primary education (and pre-school education as well, in the view of some participants), the majority of adults as candidates for literacy education, the unemployed and under-employed adults and youths as candidates for fundamental training in production or marketable skills, small farmers as candidates for advisory and support services, and all families as candidates for primary health, nutrition and childcare education (and, in the view of some, help in family planning), as well as individuals and groups in society, like the handicapped, who have suffered neglect.

This all-embracing view underlay the vehement rejection by several participants of the notion that women should be singled out for special educational treatment. There is a fine distinction to be made here. It was not suggested that women had not suffered educational neglect which ought to be urgently remedied. That proposition was undisputed. Rather, the argument was made that women's needs were not to be isolated from the mainstream of educational provision. There must be no hint of sex apartheid in education, said Cynthia Perry. All developmental activities needed to build in, as a matter of course, the educational requirements of women along with those of men.

There was need to analyse the issue, to quantify and document the role of women in agricultural improvement and health care, for instance, and thus (said Kebby Musokotwane) 'to analyse what it has cost us as Africa by leaving out our women folk'.

The general earning power of the society at large would not be enhanced

> by concentrating on aid to forms of education which benefit males at the expense of females, when we know that women's contribution is vital in the fight against poverty. This implies that there should be more aid for girls' education and more aid for non-formal education (of which even illiterate women can be the beneficiaries).

Lalage Bown (Glasgow University)

The fifth issue concerns the effectiveness of basic education and particularly of its formal primary education component. This proved to be a topic of such serious concern to the Conference that it deserves a section of its own.

Improving the effectiveness and quality of primary education as a major component of basic education

The issue of qualitative wastage, as Hugh Hawes called it, was raised by all four lead speakers and analysed in detail by Peter Williams. Participants representing all the Conference 'constituencies' tackled the theme either in written contributions or in discussion, and at least two of the working groups gave it special attention.

In discussing qualitative wastage in education it is often difficult to distinguish symptoms from causes. As in a medical diagnosis one is likely to find both primary and secondary (or consequential) symptoms, any one of which may have both primary and secondary causes. The Conference did not dwell on these distinctions but it is just as well to bring them to mind, as the list of 'symptoms' identified by the participants is very long, while the list of 'causes' is rather brief. How should one classify the observed decline in educational management, for instance — as a symptom or a cause of qualitative wastage? It is clearly both or either depending upon which part of the anatomy of the education system is being probed.

One should also be reminded that all generalisations about educational conditions in the subcontinent are bound to conceal significant differences both between and within countries. In fact, as Tony Somerset (EDC) suggested, the extreme variation in the examination performance of primary schools within any one country is itself a symptom of inequity in school quality, a condition which is in need of more study and remedial action. But a striking aspect of the discussion was the similarity of the problems of qualitative educational decline, whether reported from Zambia or The Gambia, or observed by aid officials from Washington or Bonn.

Using for convenience a simple division of internal and external indicators of educational quality, the symptoms noted at the Conference can be arranged as follows:

1 Internal indicators

a *Physical infrastructure:* buildings, plant, equipment and furniture lacking or poorly maintained; likewise transport

b *Educational materials:* library resources, textbooks, readers, teaching aids and supplies lacking, scarce, obsolete or in poor condition; also materials for post-literacy and non-formal development-related education and training

c *Teaching staff:* high rates of under-trained and untrained teachers; decay of professional morale (absenteeism, moonlighting, lack of accountability, high wastage); poorly-developed in-service programmes; erosion of public confidence and respect

d *Supervision:* inspectorates poorly staffed, grounded by transport difficulties; loss of hope and enthusiasm

e *Management:* administrative bottlenecks; political interference and nepotism; departure of skilled officers for other fields

f *Organisation:* increasing class sizes, shrinking length of school year; lack of linkage between formal and non-formal education, and among non-formal programmes for out-of-school learners

g *Student flows:* poor attendance, low survival rates (high dropout), high repetition rates.

2 External indicators

a *Performance standards:* decline in scholastic attainment levels

b *Backwash effects:* examination requirements dominate curriculum and teaching strategies

c *Dichotomous development:* élite schools maintain high-quality facilities and performance while system declines overall

d *Relevance:* learning in school not geared to the social, economic and cultural environment of school leavers.

Three underlying causes of these inter-linked conditions were given special mention by many speakers. Two can almost be taken as read. The first is the unprecedented expansion and elaboration of educational systems whose requirements have outstripped their own managerial and professional capabilities. The second is the economic recession, and especially the effects of the prolonged squeeze on budgetary appropriations, high inflation rates and severe restrictions on imports, which have driven down real educational expenditures and starved the systems of essential resources. Taken together these account for a high proportion of the damage.

The third cause suggested at the Conference is less obvious. It is the long-standing lack of political commitment to educational quality. Aklilu Habte considered that African education authorities and donors alike bore a very heavy responsibility:

Since the 1961 UNESCO Addis Ababa Conference, countries and donors alike did not pay as much attention to the quality of learning as they did to the expansion of the school system. In retrospect this is a major leadership *faux pas*.

Arthur Porter drew a caricature to drive home the same point:

Ministers of education took pride, and I think some of them still do, in having their wallcharts behind their backs and putting in pins every other day as new schools were established. ... But we and they know that the standards are falling. ... But we go about making the same noises about expansion and patting ourselves on the back whilst we know that many of the schools don't even have chalk.

An insidious process has been at work. As Peter Williams pointed out, education systems embody many possibilities of 'subtle adjustment and dilution' or 'qualitative erosion', which have enabled the slide into educational mediocrity or impoverishment to pass without political notice, while quantitative expansion has continued to bring quick political rewards.

The question arises whether improving the quality of basic education can become politically important. At least three ministers of education at the Conference expressed the conviction that a turning point had been reached, and that governments could no longer postpone decisions on qualitative improvement and the re-orientation of basic education. One working group asked itself whether the quality of primary education was really a matter of public and political concern and on balance answered yes, if only because parents are so anxious about securing the best chance in life for their children. Whether or not such anxieties can be translated into the required political action may depend upon whether the remedies available are plausible both to the public and to their political leaders.

This point recurs often in Peter Williams' paper:

So many objectively sensible ideas, particularly in the area of closing the resource gap of education, founder not so much because of lack of implementation, technique and organisational machinery — although those are really very important factors I think — but because insufficient attention has been given to what we might call the social psychology of the situation in education.

Having a vision of what the education system should become was essential, but actually communicating that vision to other people and getting them to accept it was even more important. The vision of A A N'Jai (The Gambia) like that of many others at the Conference, entailed a change of orientation of primary education from its single-minded obsession with examinations and modern-sector employment, towards the needs of the impoverished and ecologically threatened rural communities where almost all the children in his country live. He wanted the Conference to emphasise

the importance of strengthening basic education to improve the quality and to improve this in the face of dwindling resources, again compounded by rapid expansion in terms of population and number of schools. ... Everybody sees his child getting to the top, aiming at white-collar jobs which clearly are beyond the ability of the majority of the people. This Conference should really worry about how to change attitudes. We must make changes in attitude otherwise I cannot see us making a breakthrough.

Time and again the participants acknowledged that major political decisions on educational policy could succeed in practice only if the leaders carried the public with them. At the same time, the public's view of education was quite unlikely to change without clear political leadership. The best policy would be for government leaders and education authorities to take the public and the teaching profession into their confidence and, to 'create systems of management and incentives which return to communities, teachers, parents and students greater control over the education process'. (Peter Williams)

This involves a type of political action which will vary in form from country to country. But its success will require a supporting process of educational development addressed to the strategic qualitative deficiencies we discussed earlier. The working groups gave detailed attention to this requirement. The question of improving management systems was considered to be of fundamental importance by the Conference and this will be discussed later. Apart from management there are vital pedagogical issues which need a fresh look, and on which African countries can help each other (if only by sharing information and experience). There seemed to be widespread support for action in the following areas in particular, identified by working groups:

1 Clarifying quite rigorously what we mean by 'quality' in basic education, so as to achieve a set of operational targets in terms of
   a Input criteria (teacher-pupil ratios, textbook-pupil ratios, teacher qualifications, etc.)
   b Process criteria (teacher-pupil relationships, motivational and learning behaviour)
   c Social criteria (school-community links)
   d Output criteria (what cognitive and psychomotor skills, at what levels?)
2 Understanding the trade-off between the length of the open access schooling cycle (six, seven, eight, nine or ten years), and the resources available, in order to maintain acceptable quality of instruction and learning at given enrolment rates
3 Investigating the factors which influence school performance under conditions of severe difficulty, especially the role of the head and the inspector, and the conditions under which teachers are able to achieve a sense of professional worth and accountability to their communities
4 Sharing information on successful links between the schools and non-formal education programmes, on deformalising primary education, and the inter-relationships of educational tasks for out-of-school learners
5 Recognising the crucial need for examination reform in basic education, aimed at using the backwash effect on curriculum to advantage, by testing process skills (like problem solving) along with content, and using examination data as a tool to monitor educational quality
6 Developing appropriate instruments to measure literacy and numeracy in various languages and cultural settings.

The list of priorities is almost limitless, and even these six tasks would pose formidable difficulties for many African states. This highlights the importance of collaborative work among African countries, perhaps on a regional basis, and between them and the aid agencies, in order to economise resources and time.

Hugh Hawes believes that, notwithstanding shortages of funds,

> we are making insufficient attempts to make the most of what we have. Much of our effort at this level is still hampered by unreasonable expectations, inappropriate methodologies, lack of basic information about the professional context, and lack of simple instruments to diagnose it, as well as by a great dearth of expertise at the crucial 'middle level' which is so critical for the monitoring and maintenance of quality. Consequently, qualitative wastage exists on a massive scale.

To deal with these three main tasks, he proposed identifying national centres of primary pedagogy, charged with undertaking:

1 Action research into the development of an appropriate pedagogy and materials suitable for use in current conditions, to improve quality in first-level education.

2 Simple usable and communicable research into ways of assessing needs of learners and of monitoring their achievement; emphasis to be placed on instruments which can be used by teachers and 'middle-level' personnel.

3 Training middle-level manpower so that they will have the skill and confidence both to provide professional leadership in current circumstances and to generate new ideas for the amelioration of practices at local level.

'What is needed' he concluded, 'is not new structures, but new emphasis and new urgency,' and probably some international stimulus and co-ordination.

It would be agreeable to leave the issue of quality on this note except that a sombre question remains. Can improvements in the quality of basic education be achieved without reducing or temporarily halting the pace of quantitative expansion? Among many participants there was a strong presumption that the rate of expansion had to be curbed.

> African governments will have to decide on whether to promote mass education, with its attendant low efficiency and high cost, or to be more realistic and place more emphasis in the short term on improving the quality of education that can be provided with the limited means that will be available for the education sector in the years ahead.
>
> *Dorothy Njeuma*

But as Manzoor Ahmed and others reminded the Conference, the extent to which any country can afford mass basic education will depend not only on the resources it makes available but also on the nature of the programme it chooses. In this view even an efficient system of universal primary education of a conventional kind may be irrelevant to the society's needs, and therefore wasteful and unproductive. The quantity, quality, relevance and affordability of basic education are therefore intimately related. Moreover, each government which wishes to redefine basic education to achieve a meaningful integration between primary schools and non-formal education programmes, both being related to the survival and development needs of the community, will have to submit its ideas to the test of public acceptability.

Basic education may be the main priority for African education, as the Conference believed, but it is not the easy option.

Extending technical and vocational education

We want people who can do things.

Joseph Kotsokoane

This sentiment ran right through the Conference discussion. Africa needed people who could make and do, produce and create, fix and repair, improvise and innovate, grow, process, design, erect, maintain and make good. Africa's education systems were not delivering the goods, hence the priority which should be accorded to technical and vocational education. Yaya Mede Moussa ranked as 'priority no. 1' for his country: 'development of middle level technical education and professional [vocational] education, as well as introduction to productive skills'.

> This priority seems to follow from the need to assure the training of necessary technicians for development in the economic sectors, both agricultural and industrial. It should also include all those non-formal elements which contribute to consolidating the economy, as well as the use of a literacy campaign as a possible alternative approach to the problems of development.

His remarks indicate the broad scope of the field. Every contributor to discussions on this topic took a similarly comprehensive view. There is a spectrum of skills training and education which should run from the basic education stage throughout the system, embracing both non-formal and formal modes: from functional literacy to integrated rural development projects linked to non-formal skills training in primary schools, to community-based projects for school-leavers, practical courses at secondary school level, craft training in and out of institutions, and so on up the ladder of technological sophistication. None of these components was analysed in detail, but the direction of the discussion is of some interest, and two specific points deserve mention.

Firstly, considerable respect was shown for non-formal approaches to skills training and technical education, and not only at the basic level. Both Arthur Porter and Philip Coombs invited the participants to look around their countries and study how skills were actually being acquired by the majority. Arthur Porter referred to indigenous apprenticeship systems for craftsmen, which seem to succeed in imbuing 'the kind of independence, the aptitude for inventiveness and innovation and self-help which are required' but which do not seem to characterise the craftsmen trained in costly technical institutes.

Formal technical education had its advocate in Arthur Kambalametore (Malawi) who pointed to its role in advanced manpower training. But as a national system for occupational training it was viewed with considerable mistrust by others.

The message they wanted to get across was that local, homegrown systems of training should be studied with a view to assessing their

45

Technical education has come up again and again. What kind of technical education? For whom? What form? If you look back over the last 30 years, not just in Africa, but in Asia and Latin America, the World Bank and various bilateral agencies have spent millions and millions of dollars on formal vocational technical secondary schools and higher technical institutes. If you look back at the record of those largely transplanted models, it is not a record that would inspire you to do more of the same. We have learned a lot about what works and what does not, and why not. Yet all of your countries, as you have emphasised, require the preparation of young people to be producers and for this they have to learn some skills. It is interesting to look at how the skills in your countries and others are being generated today. There are lots of skills there. There is need for more but there are indigenous processes going way back that are doing more to produce, let us say, automechanics than all of your formal vocational schools, and in many ways producing more versatile mechanics. Perhaps we should look hard at what might be built on that basis rather than going directly to the expensive, but not necessarily cost effective, western models of technical education.

Philip Coombs

effectiveness and seeing how they could be assisted to improve. The role of existing technical institutions should be carefully analysed in order to enable them to become more cost effective and socially relevant. In particular, they should consider diversifying their functions and offering their services to a wider clientele, especially school-leavers and adults requiring re-training or skill-upgrading. At the same time, as Arthur Kambalametore made clear, the basic educational level of the work force is continually rising, and this has important implications for the trainability of employees within industry. Employers should be reminded of their responsibilities to provide such training to their employees, and should be advised and assisted by governments in doing so.

Secondly, several speakers referred to the legacy of negative social attitudes to skills training which puts a brake on educational innovations in this field. Isaac Ojok (Uganda) spoke of a situation where 'for a long time, people were brought up to dishonour the whole idea of technical skills, even to look down upon it, and to fear it, especially for the girls'. This matter is rooted in the colonial experience of most African countries, including the operation of racially discriminatory employment practices and pay scales, as well as the traditional premium which clerical and administrative posts have enjoyed in government service. A A N'Jai identified the syndrome as the most important barrier to successfully diversifying second-level education, and made it clear where the influence of the education authorities ended and the responsibilities of others began.

Until there is far more parity between the 'white collar' and 'non-white collar' workers, with the latter able to make a reasonably comfortable living, the pressure to set foot on the road that leads to the Sixth Form in Gambia High School will continue. We must tackle the cause and not just the symptoms, and a purely educational remedy will not suffice. Social, political and economic factors are involved and must be taken into consideration by those areas of Government concerned. Education cannot be left to cure all the ills of society entirely alone.

Developing African universities

The Conference gave priority to university development but not necessarily to university expansion. It is true, as Aklilu Habte observed, that the presence of so many expatriate professionals and consultants in Africa is *prima facie* evidence of the continuing need for additional university-trained African manpower. But it was the qualitative not the quantitative contribution of African universities which drew the attention of the Conference. It was emphasised that there was no contradiction in identifying both basic and higher education as priorities. Development could not dispense with the special contribution of each.

This did not imply an indiscriminate support for university education as presently organised. Cynthia Perry reported on behalf of her working group that unit costs were excessively high and should be reduced. The pattern of evolution had favoured a large number of unavoidably small institutions which took a high proportion of national budgets but were unable, for reasons of scale, to offer the full range of faculties and disciplines. Considering the negative history of regional universities in the subcontinent it was necessary to strengthen national universities and enable them to better serve regional requirements on a co-operatively planned basis. And a strategy must be found, said Aklilu Habte, to overcome these constraints and promote 'the development of quality institutions and centres of excellence'. One working group thought this might involve incorporating the network of free-standing government-sponsored research institutes into the university system and building up the links between the research base and the users of data and advice.

Arthur Porter and Aklilu Habte both emphasised that universities were unique repositories of intellectual strength in African countries and ought to regard themselves, and be regarded by governments, as an essential resource in the development process. 'The problems of our increasing or continuing under-development' as Arthur Porter called them, should be on a permanent agenda of discussion between governments and universities. This implied a degree of confidence between the two parties which had not always been present. It implied also that universities, as *thinking* institutions (as distinct from manpower training units), would be in a position to offer data, analysis, criticism and advice of convincing quality. It is not just a question of universities having the right kind of expertise and experience and a strong engagement with national needs. It requires as an essential precondition that governments safeguard the intellectual liberty of their scholars, and if possible take pride in doing so.

The uncomfortable truth, as some speakers noted, is that many university campuses have become potential or *de facto* centres of political opposition, among either academic staff or students or both. Sometimes university communities have been in the forefront of popular mobilisation against oppressive and corrupt regimes. In other cases, even constitutional governments have mistaken brave and forthright criticism for subversion, and have responded with displays of force. In brief, the essential concordat between governments and universities is still in process of evolution in many countries in Africa. However, once the credentials of a university and government, and a satisfactory working relationship between them, have been established, universities will be in a position to sponsor round-table discussions between different ministries which would otherwise find difficulty in dealing jointly with issues which cut across portfolio boundaries. Universities could thus become places where key information is gathered, where people involved in development can meet, where ideas can be talked through, serving not only as leading intellectual resources for development but as brokers or catalysts in the process of policy review. As Aklilu Habte noted wryly, if universities continued to cost governments so much (as in general they both would and should), then governments should get their money's worth.

In the same spirit, universities must continually improve the relevance of their work to national needs. They must be brought closer to the development process and become more aware of their importance in the community. This has many implications. Among those mentioned were:

1 The need to concentrate far more research and action on the essential priority of food production and food security

2 The role of universities in promoting the adaptation of technologies, not only in developing items of equipment, but in devising appropriate technological approaches to meeting local needs

3 The broadening of universities' role in non-formal education, through extension activities which would bring appropriate university specialists into closer touch with communities, in response to their requirements for knowledge or understanding of development problems

4 Finally, achieving a greater degree of flexibility within universities in responding to manpower needs, sometimes for the training of very small numbers of specialists.

Improving management systems in education

Development is a long-range process and we all know it. But we keep on and on responding to immediate pressures. The short-range frustrates the long-range because what is done today does not contain the developmental seed for tomorrow. As a result, the long-range developmental impact that we all aspire for Africa never comes. Can this be changed? Should it? By whom? How?

Aklilu Habte

These words capture the mood of educational leaders whose sense of their nations' strategic incapacity was a recurring theme of the Conference. Africa's education systems need both visionary leadership and well-informed, clear-sighted, professionally committed and resourceful managers at all levels: men and women who by degrees will turn the tide of decline and achieve a revival of educational quality and relevance. The need and the hope are easy to express, but it cannot be doubted that the management task in African education is one of exceptional difficulty.

It is not just that the scale of education systems is so vast. Most systems have been starved of funds for years, while enrolments have continued to rise and demand has not slackened, with consequences which have been amply described elsewhere in the book. Accompanying the impoverishment of large tracts of the subcontinent's education systems has been a corresponding decline in administrative performance. Some participants also referred to a growing trend of political intervention in civil service appointments, resulting in unnecessary breaks in continuity and a paralysis of initiative by career officers. But what troubled the Conference most was the pervasive lack of management capacity throughout the education system. Participants did not give much attention to the causes of this problem or assign reponsibility for it. They simply asserted the priority of building capacity in management and planning as a matter of great urgency. This meant, among other things, strengthening national or regional management training institutes, so that Africa's capacity to build her own management capacity would be enhanced. Part of the frustration reflected in the discussion may be attributed to the fact that countries with poorly managed education systems are not only less capable of self-reliant development, but lack many of the means to make themselves more capable. It followed that participants saw the strengthening of management capacity as a principal field for external assistance. Much of the discussion of management was therefore linked to aid and will be reported in the next chapter.

The Conference took a comprehensive view of management needs. One working group thought that such needs were 'virtually limitless'. However, they identified the following management functions as particularly important, noting that they were all inter-related in principle, although in practice the connections were often weak or absent:

1 Quantitative data collection, analysis and use
2 Qualitative data collection, analysis and use
3 System analysis, planning and evaluation
4 Project planning, management and evaluation
5 Management of maintenance systems
6 Procurement and distribution of educational materials
7 Stock control
8 Financial and cost analysis, planning, management and accounting
9 System administration
10 Institutional management
11 Educational supervision
12 Use of research as a tool of educational management and qualitative improvement
13 Personnel management and industrial relations.

The working groups and plenary discussions gave particular emphasis to the planning function, which was seen as a necessary common factor in almost all the management tasks within education systems, and a necessary link between education and overall national or local economic and social planning.

Effective planning at any level requires skills of analysis and interpretation, the ability to monitor events, diagnose errors and propose corrective action, to make educational objectives operational, and estimate what resources would be required and how they should be obtained, and to map out procedures for implementation and review. Such skills must be widely developed:

> Planning functions should be considered as an integral part of management and not as marginal activities undertaken mysteriously by experts, foreign or local. Planning and management start in the classroom and are needed in all levels and all sectors.

Working Group 2. Report on Theme II
Chairman: Sam Aleyideino (Nigeria)

A fundamental prerequisite for these joint planning and management tasks is access to comprehensive and reliable data.

> Again and again the point was made that we need better management, but you cannot have effective planning or management unless you have facts; not all the facts in the world, but the minimum essential facts to know what is going on in education, to be able to evaluate it, to identify shortcomings that need to be corrected. That is the function of management. But we need information systems that will let us know.

Philip Coombs

Unfortunately, the data available to planners is often incomplete or inaccurately reported from the source and not verified. Those responsible for storing it may not be able to retrieve it easily, or to interpret it fully, and explain or present it to those who need to use it. These are technical deficiencies which training can help correct, and it is needed on a very wide scale, much of it at institutional and local level. What requires equally serious attention is the frequency with which staff with planning responsibilities are moved about, destroying continuity in data management and control, and the low status or marginalisation of planning staff within some ministries, which effectively depreciates not only the advice they may be able to give, but the information at their disposal. The remedy lies squarely in the hands of the governments concerned.

However, it must be stressed that skilful record-keepers, data managers, and analysts are needed throughout the education system, in each school, college and education office, not just at the headquarters where the statisticians are employed. Moreover, effective management in the field, including the management of innovation or educational resources, requires relevant data of a qualitative nature about educational attainment or teacher competence — information which is usually compiled and controlled by examinations officials or inspectors. Unless it is analysed and addressed such data is inert and useless, but qualitative analysis should be seen as part of the normal, routine two-way traffic of information between management and the field,

> enabling vital feedback to be made to the appropriate practitioners . . . as well as illuminating the minds of policy-makers (or donors). Qualitative data on student performance could put power into the hands of inspectors and supervisors. Interpretation of examination scores could be fed back to textbook writers.

Working Group 2. Theme II
Chairman: Sam Aleyideino

In principle, these ministry-based information systems should be linked in with educational research networks comprising university education faculties, colleges and research institutes. In practice, such collaborative research was considered to be poorly developed and in need of considerably more assistance in order to secure a strong and permanent local research capacity.

Conference participants were much impressed with the need for African educationists to share experiences and information across national boundaries, if only to avoid making the same errors as their neighbours. Kebby Musokotwane was not alone in pointing out the desirability of creating 'a mechanism for the African to know about *African* education rather than knowing about education in one particular country', and two working groups saw UNESCO's NEIDA as one among several regional agencies which could be helped to fulfil this role more effectively. Going one step further, it was envisaged that African countries could identify their own cadre of advisers and 'develop consultancy services in response to our needs and reduce dependence on overseas experts' (Arthur Kambalametore).

A common impulse motivating all these concerns was the desire to redress the imbalance of information *about their own systems* between African countries and the aid agencies to whom they looked for assistance, and to boost the professional capacity available to African governments in policy formulation, project preparation and implementation. The Conference found common ground in the proposition that African governments must assume responsibility for establishing their own educational priorities. Equally it was recognised that the policy-making process would continue to be prejudiced by the continuing weakness of many African countries in data-gathering, research, planning and management. Ralph Romain summed up his written contribution to the Conference in a passage which, slightly edited, states the case both for African autonomy over education policy and a collaborative effort to put more muscle into the exercise of such autonomy:

> Let me summarise then. Determining education priorities is rather like childbirth — it takes time, it is painful, but no one else can do it for the mother. Meaningful aid and aid co-ordination can be achieved only on the basis of well considered priorities over which the country maintains close control. It follows then that ... we might devote attention to assuring and strengthening the country capacity in managing, planning and researching education, the capacity to produce first-rate development policies and plans which would in turn help to stimulate and guide aid and external as well as internal collaboration in development. That capacity has never been at once more severely threatened and more urgently needed than in the present financial crisis.

And so we turn to the second theme of the Conference: aid responses to Africa's educational priorities.

Chapter 3
Aid

This chapter examines

The nature of the aid process

1 Historical forces which have affected present provision and policies in aid (p. 53)

2 Some aspects of present policies; the difference in style and emphasis betweeen individual aid donors (p. 54)

3 Some lessons from experience explicitly stated at the Conference and implicit in its choice of agenda for discussion (p. 56)

4 The political dimension of aid, and its importance (p. 57)

Some directions for aid assistance

1 The role of aid to education in

   a Strengthening the base of information from which policy decisions derive (p. 59)

   b Helping systems to define and clarify policy priorities (p. 63)

   c Strengthening structures and improving expertise in management at all levels in the education system (p. 64)

2 Three sectors in greater detail

   a Basic education (p. 66)

   b Agricultural education (p. 69)

   c University education (p. 70)

The efficiency of the aid process

1 Better management of aid projects (p. 71)

2 Achieving greater continuity and flexibility in the provision of aid assistance and in its management (p. 72)

3 Facilitating co-ordination between sectors such as education, agriculture and health (p. 74)

4 Making the best use of funds available for training through examining its nature, type and location (p. 74)

5 Harmonising aid agency efforts (p. 77)

This chapter summarises two and a half days of rich and frank discussions about the role of aid to education in Africa in the light of the priorities identified in the previous days. As with the second chapter, little attempt is made to draw firm recommendations, but where there was a very high level of agreement we have attempted to signal the consensus.

Readers of this chapter may do well to approach the report, as the participants did, by reading first the two lead papers by Dorothy Njeuma

This chapter has been written by Kevin Lillis and Hugh Hawes, drawing on a wealth of material mainly but not entirely from Theme II of the Conference: lead papers, plenary sessions and group reports as well as 'think pieces' from participants, and papers submitted by aid agencies.

and Kenneth King which so effectively launched the Conference into its plenary and discussion groups, together with the analysis of policies and priorities of a selected number of aid donors, made available in Ian Clifton-Everest's background paper to the Conference and also reproduced in the second half of this report (p. 149)

This chapter is divided into four parts. The first reminds us that the map of aid provision is not a simple one. Present provision is influenced by past policies and concerns, and the whole process is naturally influenced by the social, the economic and the political traditions of the countries that are providing the aid. In particular, the Conference emphasised that the aid process cannot be divorced from political influences and political decision-making.

The second part examines the theme 'directions for aid', and looks at possible aid responses to identified priorities, both in respect of making systems of education more relevant to needs and efficient in their operation, and also in terms of allocating and maintaining resources in one level or sector against another.

The third part summarises discussions on how to improve the processes of identifying priority areas for aid, discussing them, negotiating aid and managing it.

The last part of the chapter deals with the compelling need to harmonise the efforts of the different aid agencies so that they work to the benefit of the African partners.

Past policies, present concerns

The legacy of past aid policies

To understand present patterns of aid provision requires a historical perspective as well as a comparative one. Ian Clifton-Everest's paper emphasises the enormous diversity within the donor fraternity of forms and styles of assistance. Some donors' policies such as those of Sweden have remained relatively constant while others such as those of the United Kingdom have evolved significantly over the years. In particular, those of the largest donor, the World Bank, have changed from being committed to secondary and further education in the late 1960s, to a priority on first level education and on the improvement of educational management in the early 1980s.

These developments, in turn, need to be set in the time frame of world economic and political events — and very momentous and disturbing events these were. They affected not only the direction of aid but also the urgency of demands and the amount of provision. For the period spans times of growth and optimism as well as times of economic crisis and near despair.

The provision of aid and its use are not normally sudden and spontaneous phenomena. It takes time to generate proposals, time to set up and operate aid-assisted projects, and yet more time to change emphasis from one priority to another. Nor is it easy to withdraw from commitments already entered into. Projects achieve their own momentum, and it is virtually impossible to 'choke off' demand for a certain type of educational provision once it has been offered. Hence aid projects in the present live with the policies of the past. Both donors and African governments have a great deal less room to manoeuvre than one would think.

The understanding of these historical forces is essential to partners in the aid process and for this reason, international analyses such as Phillips'* and Clifton-Everest's, as well as others produced nationally, are particularly valuable. Ian Clifton-Everest suggests, modestly, that his paper could form the basis for someone to undertake a more detailed and comprehensive survey of the field, and the commissioning of such a work could be a useful additional outcome of this Conference.

Present priorities

The variation in mode of operation between the bilateral and multilateral aid agencies represented at the Conference is evident from a reading both of their own literature and from Clifton-Everest's summary of it. It was also made very clear by the donors themselves in their contributions to the final two days of the Conference. Donor policies vary as to the countries to which they give a greater or smaller proportion of aid; as to their preferred modes of operation (some donors favour increased rigour in the devising and monitoring of their projects while others would seem to favour a move towards greater flexibility); as to the amount and quality of data which they require as a preliminary to embarking on an aid project; and finally — of vital importance to those attending this Conference — in the sectors and activities which they would characterise as particularly aid-worthy.

Consider the statements offered by participants from four aid agencies on the final day of the Conference.

1 The World Bank

One-third of the Bank's education projects and one-quarter of its expenditure on education go to Africa. The Bank lends to all sectors of education.

> If anyone has the feeling that the Bank *a priori* is not going to finance this sector or that sub-sector, he is absolutely wrong. The Bank's policy allows any country to borrow in a broad spectrum of ideas. What is needed is to make sure that what you are asking for is fully justified and falls within the country's priorities.
>
> *Aklilu Habte (The World Bank)*

Nevertheless, the Bank has maintained certain emphases. In the past three years these have been on primary education and technical education, and reviews have recently been set in motion with the Bank to look into ways in which, among other things, the emphasis on training could be increased, particularly in Africa.

2 UNICEF

UNICEF is in many ways different in character from the other agencies represented, since its funds derive from countries in both the North and the South. Its programmes are particularly slanted towards achieving a whole and integrated approach towards the betterment of young children. Hence UNICEF emphasises basic education, which is so much wider in

---

*H.M. Phillips, *Educational Cooperation between Developed and Developing Countries* (New York: Praeger, 1976).

conception than mere primary schooling, and any programme which promotes co-operation both intersectorally and internationally for the benefit of children.

> Perhaps we should talk about international co-operation rather than aid and donor and recipient. This is not just a semantic matter, but perhaps a new frame of mind we need to think about.
>
> *Manzoor Ahmed (UNICEF)*

3 USAID

For USAID, a clear current priority is the improvement of food production in Africa and the development of institutions to help achieve this goal. This implies strengthening university level programmes in agriculture, and the provision of further assistance to established institutions such as Makerere, Njala, Ibadan and Nsukka Universities which USAID had supported in the early 1970s. Thus agricultural education becomes a vehicle for the wider priority of improving quality in university level institutions.

At the other end of the educational spectrum, there is concern with basic education as a means for achieving food production and food security — with the question, as yet open, as to whether basic education in its present form represents the surest means to achieve this end.

> There is a question in our own minds as to the role that basic education plays in food production. Is it a long-term investment? . . . Questions of desertification, water management, reafforestation, crop research to increase yields, dry land farming, food security: are these being addressed by basic education? Are they being addressed anywhere in the spectrum of education? . . . We are talking of putting assistance over a period of 25 years, not five or ten years, to developing institutions to achieve these things.
>
> *Cynthia Perry (USAID)*

4 GTZ

The emphasis of West German technical co-operation has traditionally been upon technical and vocational education, though an analysis of some of their latest policy statements reveals other emergent concerns such as the development of local capacities for curriculum planning at all levels. One key need currently identified is to help alleviate the crisis of school leaver unemployment at all levels, thus making a more rational and co-ordinated transition from school to work.

> GTZ would very much like in its projects, especially in the large-scale regional development projects with various countries, to link education with other sectors — which means putting an education component especially into integrated rural development projects. For example, strengthening the teaching of agriculture, domestic science, art and craft at primary school level, and linking these in with rural development schemes so that there could be a co-ordinated approach in extension work in health, agriculture and other sectors parallel to primary education.
>
> *Herbert Bergmann (GTZ)*

A fuller statement of national priorities for these agencies and others such as ODA is to be found in Ian Clifton-Everest's review in Part II of this report. But these four examples illustrate the differences in emphasis and of style of the various agencies.

For the Conference participants, such insights into aid agency priorities and styles was a major outcome of the four days.

Lessons from experience

If the present evolves from the past, how far has our experience of the past decades of educational assistance helped us to re-evaluate present approaches? The mere fact that the Conference was taking place indicates a concern to reappraise and review the past. Indeed, there were those present who were deeply critical of the previous approach and orientation. As one participant stated

> If aid will continue in the form that it has been to education, in the form that it is to our countries, we can forget about it. . . . We have to change the format.
>
> *Joseph Rugumyamheto (Tanzania)*

The priorities identified by the Conference also indicate concern. Saying that something needs to be done now, indicates that it was not done or not done adequately in years previously. Thus the Conference called

1 For increased emphasis on information gathering and information sharing *because* aid decisions in the past frequently lacked such a data base
2 For increased investment in human resource development *because* earlier projects had often concentrated on physical plant rather than people
3 For increased attention to the training of personnel in planning and management at all levels *because* of the enormous gaps which have opened up between educational intentions and educational reality.

Many such judgements born of experience were implicit in the contributions made to the Conference, others were explicit. The World Bank's Operation and Evaluation Department, for example, had identified at least three lessons related to project implementation which seemed to repeat themselves year after year. Aklilu Habte summarised their conclusions:

> One is that projects which from the very beginning did not have the serious commitment of the country, projects which have been imposed or unduly influenced by donors . . . have generally been failures for one reason or another.
>
> Secondly, many of the projects have not been too successful, not because the capital was lacking, not because the equipment was lacking, but because the human skill, the human and institutional capacity was not in place.
>
> Thirdly, it has been said that agency bureaucracy takes a long time to generate a project. But let me tell you the other side of the picture. Projects which have been prepared too quickly and have not been well thought out will also tend to fail.

It would be naive, therefore, to maintain that the aid process does not evolve with time or that discussions such as those which took place at Windsor were not powerful instruments to help in such evolution. The key question, however, is the speed at which it can evolve given the urgent agenda sketched out in our first two chapters, or more starkly in the World Bank's own document *Toward Sustained Development in Sub-Saharan Africa* (1984). That speed is also closely affected by the political process, which profoundly influences both the requesting and the provision of aid.

The political dimension of aid

The political nature of the aid process was underlined in the last two days by participants from Africa, who emphasised in no uncertain terms that this issue had been insufficiently weighted by the Conference organisers. Politicians from donor and recipient countries are ultimately responsible for decisions on who to offer aid to and seek aid from, on aid priorities, and linkage with short- or long-term trade and political relations.

Bilateral political and economic relationships are often sensitive, and for this reason multilateral education aid retains strong appeal for African governments. It could be pointed out, and was pointed out by Ian Buist of ODA, that international agencies, in particular UNESCO, may have become slow and bureaucratic in comparison with the comparatively smoother operation of national aid bodies. But African participants were unimpressed if the corollary of this argument was that UNESCO had forfeited its claim to support. Speaker after speaker, including most of the ministers present, made special reference to the issue. Not one voice from Africa was raised to support the possible withdrawal of Britain from UNESCO.

In relation to bilateral negotiations, it was also clear that no men and women of maturity and goodwill expected the aid process to be either wholly self-interested or wholly disinterested. Benefits from the aid process flow from South to North as well as North to South. Aid belongs among the cultural, political and trade links between countries and groups of countries which are vital to all partners, not least the donors.

Because of this political quality of the aid negotiation, three lessons emerged from the discussion. The first is, very simply, the importance of involving politicians, executives and professionals together in the discussion of the aid process. One suspects that this is not done as frequently as it might be. The plan is frequently prepared *for* and not *with* political leaders. The depth of understanding gained by early involvement of politician and professional together strengthens any proposal and the possibility of its success.

> I do not agree with the paper by Arthur Porter which speaks of political interference in planning. I want to think of the politician as part and parcel of the planning process.
>
> *Kebby Musokotwane (Zambia)*

The second lesson is the need to cultivate a high level of mutual understanding and reciprocal exchange between leaders at the political level. The point was emphasised in the plenary discussion by several African ministers. Much as they valued the opportunity to get to know senior aid agency officials at the Conference, this was no substitute for free and informal discussions between ministers involved in the aid relationship. In particular, political initiatives in aid policy by donor governments (such as the questions of overseas student fees and UNESCO reform) call for consideration and response by the appropriate political leaders of the recipient governments. In future, no reasonable opportunity should be missed for mutual exchanges between ministers engaged in the aid relationship, on the basis of full reciprocity and respect.

The third lesson is the need for candour in the aid process. Many educational aid packages have covert cultural, political or economic ramifications, whether short-term or long-term. A recent example, cited at the Conference, was the large British project to supply computers to Indian schools. This project is unusual in British educational aid practice since it was directly linked to a trade promotion campaign on behalf of British exports to the Indian computer market. No attempt was made in this case to conceal the connection between aid and trade, and such openness is essential if mutual confidence between the parties to the aid transaction is to be sustained. An aid project should not be like a Trojan horse (to use King's metaphor): admirable at first sight, but containing within it all sorts of potentially destructive influences.

One welcomes the kind of honest analysis offered by Charles Bassett of CIDA:

> First of all we [Canadians] are interested in social justice, and if you do polls as we do every year in Canada as to whether you should have an aid programme, there are always two-thirds in favour of an aid programme for all sorts of vague reasons, but the common denominator is humanitarian. There is a bit of guilt in there, and there is a bit of self-serving too, because people who are as well off as Canadians are really feeling very guilty when they see on the television screens the things that are going on in Ethiopia, Mozambique and Chad. The second reason is to promote peace and stability in the world because we figure that as long as you have disadvantaged nations you are going to continue the chances of having instability. . . . The third sort of thing that we are interested in is our own national identity and national sovereignty. We want to exist in the world as Canadians. We do not want to be a former British colony; we do not want to be a dependency of the United States. We want to stand on our own feet and be recognised as such. Then the fourth thing we want in the world is that we want to do some trade. Let us get it out on the table. . . . If I look at some of the countries in Africa, for 15 years we are not going to have a big trade relationship, but maybe 50 years from now we will. Nations have a habit, you know, of having a history that goes beyond 50 years.

Directions for aid

An attempt to separate strands from two days of wide-ranging group and plenary discussions may result in a series of arbitrary and unsatisfactory divisions. But the risk must be taken in order to summarise the discussions and to highlight areas of consensus. These were significant, the more so because there was little observable difference in emphasis between members of the various interest groups who sat together to identify them.

This summary concentrates on what was debated during the last two days of the Conference, not on what was left out, however important it may be. Three themes in particular recurred throughout the Conference without being given sustained attention: population education, the role of basic education in women's development, and the training of school-leavers for productive work. Their omission from serious discussion in relation to aid reflects only the shortness of time available and not any hidden ordering of emphases.

For ease of presentation, those issues which related to the improvement of the structure and management of the education system have been separated from those which related to the different levels and sectors.

Structures and management

Three issues were discussed here:

1 The need to strengthen and review the information base from which education policy decisions, as well as decisions about aid, were taken

2 The need to strengthen the policy-making process and facilitate the identification of priorities

3 The need to improve management, including planning capabilities, at all levels in order to help systems cope more effectively with the great and conflicting demands placed upon them.

1 Strengthening the information base

Ability to make rational aid decisions depends to a great degree upon the information available to decision-makers, as well as upon their capacity to interpret and understand it. They need to know about

a The administrative structures, policies, operating procedures, and above all the conceptual maps of both partners in the aid process, for if partners are miscommunicating, the process of negotiation is built on very shaky foundations

b The conditions, needs and absorptive capabilities of countries receiving aid

c The availability of relevant expertise in donor countries.

These points are fully discussed in Kenneth King's paper. Everyone at Windsor may not have agreed with all the inferences he drew from his data, but his main points won wide acceptance for their relevance and timeliness. He identified the following weaknesses.

Firstly, *each party lacks an adequate 'map' of the other's system.* The preparation of such maps is a complicated and value-laden operation — and bears little relation to the conventional 'shopping list' of projects whose aid-worthiness is subjected to appraisal. One example will suffice. If the need for technical assistance to a particular country is being considered, such 'map-making' might include delicate issues such as the assessment of where foreign co-operation and advice would be both necessary and acceptable, an assessment of what country, or agencies within a country, provide the most relevant experience, an analysis of the roles which might be played by external advisers (for example, in teacher education, planning, the inspectorate, or curriculum development), whether such personnel should hold staff or line positions, and how much visibility or authority they should have in the host system.

At issue here is the degree of influence which independent countries are prepared to allow foreign technical assistance personnel. Hence the vital task of making such maps demands considerable sensitivity, cultural and political awareness and indeed, empathy from the cartographers.

King's second point relates to the *unequal access to information between donors and African countries.* He argues that because of their intense concentration on priority sectors or sub-sectors, the trained personnel at their disposal, and their often superior analytical capacity, their privileged access as donor agencies to local information and their sustained institutional memories, individual donor countries often know more about certain aspects of individual African education systems than local officials do. Such agencies have the further advantage of a vast store of comparative data virtually denied to single countries, and once donors begin — as they are now doing — to compare available data, their joint knowledge is very considerable. Lack of information, combined with swift turnover in personnel and lack of training and experience in national ministries, put African countries in a weak position when aid negotiations take place.

Such imbalance was recognised in discussion, but it was also very clear that there were areas where nobody — least of all the donors — has sufficient and credible information. Two categories were mentioned, the first being educational statistics. In many cases, statistical data are barely acceptable as a basis for credible planning. What may be needed in such cases, in order to permit informed decisions to be taken, is to develop reasonably reliable and easily-applied techniques of sampling reality, in which national officials might if necessary receive technical assistance from aid agencies.

The second category relates to qualitative information about systems. We may know how many schools there are, and sometimes what they are supposed to teach, but we are often ignorant of what they teach and how. We may have statistics of marks in examinations, but little idea of what these marks are supposed to measure, whether they have actually measured it, what are the implications of an analysis of the results, and a host of other essential data.

Hugh Hawes presented the issue in story form:

> An inspector in Sierra Leone, conscientious and concerned, forms a shrewd suspicion that nearly half the Class III children in his area can't really read (as distinct from knowing their class readers by heart). But he has some difficulty in proving this since no one seems to be able to tell him what reading attainment at this level could be expected or how to measure it. He consults the Institute of Education in Freetown and discovers that no standardised reading tests have been developed in Sierra Leone or anywhere else in anglophone Africa. He shrugs his shoulders and busies himself with something easier to manage — like checking enrolments.

At a more descriptive level, we have very little idea of the sociology of education in the communities for which it is provided: the aspirations, motivations and priorities of the communities. This gap is serious enough already, but becomes even more significant once we begin to think of greater community participation in education.

King's third point *suggests that both donors and recipients lack knowledge of what experience and expertise in donor countries can be most usefully shared.* Often, he claims, 'experts' working for donor agencies are more experienced in educational practices in Asia or Africa than they are in those of their own countries.

This lack of knowledge on both sides would not particularly matter if the donor were simply giving financial aid to supporting local educational structures, but very often aid is given to transfer or implement a particular project for primary school improvement, for vocational training or decentralised management. So it does become important whether the 'export model' has any relationship to the well-tried system which the aiding community has grown up with or whether it is an experimental model which perhaps makes eminently good sense to the aid community but exists nowhere in the form that is being suggested.

From the analysis of the issues presented and the discussion which followed, a number of strategies for action emerged.

Sharing

There is need for greater sharing of information between partners in the aid process. At one level, it is obvious that greater access to comparative data on projects needs to be encouraged. Far more subtle is the opportunity for deeper knowledge and understanding at regional meetings of the type held in Windsor, or by arranging attachments of senior officials between the partners in development co-operation. (SIDA, for one, has arranged such attachments.) Donors differ at present in their willingness to allow others access to their own procedures and information.

One aspect of sharing identified at the Conference is relatively easily accomplished. That is the collaboration of donors in their requests for information from African countries. Too often, hardworked officials find themselves being called upon to produce virtually the same voluminous sets of information for different agencies, though in different formats and with different emphases.

There is a strong case for proposing, as did one working group

i That donors working in the same sector in the same country should do all they can to harmonise their data requirements, show willingness to use sector reviews prepared for or by other donors, or preferably collaborate with each other and the government in deciding the coverage and frequency of such reviews

ii Donors should as far as possible standardise formal project documentation and reporting procedures and

iii Donors should seek the recipient government's approval, which should not unreasonably be withheld, to publish and widely disseminate all useful reports which they had commissioned on aspects of the recipient's education system.

Working Group 2. Report on Theme II
Chairman: Sam Aleyideino (Nigeria)

This touches on the very sensitive issues of dissemination of reports and raises the question of who controls the release of documentation (and to whom), and what roles the various stake-holders have in the process.

Redefining

There is an urgent need to redefine the kind of information that could profitably be collected. The need for an up-to-date statement of the purposes, priorities and modes of operation of different aid agencies has already been mentioned, as well as the 'aid topographies' suggested in King's mapping exercise.

Next there exists the problem of defining the qualitative information so sorely needed, including the politically sensitive sampling of reality especially in remote or otherwise difficult areas. Although seminars and conference reports, in their wordy way, have addressed the issue of qualitative aspects of educational planning, simple manuals of value to the hardworking planning officer or aid administrator have yet to emerge.

It would also be profitable to re-examine *who* collects the information. If expatriate researchers funded by aid agencies have collected material about African schools and their communities, it is certainly not because they are the most suitable persons to do so. It is because the information had not been collected locally. Hence a very considerable challenge is presented to African universities and to those who support them. This issue is taken up in greater depth in another section.

Strengthening and training
In discussing how the collection of information could be increased and improved, working groups recognised that the process could well start *internationally*. The activities of existing agencies which collect data could be strengthened, particularly those which offer training of trainers (often in-country), both in the wider area of planning and in the narrower one of data collection and analysis. Networks such as NEIDA, bodies such as UNESCO's Department of Educational Statistics, IIEP in Paris, together with UNESCO's BREDA in Dakar were mentioned.

Nationally, there is need to support bodies charged with the collection of information. This might extend to the provision of support for new units or centres. In addition to the provision of increased staffing and training, there is need to initiate discussions on which kinds of information should and could be collected, and for what purpose.

An essential feature of such centres would be the capacity to acquire, store and use relevant international data — and here bodies such as UNICEF, UNESCO and the World Bank have vast resources to offer — and also to gather all relevant information within national systems. For example, they should house data on non-formal as well as formal education, information on demography, on agriculture, on health, those bodies of knowledge so essential to development and so related to education, but so frequently unavailable to decision-makers because they are encapsulated in many separate ministries.

One footnote needs to be added to the issue of training. The collection of information on which to plan is not the purview of a particular breed of experts specially trained and brandishing certificates to prove it. Such beings are necessary, but largely to collate and analyse the information which other people collect. At the end of the line it is the field worker, the teacher, the head, the education officer, the inspector, who controls the quantity and quality of the information on which vital planning decisions are made. Unless planners are able to convey to these practitioners not only how to collect information, but why it is important to collect it, and unless they are convinced that the information that they have so laboriously collected is used effectively, these individuals will neglect its collection, or, if they are of an imaginative turn of mind, they will make it up. Hence the strengthening of *local* management and training is central to the information process.

2 Defining purpose and priorities

The need to define purpose and priorities is common to all partners in the aid process. In particular, it is essential to countries seeking aid assistance if they are to maintain true control of their own educational policies. A country which has vague or conflicting ideas of its educational development is clearly more susceptible to the influence of its aid partners who themselves can be swayed by trains of thought within the international aid community. The following contribution from Ralph Romain (World Bank) points the argument:

> The basis of aid co-ordination is a *solidly conceived and articulated notion of where the system is heading.* It is not an *ad hoc* inspiration of the occasional expert or team of experts. Occasional views are in fact better received and accommodated within a strong setting, within a sound knowledge of priorities.

Vital though it is, the determination of priorities is not easy. Those who fight to achieve it have to negotiate a whole defence line of autonomous institutions, bureaucratic structures, self-interest and lack of knowledge about the system as a whole. There are also, as Kenneth King pointed out, inevitable differences in emphasis between the priorities perceived at political and at professional level in respect of both donors and recipients.

Increasingly, moreover, educational priorities may have to be related to and sometimes even justified against other sectors of the economy, particularly in times of crisis. Indeed, there were some participants at the Conference itself who saw reason for questioning the priority of educational provision against the urgent demands of agriculture and communications.

> By acceding to a popular demand for education, scarce resources have been diverted from these tasks. The starving masses in Africa need food, not textbooks. It is time to put first things first. Schools can come later.
>
> *Paul Hurst (EDC)*

So the administrator of educational projects in an aid agency may have to justify his case to others (often economists), while the minister of education in Africa has to make his case to the whole cabinet and especially the treasury. This is complicated sometimes, as one minister observed, by the fact that aid officials may be visiting different ministries, stimulating them to make cases for the priority of their particular programmes and thus promoting competition between ministries for scarce resources. In one sense, those seeking to justify expenditure on education are frequently at a disadvantage. The eventual outcomes are far less easy to measure and take far longer to become apparent than the provision of roads or dams.

To talk, as we educationists must do, of a process that goes further than merely to produce *trained* personnel to meet some specific development need, but rather develops *educated* men and women who are able to identify and find ways of meeting future needs, is to invite polite agreement but little hard commitment. Indeed, it can be envisaged that if political and economic situations become yet bleaker it will be increasingly difficult to justify education in its wider and more holistic sense — a profoundly disturbing conclusion since it is only that wider and deeper education which will free cultures from intellectual dependency.

Three main implications for aid emerge from discussions on policy and priorities.

The first is the importance at individual project level of the full and careful analysis of the objectives of a programme or project set within a wider context of overall priorities. Such an analysis would need to be done co-operatively between the two aid partners with the national representatives in the major role. Strange though it may appear, this process is *not* always followed, though agencies such as GTZ are now beginning to include it as a major component in project preparation.

The second is the promotion of opportunities for broad and deep discussion of priorities at national and, in some cases, at regional level, together with discussion of the implications of these priorities. Such a process needs to be carried down to the level of local implementation. If, for instance, it is agreed that the promotion of self-sufficiency in food is an overriding priority in the content and structures of educational programmes, there would be need to discuss how *all* educational agencies (teachers, heads, administrators, inspectors, examinations organisers) in collaboration with the vitally related sectors such as agriculture and health, could contribute towards this goal. A similar set of discussions could follow an organisational priority such as the improvement of management practices.

The third is, as ever, for training. Here there is an urgent need to lift training courses above the level of the mere preparation of educational technicians. It is vital that the issue of priorities — and priorities seen in their widest sense — should be deeply considered in any training offered to educationists of experience. Techniques of curriculum development, organising planning units, or heading institutions are themselves of very limited value unless they are fundamentally linked to this issue of priorities.

3 Strengthening national capabilities for planning and management

The importance of aid assistance in developing planning and management skills may seem so obvious as to need little elaboration. It is a common feature of all agency reports, as well as an issue where one sensed complete unanimity during the Conference. But in addition to stressing the urgency of the task, there was also consensus that the nature and scope of that task had to be redefined, with important implications for the aid process.

Certainly, inefficiency in the management of resources, which is wasteful at any time, must be strenuously resisted and overcome. Yet there is a widespread conviction that the regular administration of ministries of education and schools in the region is deteriorating not improving, and both governments and donors may need help in understanding what is occurring before effective remedial action can be applied.

In fact, the inclination of the Conference was to urge a much wider field of action, with a central emphasis on developing the autonomy and decision-making capacities of managers, including those at local level. For the scarcity of resources requires not only better husbandry, but also the ability to envisage alternative solutions (many of these, inevitably, being local solutions).

In these circumstances, educational managers will need to cultivate an openness to unusual influences and a breadth of understanding in order to reformulate both their priorities and the implications for educational practice. The Conference therefore advocated a review of conventional conceptions of planning and management, as well as a concentrated effort to improve practice and develop skills.

The scope for donor assistance towards improving planning and management attracted detailed consideration. Two related aspects were discussed. The wider issue, that of assistance to national and local capacity-building in management, is considered briefly in this section. The more sharply focused topic of how specifically to improve the management of aid projects is dealt with in the second part of this chapter.

Training in management planning and data collection was identified as one of the major areas where overseas assistance could make a timely and significant impact. Donors have roles to play in staff development in all the management and planning fields outlined earlier in this section at both central and local levels.

At *central level*, assistance would be welcome in the following fields:

a Strengthening and supporting in-country training initiatives sponsored by specialist agencies of UNESCO, such as the IIEP (this was referred to above).

b The provision of fellowships to these and other training programmes specially constructed to meet the needs of the region.

c Help towards the establishment and strengthening of national capacities for training in educational management, and assistance with operational support, such as the production of training materials.

d Enabling certain of such national institutions to serve sub-regional or regional training needs, in accordance with appropriate inter-governmental decisions.

e The provision and appointment of short-term consultants (local or foreign) to serve as catalysts by working with ministries or departments on the solution of specific management problems.

f Facilitating longer periods of productive discussion between invited consultants and local officials relating to management and planning problems, thereby enabling consultants to play a catalytic role rather than being seen as fleeting visitors with a superficial understanding of local needs and conditions. Much of the work of project formulation currently done within donor agencies following a sector analysis or project review might more profitably be undertaken in the country where the project was actually going to take place.

At *local level* the main need in staff development is to train the 'enablers'. Emphasis on management training is nowhere more vital than at local level for it is that crucial group of middle level personnel who probably exercise the greatest influence on quality: the teacher trainers, inspectors, education officers and, above all, heads of institutions. Indeed in his 'think piece', Tony Somerset (EDC) offers compelling research evidence to support what most experienced educational workers have long suspected: the dramatic effect that selection, training and motivation of local education officers and school heads can have on school quality.

He presented a profile of achievement from one district in Kenya, showing not only how the district had suffered rapidly and dramatically following the transfer of a well-motivated and competent district education officer, but also how individual schools suffered or benefited from good leadership where

> extremely high levels of performance have been achieved in the most successful schools despite the fact that few if any of their pupils come from economically or educationally privileged backgrounds.

A key role for aid is, therefore, to help governments establish systems to train such personnel and to support them in the field. A field manager's life is both lonely and taxing. Simple, short training courses are badly needed but without a lifeline to the field will hardly serve to keep enthusiasm and commitment alive in difficult circumstances.

Multiplier-type training using the so-called 'cascade system' is often favoured. But too often those at the bottom of the cascade barely get wet. There can be few more vital challenges to aid than finding an alternative: a management support system which will build up the skills of local personnel who in turn can support their own local teachers.

Such training, as Lalage Bown pointed out, would have to redefine the scope of administrative practice in order to encompass techniques of local needs analysis and programme-building to suit local realities. Training must also include skills of human relationships which are essential in working with teachers, parents and local communities who will take an increasingly large part in shaping their own educational provision.

Sector priorities — the role of aid

Aid responses to three educational priorities are examined here. These are basic education, agricultural education, and university education. Since the participants often refined their ideas on educational priorities by reference to aid requirements, parts of the discussion intersect with Chapter 2. There is also some inevitable cross-referencing to the earlier discussion of management, since the promotion of relevance and efficiency were woven into the debate on sectoral priorities and aid requirements.

Basic education

The following major characteristics of basic education have already been identified:

a It is a vital basis for development, particularly through its potential for education of women

b It involves many different delivery systems, incorporating not only formal primary education but also formal and non-formal educational opportunities, in basic literacy skills and other developmental activities such as health and agriculture. Distinctions between formal and non-formal education are by no means sharp and could become even less distinct through a process of 'deformalising formal education'

c The importance of basic education lies in its content rather than its structures. What is significant is *whether* individuals in school and out of it meet their minimum learning requirements, not *how* they do so.

66

With these fundamental aspects of basic education in mind the Conference considered ways in which aid could help develop and promote it.

Strengthening the information bases

The strengthening of data collection has already been mentioned. What is particularly important is the process of information sharing, especially in relation to different types of basic education and the experiences of 'deformalising' primary education. Hitherto we have been dependent for knowledge of the latter on descriptions of innovative projects, often aid sponsored. As pressure on basic education provision is intensified and local initiatives are encouraged, a host of other experiences are likely to emerge. Aid could, therefore, sponsor the collection and collation of such data and the provision of study tours and visits so that first-hand information could be gathered and exchanged within and between countries.

Discussion of purpose and priorities

No one denied the importance of providing basic education through a variety of agencies, and there was strong support in written contributions and working groups for a process of 'deformalising' formal basic education. But there was no unanimity, either on the desirability or the content of such a shift. Nor would there be at national level. Basic education has in the past been an exceptionally sensitive issue since there is always a suspicion that it represents second-class education for second-class citizens. Consequently if new initiatives are to emerge (as the pressure on resources set against the insistent demand for basic education seems to demand), then the nature of alternative patterns must be fully discussed and the implications of policy alternatives carefully examined. The funding of such discussions would be a very proper target for assistance.

Promoting liaison between basic education agencies

Aid agencies could support this difficult task through

a Helping different ministries to find common ground in their curricular objectives and content and build collaborative procedures among field workers, teachers and community leaders

b Providing support for in-service training centres to develop common approaches

c Providing support for common services such as resource centres and evaluation teams.

The management of basic education

We have already emphasised the key importance of training field personnel in skills of management and evaluation.

The training of teacher trainers

The provision of teachers who have not only the skills but the understanding of what it is that they are trying to provide lies at the heart of successful basic education. The task of redefinition of objectives is crucial. Mere support for mass programmes of teacher education which serve up the same fare provided to current college students — but in smaller quantities! — would not represent a prudent use of funds.

67

Support for curriculum development and examination reform

The two processes are closely linked. Since the provision of a content relevant to needs is at the heart of basic education, it follows that much material must be local and indigenous and that skills need to be developed to produce such local material. Since numeracy and literacy, particularly in the mother tongue, are central to basic education, aid agencies could have a critical role in collaborating with national centres to develop instruments for measuring literacy in various languages and numeracy in various cultural settings. There is also the formidable task of devising, operating and monitoring examination reform in basic education, as a means of propelling urgently needed, development-related curricular and pedagogical reforms. Aid agencies should be receptive to invitations to help in this endeavour.

Provision of material resources for basic education

Here a fundamental dilemma can be identified. On the one hand, there are countries in Africa where pressures of numbers upon resources are so great that schools lack almost everything except children. In these circumstances it would seem that external assistance should now move into providing basic necessities for learning in order to meet the crisis. Yet some argued that the provision of such handouts increases the fundamental dependence of African educational systems and intensifies the 'donor to recipient' relationship rather than one based on partnership.

> I myself feel that if we ask for assistance to help us improve our capabilities and capacity to analyse, this perhaps would be acceptable, but where we are asking for aid for chalk or pencils or textbooks, it seems to be embarrassing. . . . It is going to create a situation of dependence.
>
> *Arthur Porter (Sierra Leone)*

Others thought that the dependency issue did not provide an appropriate framework for aid policy in a situation of extreme gravity:

> Many countries today have built up and invested heavily in basic education, and the problem is now foreign exchange for the running of that system. I think we should make a plea, and I hope you will make it from this meeting, that donors should be more open to assist. Investment in education does not stop when the building is finished. Investment in education is to train the people, and if it stops after the building has been finished, then you run into problems. . . . I can say that Swedish assistance in many countries today is almost 100 per cent in what you could call recurrent. We call it investing in education.
>
> *Lennart Wohlgemuth (SIDA)*

However, one working group pointed out ways in which aid agencies could assist through

a Strengthening existing materials production units, where these exist

b Providing finance and technology for setting up industries for production of educational necessities such as paper, chalk, rulers, where these are economically viable

c Providing finance and equipment for local school furniture production.

Special needs

The final area of support was in helping nations seeking the universal-isation of basic education to identify needs of handicapped children and adults, and ways of meeting them, possibly by

a Financing need assessment surveys and studies of how provision could best be made

b Supporting teacher training in this area

c Supporting the provision and expansion of appropriate facilities for handicapped learners.

Agricultural education

Although no specific group discussions at the Conference focused solely on the role of aid in the promotion of agricultural education, the theme underlay nearly every aspect of the last three days. Implicit in all the discussions was a certain perspective — and a vitally important one. This was to conceive the promotion of agricultural production, food self-sufficiency, effective nutrition and soil conservation, not as a set of specialist vocational knowledge, but as a vital component of general education at all levels, fostering skills of practical enquiry, problem-solving and self-reliance.

Hence we are not talking only of the strengthening of agricultural programmes *in* basic, secondary and tertiary education, but also of the strengthening of basic, secondary and tertiary education *through* agricultural education, because agricultural education, properly conceived, is an excellent means of helping to develop that independence of mind and ability to link learning with living which all at the Conference sought to promote.

Many agencies spoke of programmes in this field and Cynthia Perry of USAID submitted a background paper on this subject, which is her agency's major priority.* The paper presents the different levels and modes of proposed assistance with force and clarity, stresses the key role education needs to play in developing knowledge and skills in agriculture, and lays particular emphasis on the need to educate women at every level both as agricultural professionals and as 'receivers of services to farmers'. The paper continues:

> Increasing agricultural productivity and human resource development are complementary objectives to the overall goal of reversing the deteriorating food production capacity in Africa and achieving agricultural development. Furthermore, agricultural education needs address every dimension of the agricultural sector from training policy makers and scientists to basic education for the farm family. Therefore, a comprehensive approach to agricultural education must be developed.

This approach envisaged five related strategies:

1 Institutional development in selected higher and intermediate institutions, with an additional emphasis to promote agricultural extension

2 Participant training with particular emphasis on faculty training for local institutions, especially for building up research skills, training of key extension personnel, and project-related specialist training

---

*C.S. Perry, 'Agricultural Education and University Building in Africa: A Development Strategy'.

3 Strengthening agricultural education in the basic educational curricula through new emphasis on problem-solving skills and using local environments as a resource and reference, together with appropriate teacher education —

4 Strengthening regional agricultural instructional materials centres attached to strong regional universities for production and distribution of low cost learning materials, and

5 Support for professional associations of agricultural educators in Africa, to provide a support mechanism and a publication service.

University education

Amid the strong support for qualitative improvement of university education, there was considerable unease about the relationships of aid negotiators (national and international) to universities, and the relationships of the universities themselves to the process of educational and national development.

Academics and government policy-makers have strongly conflicting ideas on the issue of foreign assistance. In particular, opinions may differ strongly as to what aid should be accepted, who to accept it from and even, in some cases, the wisdom of accepting aid at all.

Some universities are less than co-operative with governments, less prepared than they should be to put their intellectual resources at the disposal of the nation's development, and less committed than many would consider necessary to review their own programmes and practices in the light of national needs and priorities. On the other hand, as was noted in Chapter 2, some governments have demanded docile obedience from their university communities, under threat of overt force.

Because of these uneasy relationships, donors and ministries may be tempted to deal directly with each other and ignore the pool of human resources at their doorstep. Despite the difficulties and frustrations which all parties face in achieving a strong working relationship, one wise participant noted that

> universities probably are the centres in any of our countries where the largest number of highly educated people are concentrated in one place. . . . We must find a way of utilising to the fullest our universities as centres of learning.
>
> *Aklilu Habte*

While the role of aid in promoting university involvement in development may in some ways be limited, there are steps which can be taken. They include

1 The provision of support for university-organised seminars and reviews of national policies in collaboration with political leaders and government ministries (as in Sierra Leone)

2 The encouragement and assistance of new university programmes directly linked with national development priorities, such as the programmes in agriculture already mentioned or programmes in education to develop leadership cadres in primary/basic education (such as that already financed by USAID in Botswana and the one under development at Kenyatta University and supported by ODA)

3 The development and support of university-based research units and projects which are directly linked to the provision of relevant information for policy-makers, and the training of staff to work in them; as well as, more generally,

4 The building (and in cases such as Makerere, rebuilding) of established universities as international centres of excellence, capable of providing a basis for research and teaching specifically centred on the development needs of sub-Saharan Africa.

Making the aid process more efficient

Five aspects were considered by the Conference and are reported here. The first relates to the management of the aid process. The second and third discuss the broadening and deepening of the role of assistance to education, by encouraging partners in the aid process to take a longer view of programmes and projects, and by attempting to break down the boundaries between individual projects and between sectors' contributions to national development. The fourth considers the organisation and location of what is arguably the most important component of aid — human resource development through training. Finally, and appropriately for such a Conference, we report discussions on how better to harmonise the efforts of different aid agencies.

The management of aid projects

Improvement in techniques of data collection, planning and management, together with the identification and training of local personnel in these areas have important implications for the efficiency of the aid process itself.

But further specific steps could be taken to improve project management, as one of the working groups recommended.

1 Preparation of projects

Government and aid agencies should:

a Ensure that they are planned jointly from the outset by local staff with donor co-operation to ensure a coherent approach to project planning and implementation

b Ensure that the planning component of a project provides for the training of local staff, and for supporting them to visit other countries to study comparable projects and to assess the conditions contributing to their success or lack of it

c Avoid rigidity in objectives, methods and time frames, as well as building flexibility through periodic reviews and, if necessary, mid-course corrections

d Control 'alliances' of local and foreign specialists who may enthusiastically recommend unnecessarily lavish or even inappropriate facilities or equipment which might later prove a barrier to implementation

e Simplify the language of project documentation into step-by-step procedures for implementation, with the stages broken down into

71

operational form. Too often projects are in such sophisticated jargon that those who seek to implement them at local level cannot understand what it is they have to do.

2 Control of projects

Projects should be placed firmly under the control of local directors. It is important that such a local director continue to receive the appropriate local salary and allowances and not be paid an international salary or be taken out of the line of management. Once the leadership of the project is clearly in local hands, the staff of the project, whether local or foreign, should be provided with appropriate working roles, avoiding redundant and invidious 'advisory' positions.

3 Qualitative analysis and evaluation of programmes and projects

These should be seen as normal routine necessities of management, enabling vital feedback to be made to practitioners in the field as well as illuminating the minds of policy-makers and donors. Donor-assisted evaluation should be undertaken co-operatively, with genuine and not 'cosmetic' participation by recipients. As a matter of general practice, universities should be involved in the evaluation of such programmes and projects.

4 'Honourable withdrawal'

One further issue was discussed, that of the possibility of either party being able to withdraw honourably, with reasonable notice, from a project once it had started. In some cases, projects have continued after they should properly have been terminated because they were not achieving their objectives, or because force of circumstances prevented one partner or the other from being able to make a planned input. In others, withdrawal may have been forced on one of the parties by international circumstances with considerable loss to the educational institutions for whom the project had been intended. It is obviously desirable that conditions of trust and cordial working relationships should exist so that such questions could be frankly discussed and acted upon. The Conference was advised that some donors were in a position to step in at short notice and provide supplementary support if required, or 'take over' a viable project from another donor.

Greater continuity in the aid process

The improvement of project management is only one aspect in the very much wider issue of improving continuity in the aid process. The process has traditionally suffered from the shortness of its time spans and the rigid nature of the boundaries which are drawn when particular 'packages' of assistance are being negotiated. Hence the 'project' often seen as central to the negotiation of aid may come to be regarded as an island of its own with a committed but sometimes partisan population separated from the mainstream of planned activities. A major focus of discussions at Windsor centred on how continuity and integration could be achieved, while both partners in the aid process maintained their independence in decision-making and action.

Yet again the process starts with the building-up of capacities, to collect information as a basis for decision-making, to assess long-term priorities and to manage change. Once such capacities are built up it seems natural to think of programme support over a longer term for certain broad strategies rather than small, discrete, limited projects to meet immediate needs.

Plenary and group discussions identified the following important issues.

1 Commitment to longer-term programmes

The World Bank in particular has announced a policy of sector or sub-sector programme aid which in principle should allow greater flexibility in the use of external resources and allow the recipient country more scope to take the initiative. Such a trend is also evident in the very long-term view being taken by USAID in its programmes for the development of agriculture. SIDA, too, favours long-term commitments in order to achieve continuity and help build capacity. Not all donors as yet adopt the same policy, and there is a parallel movement, as competition for scarce resources becomes ever greater, to insist on very tight accountability by the recipient government, which to some extent implies very detailed project or programme specifications. Lennart Wohlgemuth also reminded us of the Swedish view that long-term programmes may sometimes actually curtail the freedom of action of recipient countries by tying them to policies for a longer period than they may care to commit themselves to. Hence, though a longer and broader view of aid planning may be desirable, there are many contrary forces to reconcile as negotiations take place to achieve it.

2 Shared understanding of objectives and resources available

We have stressed the importance of understanding and agreement of programme objectives which have been identified, in the first instance, by the country requesting the aid. Equally important is a deep understanding by both parties of the amount of resources which can be committed by both sides, the way in which these resources can be committed, the extent to which the donor agency is intending to monitor the operation of the programme and to insist upon conditionality, together with the amount of technical support and training which is likely to be available. All these issues are closely bound up with the question of understanding the 'maps' of both partners raised by Kenneth King.

3 Aid provided at critical times to support policy formulation

The importance of such timely support, backed up with research, data-gathering and training components, has already been mentioned. Aid to support policy formulation is particularly needed when countries are reviewing their system or moving in new political, social or economic directions. Multilateral aid or some form of co-ordination among donor agencies under the recipient country's lead is particularly helpful at this time.

4 Maintaining continuity

Once a programme or project falters due to weaknesses in its planning or execution, expectations wither and are hard to revive. Many good initiatives have come to grief for this reason. It becomes essential therefore to maintain as much continuity of approaches and of personnel as possible throughout the implementation of a programme. This has implications for the staffing not only of ministries within African countries, but also of aid agencies themselves.

73

5 Flexibility in the operation of projects

Continuity in approach and staffing is not the enemy of flexibility, but each requires the other. Given the pressures and financial stress affecting nearly all educational projects it is essential to maintain flexibility in the way that goals can be implemented, and in the management of scarce resources in achieving these goals. If alternative patterns of delivery seem appropriate, if new methodologies appropriate to achieving 'more with less' can be suggested and agreed jointly between the partners in the programme or project, they should be adopted.

Similarly, there are occasions when a programme needs material input to sustain it during a difficult period. Such inputs might include provision of cheap vehicles to enable monitoring to take place, or provision of basic office equipment with maintenance back-up. On such relatively small inputs, success or failure of important programmes may hinge, and flexible responses to such familiar contingencies would be highly cost-effective.

Continuity across sectors

Implicit in all discussions was the necessity of taking a view of the aid process which cuts across sectors. Thus the functional separation of 'health', 'population', 'agriculture', 'industrial training', or (even more bizarrely) 'rural development' from education makes little sense. Yet they are routinely separated in both African administrations and in aid agencies. While communication does take place, it is often a matter of exchanging information rather than seeking joint programmes, and indeed there is often, in a more or less subtle way, competition between programmes and sectors for scarce resources.

Improvements could be made through increased dialogue within agencies, hopefully leading towards greater complementarity between projects and increased support for existing intersectoral projects. Both SIDA and GTZ (for example) have a declared policy of promoting such co-operative planning. Agencies should also consider funding of seminars and joint planning meetings to consider how initiatives within African countries on issues such as population education, food production and primary health care could be emphasised through co-ordination of many sectors and programmes. In every instance education, in its widest sense, would naturally be seen as central to spreading knowledge, developing skills and changing attitudes inherent in each of these priorities. An essential component of such meetings is that they should lead to a defined and monitored programme of action rather than merely serving as a platform for theoreticians to exchange ideas — a further challenge to the universities which, as we have noted above, are uniquely placed to initiate such debates.

Approaches to training

So far in this chapter discussion has centred on the organisation of aid programmes and projects related to identified priorities. In every case there are training implications and in some there are specially focused training elements. But the issue of human resource development extends far wider than mere project related training. It is arguably the most important function of aid to education, and as such it was the focus of a good proportion of the discussion over the last days of the Conference.

In the summary of discussion which follows, we have somewhat arbitrarily divided the issues under three sub-headings:

1 Who should be trained
2 How training can be made most effective
3 Where training can be most profitably located

There are significant overlaps between all three sections.

Who should be trained

The term training itself is a misleading bit of shorthand covering all sorts of educational experiences from those which are highly vocational such as learning to operate a computer or diagnose plant diseases, to doctoral programmes examining the conceptual development of learners or the application of management theory, to even more broadly-focused opportunities (through attachments, study tours or seminars) to enable senior men and women within a system to gain the breadth of vision and the comparative perspective they need to do their demanding jobs better. It is therefore exceptionally difficult to assign priorities.

Nevertheless, we can isolate three principles which emerged from the discussions. Firstly, merely to identify training needs by skilled manpower categories is not in itself sufficient. There remains a need to provide opportunities for young men and women of the highest abilities to prepare themselves for intellectual leadership. Otherwise Africa will remain dependent.

Secondly, a significant amount of training must be directed towards training 'enablers'. This category includes those who train others. The mode in which they do so must be very carefully monitored, so a significant aid commitment needs to be invested in ensuring that two- or three-stage training systems are designed to work effectively. It also includes those who make things happen efficiently: the managers and implementers as well as those who monitor and evaluate progress of programmes and individuals.

Thirdly, comparative perspectives in training are important; so are problem-solving approaches. A course which widens an individual's experience by giving him the opportunity to see a variety of solutions to problems, and to mix with others who have different experiences to share, is more valuable than one which merely presents a single preferred way.

How training can be made more effective

In addition to the debate on the management of 'multiplier' training, a number of other issues were raised. For one thing, overseas training would be more effective if it was cheaper and more students could, therefore, benefit from it. In this regard, the British policy to charge economic cost fees to students from outside Europe is still deeply regretted by African countries. The British decision, as Dorothy Njeuma pointed out, was somewhat at variance with the announced intention 'to help us in developing our education system' and 'to train our badly needed manpower'.

Equally regretted were instances cited by participants where individual institutions were alleged to charge exceptionally high fees to overseas students in order to help compensate for shortfalls in income from home students. Such practices had resulted in an affected African government withdrawing its students from a particular institution and listing other institutions with similar charges.

Ironically, countries with very limited resources had become entirely dependent on aid support from Britain to keep some students at British universities.

> We have no people coming here this year except those who are coming on an ODA award. We can no longer afford to send people to train in Britain because of high tuition fees demanded. In fact we have people who are already here and who have not been registered by their colleges because we just cannot afford to pay the tuition fees for this or last year.
>
> *Ahmed Bushra Ibrahim (Sudan)*

Where training can take place

A considerable debate took place on the locus of training, with discussion centred particularly on the possibilities, the effectiveness and the popularity (or lack of it) of third country training.

On the other hand, the debate revealed that within certain parameters, third country training could be funded by bilateral aid donors — including the United States, France, West Germany and the United Kingdom. Sweden has, for years, offered the vast majority of its training fellowships in other countries. With the exception of Sweden, and in rare cases West Germany, such third country training applies to training in Africa. USAID would not, for instance, accede to requests to fund Zimbabwean students to study in Britain. Certain categories of students, such as doctoral students, are not usually eligible for third country training.

On the question of what kind of third country training is most feasible and cost effective, considerable evidence seems to favour the strengthening of existing institutions rather than the creation of new ones, particularly regional bodies specifically set up for training purposes. These tend to be expensive, difficult to manage and monitor, and politically sensitive. Many clearly supported the view expressed by Aklilu Habte that

> rather than start with a regional centre that is owned by everybody, it is better that we start with a national project which is owned by at least one country and which makes its facilities available to a group of countries.

But the issue of third country training is more complicated than it may appear. Sometimes it could actually cost an agency more to finance African students in another African country — such as Algeria, for example — than in the United States. Often African universities have little spare capacity for non-national students. Sometimes there are political overtones to students wishing placement in other countries, since they might prove not to be welcome back in their own. Finally, it is necessary to face the fact that overseas degrees often have more glamour attached to them (and sometimes a greater social cachet) than degrees from African universities. Nevertheless, the principle of third country training is an important one to develop, not for economic reasons, but because it is potentially valuable in increasing relevance, building up regional co-operation and developing the potential of African universities.

76

We are talking about narrowly providing a few scholarships. That is short range. The longer range is that we support the regional and national institutions not just by giving scholarships, but helping them get more teachers, professors, teaching materials. This will strengthen them and consequently turn them into centres of excellence.

Aklilu Habte

One final, and very profitable, strategy needs to be further examined. That is the provision of joint or 'split' programmes of training in which some parts of a programme of study can be arranged in an overseas country, or a third country in Africa to strengthen or complement studies in the participant's home country. The ODA favours further extension of this mode of training.

Harmonising the efforts of different aid agencies

A final cluster of issues, particularly appropriate to the theme of the Conference, related to harmonising the efforts of different aid agencies through the following measures:

1 The exchange of information and sharing of views and policies between donors — with participation of their partners in the aid process
2 The collaboration of more than one donor in major projects and the provision of opportunities for donors, where appropriate, to take over responsibility for each other's projects
3 Co-operation in regionally organised projects and institutions
4 The co-ordination of efforts and activities by separate donors working in a particular country, such co-ordination being organised on the initiative and under the aegis of national governments.

Exchange of information among donors

Many opportunities are already provided for this purpose, including, just prior to the Conference, the meetings of DAC and the post-Bellagio group on basic education (both in Paris). It could even be argued that such frequent meetings of donors constitute a threat to the autonomy of African countries, since the pooling of policies and information might lead to a common donor position which is neither shared, nor fully understood, by countries in the region.

In fact, such meetings are often neither as effective nor as informative as they might be, partly because the 'show and tell' nature of the proceedings often fails to reveal the deeper issues of policy, the constraints, and the pressures which agencies face. Political issues are rarely discussed.

There is a need to consider firstly, how such dialogues could more substantially involve other partners in the aid process — as partners in discussion. The style set in the Windsor Conference might prove a pointer to future meetings. Discussions on how to provide aid to education in Africa which take place without significant representation of African officials and experts cannot easily be justified.

Secondly, it should also be considered how donor meetings could be more carefully focused to deal with particular issues rather than more general ones. This might argue in favour of smaller working groups meeting for longer periods rather than large, broad-based and hence formal sessions.

Donor collaboration in projects

Is there an arrangement whereby donors combine together or collaborate together to meet the needs of projects that are larger and which are situated in large countries? Secondly, is there an arrangement whereby a country that has started a project in one place could transfer the aid obligation to another country in case they wanted to do so?

Sam Aleyideino

From the point of view of an African country, the primary issue is the success of a particular education programme or project, and not who made it successful. This may also be the chief preoccupation of any aid agency, but often there are other factors that inhibit the sharing or transfer of responsibility for assistance. They include, for example, historical, political and economic ties, future commercial considerations, procedural and budgetary constraints, and differences of strategies, priorities and operational styles among the different aid agencies.

Yet there is ample evidence that such collaboration has occurred, could occur, and indeed should occur more often. At least one agency, the European Development Fund (EDF), collaborates as a matter of major policy. Others, such as USAID in its new agricultural education policy, are actively trying to seek links and working relationships with other donors such as the World Bank.

Regional projects, regional institutions

A further avenue for co-operation is through regional projects (where national institutions are enabled to serve regional needs) and regional institutions (which are internationally owned and managed). The two need to be separated, and discussion appears to indicate that there is less consensus on the value of the latter than of the former.

There are considerable funds available for soundly-based educational initiatives benefiting more than one country — or indeed for institutions which tackle problems of a more global nature. However, the question of control and financial authority seems crucial. Both the EDF and the French Ministry of Co-operation and Development (among others) specifically favour support of regional projects. Yet it has proved difficult to get the specific political agreement necessary to finalise as many projects as might have been hoped for.

If we took [the Sahelian] countries together we could have a Sahelian institute that could look at the problems of lack of water, solar energy, the problems of pasture, migration and so on. But that means that these countries would have to participate in the institute financially, technically, and in terms of manpower.

Iba Der Thiam (Senegal)

Asavia Wandira of Uganda cited the difficulties of the Association of African Universities in liberating aid funds:

When you ask countries and university institutions to provide signatures of two presidents before the money is released from the EEC, you are prescribing a formula for keeping the money in the budget and never spending it. Inflexibility in negotiations for inter-country co-operation as a condition for release of money makes this impossible. Those institutions which cut across these inflexibilities demand more support.

Regional institutions owned by several governments have had a mixed track record in Africa. To cite only anglophone African experience, the regional universities of East Africa and of Lesotho, Botswana and Swaziland have broken under the stress of centrifugal national policies. On the other hand, the West African Examinations Council has had a long and respected life. Clearly, if support is to be provided to such institutions, they must be strong, well-funded and staffed, and have a clearly-defined purpose which is approved and supported by all countries which participate in them. Much interest, including substantial donor support (which is itself — with the Nordic Initiative — showing signs of regional mobilisation) is being shown in the flexible model of the Southern African Development Co-ordination Conference (SADCC), which groups nine countries' efforts in regional co-operation, including the field of manpower development. Though it is one of the biggest programmes in Africa,

> it does not have a regional bureaucracy. It has a very, very small secretariat. The focus is on the individual country members, which looks like a promising way to proceed.
>
> *Charles Bassett*

In-country co-ordination of initiatives

We end this section, and this chapter, on a point upon which there was total agreement: the value of co-operation and co-ordination of donor policies and activities *within* individual African countries.

Such an approach builds on much that has already been discussed in this chapter. It needs to be based on both trust and knowledge, by all partners, of the workings, the priorities and the 'ecology' of the participating agencies and national governments, as well as the frank sharing of information between aid agencies working in the same country. This, in turn, must have implications for the knowledge and training of those who sit down together. An ideal, all agreed, would be to see personnel from aid agencies who have a deep understanding of the culture and education system for which they provide assistance, discussing with nationals who have an equally deep knowledge of the countries and agencies with whom they are talking, and who have perhaps spent time examining the workings of these agencies.

Ideally, also, such a dialogue should evolve from a carefully articulated view of priorities, and involve politicians in the discussions as well as the approval stage. Such a process would be initiated, managed and monitored by the host country which would thus provide a regular, institutionalised forum for periodic discussions and decision-making.

Perhaps these ideals are not far from reality. In many countries, it was reported, such systematic co-operation is already being implemented. It would be satisfying to believe that the discussions at the Windsor Conference might help in some way to ensure that this process became a regular practice.

When such ideals are realised it will prove a good deal easier for us all to present an efficient and united response to the enormous educational challenges which confront sub-Saharan Africa.

Chapter 4
Reflections on the Conference

Roger Iredale

The Conference was intended to dwell on the hard choices facing African educationists, in their struggle to meet a rising popular demand for schooling with systems increasingly starved of financial support. It achieved no single balancing of primary education against secondary, of 'vocational' against 'academic' or any other simple rule-of-thumb formula. What it did achieve was a remarkably frank dialogue about the problem confronting politicians and managers throughout Africa, at a time of over-stretched budgets, debt crises, and food shortages through drought and war. If it contained one important message, that message was that ministers and senior officials are not as mesmerised by the problems of dwindling resources and finance as are donors and other outsiders. Perhaps those at the coal face are more aware, even if unconsciously, of the substantial achievements that have been made since independence; perhaps, having actually themselves lived through periods of rapid growth which are only historical phenomena — or at best faint memories — to outsiders, they are conscious that present crises are simply another dimension of difficulty to be confronted.

This chapter reflects on both the major themes: priorities, and the role of aid donors. I write from the viewpoint of an educationist within a donor agency, but my views are a personal commentary on the problems facing us, though I naturally hope that they will also reflect my colleagues' thinking. They spring not only from the Conference itself, which was a valuable catalyst for all our thinking, but from recent experience as a parent, as a frequent participant in wide-ranging discussions of education and its relationship to the needs of people in many different environments, and as a traveller in Africa, Asia and Latin America.

Education priorities

The opening stages of the Conference very naturally dwelt on the famines that are currently plaguing Ethiopia, Sudan and other sub-Saharan countries. The famines served as a cogent reminder that education is nothing if it fails to confront the five major issues of population growth, food and health, the preservation of the environment, productive employment, and the strengthening of a spirit of national unity and co-operation that enhances political and economic stability. With falling food production levels in many countries, with menacingly large population growth rates in a range of the larger nations, with a deterioration of the

---

This Conference on education was conceived in large measure by the ODA to educate itself. In this chapter, ODA's Principal Education Adviser reflects on the proceedings and their implications for his administration.

environment through excessive grazing and cultivation and the widespread random destruction of natural resources including trees, and only 20 per cent of Africa's labour force employed in the formal sector (including the public service), it became very apparent to all present that education must pay attention to the critical issues of the attitudes of young adults to family, surroundings and work.

It was perhaps inevitable that the Conference turned to the role of women and their access to education. The importance of the part that woman plays in education of the young, and in health, nutrition, family welfare, population growth, care of the environment, food production — not to mention 'modern sector' activities — does not require detailing. The most important discussions near the end of the Conference revolved around the importance of ensuring that women are properly provided for in all forms of education, but without being singled out for separate, special treatment. Discussion recognised the need for sensitivity in ensuring equality of treatment in a milieu that was patently not one of equality and in finding ways of developing female education without adopting patronising attitudes.

The widespread tendency, especially amongst 'professional' educationists, is to focus on the formal school/college system. That is where the money is spent. Moreover, there is ample evidence that what best fits a young person for productive employment, whether self-generated or waged, is a broad general education that provides the capacity to develop specific skills according to the demands of a particular job. The level of a person's general education has been shown to influence in very positive ways the health of his family, the productivity of the land he farms (through his capacity to take advantage of change and improvement), and his employability. If it is fully to repay the taxpayers' investment in it, schooling should also create responsible and caring attitudes towards the environment in which people live.

But, as the Conference recognised, education does not necessarily flow down one single pipeline, especially when it is viewed more broadly as *learning* rather than *schooling*. One of the important emphases was on the need to build closer links between formal education imparted by school, and all the other channels by which people achieve understanding: forms of youth and adult education that include literacy classes and agricultural or health extension work, correspondence colleges, informal apprenticeship schemes, on-the-job skills training, and self education. Educationists are still too tightly fenced in behind their own concepts of what education is or should be to be able to develop the decades-old dream of opening up learning opportunities to all comers at all ages and levels. For me, one of the most important though obvious messages was that as long as educational planners think exclusively in terms of what can be achieved within institutions of full-time learning to the exclusion of all other means of acquiring knowledge, skills and constructive attitudes, they will remain constrained by unnecessarily narrow perceptions of what education is really about and what it can achieve.

It is perhaps too much to expect government to take all this on board and act on it. Since 80 per cent of Africans work outside of the stockade of formal employment, perhaps their education needs to develop its own self-catering attributes: Kenneth King in his lead paper writes of the importance of model schools, a concept in which I have little faith, if I interpret the phrase to mean a government- or donor-supplied school to which everyone will pay homage and go on doing exactly what they were doing before, using physical and human resource constraints as their excuse. The true 'model' schools are those that are spontaneous and community-inspired. The best conventional secondary school I have ever visited in Africa was a community-created institution literally in revolt against the prevailing system (which happened to be apartheid). But it is not schools that I have primarily in mind: it is health centres, nutrition classes, literacy groups, self-generating charities with the potential to reach people who have by-passed the system, who are looking for a second chance, for new skills, for new perceptions, or for new contacts. One of the things that amazes me about the industrialised countries with their relatively high unemployment figures is that they have not stimulated on any significant scale the formation of self-help groups by encouraging people to develop creative skills and inducing them to exercise them for their own benefit and that of the community. One thing on which educationists everywhere need to focus more is the community dimension of skills acquisition and a low-cost means of encouraging and providing access to those skills.

All this links with the many speeches and papers at the Conference, beginning with the comprehensive lead paper by Peter Williams, that demanded a greater degree of community involvement in the school, and a greater flexibility in the curriculum. There was a feeling among some speakers that the community should only supplement government, not take its place. To me, that is a questionable proposition: it seems to me that with the problems of finance and quality control that government faces in trying to cope with formal school and college education, it has little choice but to rely more heavily on the community. We all know that the crucial element in the running of the school is the headteacher; we all know the teachers will take their lead from the head, in matters of conduct such as punctuality and in attitudes to children and parents. The training of headteachers is something to which we all pay lip service, but there must be ways of enabling the community — who are paying clients — to put pressure on an institution where there is absenteeism, slackness, poor teaching standards. While we must accept that the community can have a potential for narrowness of vision and restrictive perceptions of what is educationally desirable (as evidenced by recent fundamentalist religious constraints on Darwinian biology teaching in parts of one major Western country), there is a lot to be said for any system of community involvement in education that makes the school directly accountable to parents. Much has been said and written about the morale of the teacher, with suggestions for rewarding with promotion or bonus pay those willing to teach in rural areas. While this may be part of the answer, the reality is that there is no system-based panacea for the demoralised rural teacher (have we in Britain solved the problems of the demoralised inner-city teacher by promoting him/her?) other than adequate leadership, regular contact with a helpful professional supervisor, and a sense of community involvement and support.

But if the Conference concluded that the community's views and feelings are important in terms of the school, it also reasserted that the community in the form of society at large is even more important in terms of the university. Statistics produced for the Conference reveal that universities in Africa consume vast resources: 20 per cent of Malawi's education budget, for example. Elements of the Conference, following Arthur Porter's valuable paper from Sierra Leone, focused on the role of this highly prestigious and controversial institution. It is seriously open to doubt whether universities in Africa provide the kind of value for money that the taxpayer is entitled to expect. Certainly they provide engineers, doctors, scientists and civil servants; but when the employability of their arts graduates drops sharply — or, worse still, the growth in the number of local unemployed arts graduates puts pressure on government to expand public sector employment — and when research programmes fail to tackle important local or national issues, one has to question the university's role and its right to go on mopping up large sums of the taxpayer's money.

In one sense, the university *is* a priority sector — a priority for selective change, not untargeted support. Nor, with such rigid formal school systems, is it by any means certain that the ablest and the therefore most suitable candidates will gain access to higher learning. The freeing-up of the education system's structures is inextricably linked to the question of whether people, young or otherwise, are enabled to realise their full potential. If the university intake can really contain a country's most creative learners and thinkers rather than only those who were lucky and dogged enough to get through the school system with enough routine passes, the university will benefit in terms of its own creative role in society. Is it a coincidence that one can count on the fingers of one hand the number of university courses in the world that genuinely include some community-based activity that springs from, and is related to, the department's academic pursuits? Are the universities rigidly bound to their own narrow dogma about what constitutes success without being sufficiently aware that there are other measures of success both for themselves and for their alumni?

I will attempt to sum up this section of the chapter. The Conference served to remind us all that ministries of education are merely reference points for all those who are concerned in the educational process. Ministries of agriculture, transport, health, planning and manpower are the end users of the process of which the minister of education is only the custodian, albeit a powerful one because of his control over certification; but outside of his jurisdiction are many other educational processes concealed under other guises and serving specific purposes not normally associated with the minister of education. The formal system itself, at once both servant and engine of development, needs to loosen the rigidity of its own structures, incorporate greater community accountability into its management styles and, apart from the essential tools of literacy, numeracy and the ability to express oneself in speech, give attention to the crucial matters of health, population, job creation and the environment, including agriculture. The priorities, if I had the difficult task of selecting universally applicable ones, would include:

the university: a scrutiny of its costs, curriculum and methods, its contribution to the community, its response to the real questions and dilemmas of its society

the school examinations: their influence on curriculum, the scope for flexibility in responding to different circumstances: rural, urban, desert, savannah or forest

the structure: its rigidity, the scope for entry and exit, for late-starters or part-timers, for taking account of and giving value to educational activities not normally classed as 'education' and its efforts to promote the education of women

the management: at the top, the awareness of the close ties with agriculture, health and other human activities; at school level, the morale, competence and accountability of the institutional line manager or head teacher

non-governmental initiatives: the provision of the right climate for self-help educational activities of all kinds and at all levels to stimulate themselves without either dependence on or interference by government.

The role of the aid donor

If one thing was clear at the Conference it was the lack of information and understanding on the part of recipients of the constraints, problems and roles of the donors. This lack of understanding is not the fault of the recipients; it underlies a substantial gap in information and attitudes which the Conference did much to close. The later sessions underlined the importance of donors' accountability to their subscribers, the taxpayers, and provided a valuable insight into the processes by which donors seek to satisfy themselves of the developmental validity of a particular project. It gave one ODA representative the opportunity to explain why the British aid programme has no specific global allocation for education, how education competes country-by-country for resources that are finite and on which there are many other valid claims. Some of those present were visibly and audibly astonished at this and the idea that there was no guaranteed global allocation to education did not go down well. But the logic is one which I would defend, for it underlines the points made early in this chapter: a project involving educational support must demonstrate that it has a more valid claim on limited funds than other competing bids; if it is regarded by the recipient as an urgent priority — and one that is more important than staffing a hospital or building a road — then it proves its own validity. Moreover, by *not* making sectoral allocations, the donor clears away some of the rigidity of his own system by giving greater freedom to his professional groups to work together on health, agriculture, rural development and other areas of human endeavour where an educational element is only one (sometimes small) part of a network of integrated development. It is the crossing of such traditional boundaries that the professional groups within aid agencies need to accomplish as urgently as do the systems to which I refer in the first part of this chapter.

Nevertheless, the reservation in the conclusion of Dorothy Njeuma's paper is an important one: education is such a long-term process that it is easily set aside in favour of projects that appear likely to produce swifter and more tangible results. It is difficult to balance the apparent short-term benefits of a dam or a road with the long-term effects of education, especially where manpower supply and demand are so difficult to forecast over a longish time-span. The fact that so many donors' roads appear to lead nowhere in particular and do not always produce the benefits expected emphasises the importance of demonstrating by rigorous argument at the project preparation stage the exact benefits that are expected from any particular package of educational assistance; further, the 'package' approach is attractive to the donor for precisely the reason that he is better able to estimate costs and benefits, comparing them with other potential investments. Much as a recipient would like holes in his system plugged by a donor, often on a temporary basis, it is difficult for agencies to see themselves mainly as plumbers. An integrated plan to provide in-service training for teachers over five years or to provide a coherent staff development plan for a key university department has more appeal to those who allocate resources between sectors than a one-off request to provide a finance officer or three headmasters. These are the facts of life with which donors and recipients must learn to live.

Kenneth King's stimulating and attractive paper raised issues that go beyond the scope of education, and many I agree with. I do not, however, accept his general inference that by requiring, collecting and storing the statistics of a recipient's education system over a number of years the donor is able to gain some indefinably unfair advantage over the recipient. We must not forget that statistics are provided by the recipient who is as much at liberty to store, analyse and draw conclusions from them as the donor; nor is lack of continuity necessarily an endemic feature of a ministry of education, which — if it knows its business — should ensure that it retains an element of continuity in its staffing. Where I believe Kenneth King is right is in encouraging the recipient to challenge the credentials, experience and authority of a donor proposing to operate in a given sector of his education system. I would agree entirely that there are real dangers in contracting a major part of a system — such as teacher training — to a university group in a donor country, without the most careful scrutiny of a group's credentials, experience, competence and reliability. In this respect, the vetting by the recipient needs to be as intense, as discriminating and as penetrating as that of the donor when he appraises a project with a view to funding it. It is important to remember that while a donor agency itself may have (and usually has) the best of motives, those who obtain contracts against which aid funds are provided may be in business for cash that will enable them to extend their research base or retain otherwise redundant staff. While it is the donor's responsibility (and in his interests) to ensure 'fair trading', the buck ultimately stops with the recipient, whose system is ultimately at risk.

Underlying the Conference is the basic question: in which directions should aid to education go in the coming years? Which priorities are likely to attract the attention of both recipients and donors, and what patterns of assistance are we likely to see develop? In the paragraphs that follow I attempt to look forward to some of the developments I think most likely or at least most desirable:

1 Donor co-ordination

In future there is likely to be far more donor co-ordination, not only in education, but across the whole aid spectrum. The Conference revealed this to be an area of some concern for recipients, in the sense that they fear that donors may 'gang up' on them. This is a natural fear, but one over which recipients have a degree of control themselves by maintaining the initiative (by, for example, calling their own donor meetings). There may be considerable benefits in encouraging donors to co-operate in strengthening a part of an education system, rather than placing the sector in the omnipotent hands of one donor.

2 Inter-sectoral co-ordination

Education specialists in donor agencies will tend to work more widely with ministries other than education. ODA's manpower reviews in all sectors now involve representatives of departments of manpower and planning in their surveys of British assistance to a sector. For education particularly this is a welcome development, given the close relationship between education, training and the labour market. I hope that the time will come when closer collaboration with ministries of health, agriculture and the environment develops.

3 An innovative role

If education systems at last begin to meet their own manpower requirements by producing enough teachers to run the system, the emphasis for donors will tend to be on increasing quality and efficiency or the pump-priming of innovative elements. It is at the margins of systems that important work remains to be done, for which ministers, with their huge recurrent salary and maintenance burdens, have no spare funds.

4 Indigenous research

There must be a greater emphasis on developing the indigenous research capacities of existing institutions, by greater collaboration in the first instance between donor country institutions and those in recipients' countries with the burden for taking initiatives gradually transferred to the indigenous institutions. There are substantial built-in resistances to self-reliance in research matters. It might help if there were a conscious demystifying of research as an activity, with an emphasis on the basic gathering of information and its formulation as a basis for decision-making. People need to understand that useful research does not have to be undertaken at high levels of abstraction, that it is a practical and not necessarily complicated tool.

5 Institution strengthening

If universities and other institutions are really going to reappraise their functions with a view to better serving the community they may need outside help. This will involve donor countries' institutions in some radical reappraisal of their own functions and community attitudes, if they are capable of it.

6 Links

From the above it follows that inter-country links will be increasingly important at all levels throughout systems. This will require greater selectivity, appraisal and exiguity on the part of recipients. As suggested above, it may demand a greater degree of genuine learning and discovery — and hence a fundamental change of attitude — among institutions in donor countries.

7 Voluntary agencies

In the development of non-formal learning systems and the encouragement of local community activity, the voluntary agencies will require greater support and recognition. In British terms, this is already effected through the £-for-£ Joint Funding Scheme which channels ODA funds into a substantial number of non-formal education projects throughout the world. Government departments in developing countries may well have to learn to 'think small' and be prepared to find means of accepting greater diversity and local variation in meeting the needs of a variety of groups among the population.

8 Targeted training

The training of personnel overseas is an area of considerable ambivalence. Both donors and recipients speak of the need to strengthen indigenous or regional training facilities, with a consequent reduction of dependence on institutions in donor countries, whose courses and methods may be seen as irrelevant to the 'real' situation, and even culturally damaging. Yet there is an equally powerful groundswell of opinion in donor and recipient countries that demands the right under the banner of 'student mobility' to have free flows of students to other countries, and especially to metropolitan nations. This issue was raised and discussed at the Conference itself. Ministers reiterated the views expressed at the 1984 Cyprus Commonwealth Education Conference that Britain should take more students from their countries. Given that this flow will inevitably continue, the emphasis will tend to be increasingly on training for specific purposes at carefully selected courses, often tied in with institutional link arrangements.

9 Discrimination

As I have said already, recipients are likely to become considerably more critical of donors' claims to competence in given sectors and to take matters more firmly into their own hands. This will be a welcome development leading to a greater sense of partnership between donor and recipient, and perhaps a greater understanding that institutions in donor countries have genuine lessons to learn from their counterparts in the recipient nations.

One major problem for Britain is going to be to maintain a reservoir of overseas experience among its new generations of educationists. In the future few will have worked overseas in positions that will give them real insights into the problems encountered in a different cultural milieu; and this will affect the *quality* of assistance. It is for the agencies to think hard and carefully about the implications of the gradual substitution of institutional links for a large cadre of teachers with past overseas experience and a strong commitment to an overseas 'career'. The challenge will be to develop reservoirs of interest in Britain amongst local authorities and institutions, and to find ways of offering the returned volunteer cadre an opportunity to keep in touch with its overseas interests and return in one way or another to service overseas.

The biggest challenges will be within the structure of our own aid agencies. If education is genuinely to integrate with other disciplines in an effort to break away from total dependence on the formal structures of school, college and university, the agencies themselves will have to be prepared to adopt a more flexible response to the inter-disciplinary demands of subtler patterns of teaching and learning. It is no use advocating the possibility of a ministry of agriculture and education, or of health and education, or of work and education, as the Minister for Overseas Development, Timothy Raison suggested in his opening address, unless the agencies themselves reflect such structures. This will involve a closer and more exciting partnership between groups of professionals within donor agencies and a greater sense of integration within aid agencies.

The Conference will not lead to any obvious major change in ODA's overall educational policy. Our approach remains country-specific, and I believe rightly so. One essential issue at the Conference revolved round the problems that recipients encounter over donors' internal policies. Agency roles and guidelines on methods of giving aid are one thing that we all have to live with; but global educational policies, supposedly applicable across a whole range of diverse countries, seem to me to introduce an unnecessary rigidity. Hence ODA's education 'policy' for any particular country is to meet the specific priority educational needs of that country in relation to overall economic and social development. What will change as a consequence of Windsor will be our perceptions, country by country, of what is needed, where, and how.

We shall also, I hope, continue to root our educational expertise in the British education system. My colleagues and I are very conscious of the dangers of the expatriate who knows more about African education systems than his own. Our in-house team maintains close contact with British institutions — and we constantly encourage our aid personnel to renew their contact with the British education scene, through work or study. We shall increasingly look to British departments, such as the Department of Education in Developing Countries in the London Institute of Education, and its sister departments elsewhere in Britain, to provide a genuinely co-operative dimension to technical co-operation.

PART II DOCUMENTS

African education under siege

Peter Williams

Introduction

Consider the following statements:

> (We) cannot (be) blind ... to certain lingering shortcomings. These are both quantitative and qualitative, and must at all costs be remedied in the next few decades, to ensure that Africa may enter the twenty-first century on an equal footing of opportunity with the other regions of the world. One inescapably comes to a twofold conclusion: the Addis Ababa Plan's forecast of universal primary schooling by 1980 has not been realised, owing mainly to a higher rate of population growth and an initial underestimate of the actual population of Africa; and the number of illiterates has grown steadily greater in absolute figures. In many cases, serious disparities persist in regard to access to education, adversely affecting in particular people living in rural areas and women and girls, expecially at the secondary and higher levels of education. These shortcomings and difficulties, like those connected with premises, equipment and materials, and the widespread lack of adequately trained teachers, are attributable in many cases to lack of resources. In some cases they stem from social causes, such as family poverty. The high rates of student wastage through drop-outs and repeats, which are a cause of illiteracy and which reduce the intake capacity of education systems, are both social and educational in origin. Often, it is the very conception of education, its aims and content, its structures, the values that it instils and the spirit in which it operates that are at issue.[1]

> African education today is not a pretty picture for anybody to contemplate, and there can be few who had anything to do with the painting of it who can regard the results of their work with complacency or self-congratulation.[2]

These two statements reflect the rather sombre contemporary mood about the state of education in Africa. The first of them was made by African Ministers of Education in the Harare Declaration issued at the end of their most recent UNESCO Regional Conference, the Conference of Ministers of Education and those Responsible for Economic Planning in African Member States held at Harare, Zimbabwe, 28 June – 3 July, 1982.

The second statement was in fact written in 1969, by a British commentator on education in Africa, as part of a paper prepared for a Conference rather like the present one. But I suppose it might equally have been written in 1949, and will I fear be equally appropriate in 1989. One of the unchanging fashions in African education is to declare that it is not a pretty picture to contemplate! I shall first argue that such a statement is not really quite fair. Few if any aspects of life in a rapidly changing society — whether it be the England of yesteryear or contemporary Africa — are likely to present an entirely 'pretty' picture. The quantitative inadequacy and qualitative deficiencies of social provision will always be painfully evident in societies in the course of transition. One must not be unrealistic by expecting too much progress too fast.

For references see page 105.

Table 1. Africa: enrolment (millions) and adjusted gross enrolment ratios (per cent), 1960, 1970, 1982

	1960		1970		1982	
	No.	Ratio	No.	Ratio	No.	Ratio
First level	19.3	(44)	33.4	(57)	68.5	(81)
Second level	1.9	(5)	5.4	(11)	17.0	(25)
Third level	0.2	(1)	0.5	(2)	1.6	(4)
All levels	21.4	(20)	39.2	(34)	87.1	(44)

Source: *A Summary Statistical Review of Education in the World*, prepared by UNESCO Office of Statistics for the 39th Session of the International Conference on Education, Tables 4 and 10.

Progress

The bare facts of recent African educational expansion are remarkable. Data for Africa as a whole (including North Africa and the Republic of South Africa) has recently become available for the period up to 1982. Even if, as African Ministers themselves confirmed, the 1961 Addis Ababa targets were not all achieved, these pan-African figures (Table 1) show a really massive increase in enrolment at each level over a relatively short time-span. Opportunities for access to schooling have been completely revolutionised in a very brief period with a dramatic effect on equality of opportunity to enter school. The rise in second level enrolment is particularly great. This is significant in that a society where 25 per cent or so will have attended secondary school is going to be qualitatively different, because of the 'density' of educated people, from one with only 5 per cent. Similar conclusions might be drawn from the literacy figures, showing a drop in adult illiteracy from 71 per cent in 1970 to an expected 54 per cent in 1985, which is predicted to fall further to only 35 per cent by the year 2000.[3]

Such quantitative data are admittedly crude and partial indicators of progress. One knows for example that nominal enrolment and actual school attendance can differ quite markedly. The indicators say nothing of the quality of education given, except that the literacy figures, if true, appear to indicate some acquisition of basic skills, presumably through primary schooling for the most part. But to complete the record one must also take account of some qualitative achievements by African countries in terms of the range of educational services offered, the localisation of cadres of educational personnel, the rise in qualification of teachers on average, the unification of the previously fragmented education systems, the enhanced educational opportunities for females.

African educators may justly claim that they have wrought qualitative changes not only in African schools but in African societies too. These have become schooled societies, different in kind from pre-school societies. There is a new and greater awareness of what lies beyond the immediate homestead and village; a comprehension that there are objective truths, independent of the authority of senior kin or community elders. This marks a complete change in people's outlook. With the substitution, as determinants of social mobility, of 'achievement criteria' in the form of educational certificates, diplomas and degrees, for the 'ascriptive criteria' of inherited social status, school education seems assured of a future.

Constraints and challenges

Population and the economy

The 'crisis' in African education is largely one of physical and economic difficulty in meeting the level of education demands, and of closing the gap between population and resources.

Population growth is very rapid indeed, more so in sub-Saharan Africa as a region than in any other region of the world. The effect of this can be dramatically illustrated. Between 1985 and 2000, numbers in the 5–14 age group are expected to grow by 5 per cent in more developed countries; by rather under 30 per cent in Latin America and the Caribbean; but by as much as 60 per cent in Africa.[4] More starkly, in developed countries one in *seven* of the population will in 2000 be in the 5–14 age group, whereas in Africa the figure will be one in *four*. Not only therefore is there a bigger school expansion job to be done in Africa, but there are proportionately fewer people in the working population to carry the burden of that schooling. In the year 2000 in developed countries the ratio of people aged over 19 to those aged under 19 will be 71:29. In Africa it will be 45:55.[5] So in developed countries every 100 adults will have 41 'minors' dependent on them, compared with 122, three times as many, in Africa. The dependency ratio in Africa is thus extremely unfavourable and limitation of the population growth rate (not necessarily of ultimate population size) in sub-Saharan Africa takes on an extreme urgency.

In the face of this population growth the economic juxtaposition of low and declining income per head and comparatively high education expenditure per head is particularly serious. The World Bank's recent report *Toward Sustained Development in Sub-Saharan Africa: A Joint Programme of Action* opens with the following grim passage:

> No list of economic or financial statistics can convey the human misery spreading in sub-Saharan Africa. A special study by the United Nations Children's Fund (UNICEF), *The Impact of Recession on Children*, has documented how children have been the victims of economic decline. In Zambia's poorer northern regions, height-for-age ratios have fallen in all age categories under 15 years. Child mortality in sub-Saharan Africa was 50 per cent higher than the average of developing countries in the 1950s: now it is almost double the average. Moreover, despite the surges in food imports and food aid, an estimated 20 per cent of Africa's population still eats less than the minimum needed to sustain good health. The number of severely hungry and malnourished people is estimated to have increased from close to 80 million in 1972–74 to as many as 100 million in 1984.
>
> The illustrative scenarios in the World Bank's World Development Report 1984 suggest that, even with some fundamental improvements in domestic economic management, per capita incomes in sub-Saharan Africa will continue to fall during 1985–95.[6]

According to the Report total Gross Domestic Product (GDP) in sub-Saharan Africa — after growing at 3.6 per cent per annum between 1970 and 1980 — *declined* by 1 per cent in 1981, by 0.2 per cent in 1982 and by 0.7 per cent in 1983. It is when one remembers that population growth was about 3 per cent per annum that the seriousness of the position sinks in, for this meant that *per caput* GDP fell by 4 per cent, 3.3 per cent and 3.8 per cent in 1981, 1982 and 1983 respectively, or about 11½ per cent over the three-year period as a whole.[7] This would be a development of catastrophic proportions if it were to continue for at all long. Even though the recession will not hit all countries with the same impact, it is clear that economic conditions are unlikely to become more favourable for sub-Saharan Africa as a whole. The oil crisis, depressed prices for many of Africa's commodity exports, external indebtedness, the severe drought and accompanying famine, are all taking a harsh toll of economic development and cast a long shadow over education development prospects.

High unit costs

Cost constraints hit sub-Saharan Africa particularly hard. The unit costs of education have proved to be high compared with those elsewhere. Primary school teachers in sub-Saharan Africa are paid on average 6 to 7 times per capita GDP, compared with 2.5 times in Asia and Latin America.[8] There is tremendous variation by country. The ratios have been estimated at 4 in Ghana and 22 in Mali.[9] As the World Bank observes, the high ratios in Africa are a reflection more of their scarcity value at independence than today. Spatial factors are another contributory factor — low densities of population mean that primary schools in rural areas cannot always reach a viable size and they also necessitate boarding facilities in rural areas at secondary level. Costs of distributing materials, of providing effective supervision of schools, of holding in-service courses and conferences for teachers are high because of the great distances involved. Budgetary constraints are pressing hard on governments at the present time with revenue falling short, and much of the public budget being pre-empted by defence and other public services. Many African countries have 20 per cent or more of their budgets devoted to education. In Kenya at one point about 30 per cent of the budget was spent on education and the country as a whole was devoting 7.2 per cent of GDP to education expenditure. In Africa as a whole, public expenditure on education rose from 2.7 per cent in 1960 to 4.7 per cent in 1981.[10] The outlook for educational expenditures is bleak, not only because many African economies are in poor shape, but also because of a number of inbuilt cost escalation factors as education systems expand. In particular there is the problem that the thrust of enrolment expansion is moving to secondary and higher levels which for a number of reasons (better qualified teachers, smaller teaching loads, smaller classes, expensive plant and equipment, residential facilities etc.) are much more expensive than primary school. The ratios of *enrolment* between primary, secondary and tertiary education in Africa were 90:9:1 in 1960; but 78:20:2 in 1982.[11] When these data are plotted against *unit costs* as a percentage of GDP per capita one finds that for Eastern Africa the percentages are 16:85:1040 at successive levels and in francophone Africa 29:143:804.[12]

This highlights one of the major cost-related policy issues facing African countries, namely how to move from UPE to ULSE. The data shows that countries have made notable progress in moving to universal or near universal education at elementary level over a primary cycle of six or seven years duration. The problem now being grappled with in so many countries

94

is what happens in grades 7 to 10 and the various restructuring exercises currently in train (to 6–3–3 in Nigeria, to 8–4–4 in Kenya, to 7–2–3 in Zambia and Botswana, to 6–3–3 at some distant date in Ghana) attempt to solve the issue. There is probably much useful insight and experience to be shared on issues such as this, and one question the Conference could usefully address is how one can reduce the possibility that African countries may individually try to reinvent the wheel, instead of sharing experience and adapting solutions others have developed. How can useful ideas, practices and techniques be communicated more rapidly and effectively?

The serious obstacle to solving the universalisation of lower secondary education is the inherited model of high cost specialised secondary schools existing in many countries. The old model of secondary schools — large, specialised curriculum, graduate teachers, big compounds and often boarding attendance — cannot be afforded for everybody. Policy makers are reluctant to leave prestigious existing schools intact and to provide pale imitations as part of an overtly two-tier system of secondary schools. Parents in any case reject an explicitly dual system as the fate of Nigeria's secondary moderns and Zimbabwe's F2 schools testifies. For economic reasons one wishes to provide something local and with day attendance and therefore modest in size.

But all this poses a tremendous challenge in organisational and curricular terms if one is to create a system which is equitable, economical, and provides the kind of broad curriculum appropriate to the lower secondary level. There is a challenge here to find something which is genuinely intermediate between local inexpensive unspecialised primary schools and regional expensive specialised secondary schools. Kenya and Botswana, to name just two examples, offer interesting models of low-cost, part community financed, localised lower secondary schools; though whether these can become the basis of mainstream provision, rather than a voluntary supplementation of what government provides, remains to be seen.

Matching demand and supply

The high cost per pupil in the upper reaches of African education systems raises problems. High private rates of return to education, particularly at secondary and higher levels, are juxtaposed with low social rates of return. Education at these levels is in a sense underpriced to the consumers in relation to the private financial benefit it can bring, because wage differentials for additional years of education are so high (and protected by lack of competition in the form of jealously guarded public service salary scales). The private costs of education to the individual are a small part of total cost, and private benefits are high. To the state, costs of providing education at secondary and tertiary level are high (partly because of those same high wage differentials) and the social return in terms of actual increased productivity (as opposed to salaries paid), is sometimes low. High private pay-offs from schooling and low social benefits are a recipe for trouble for education policy makers for they suggest that parental demand for education will be high, yet difficult or impossible to meet because of lowish benefits to society. However budgets are limited and governments find it difficult to expand public employment at prevailing high wage rates. Thus even in economies with surplus labour, the message comes down to aspirants for further education that there is no 'manpower requirement' justification for their having more education.

But the task of aligning the private and public benefit is difficult politically. Dampening private demand by transferring more of the cost of education to private households and by limiting pay differentials for higher qualifications is unpopular: just as the adjustment of social rates of return through making cost savings in education and raising productivity (but not pay) of graduates is fraught with political complications.

The net result of all this is paradoxical. Logic, supported by research findings, may suggest a shift of emphasis to primary education because of its ostensible higher social rate of return, with productivity gains outweighing the cost of primary school. But strong parental demand is directed to the expansion of education levels which are most expensive to the state to provide.

Expansion-induced dilution of quality

My earlier emphasis on the achievements of education in sub-Saharan Africa, before confronting the darker side of the picture, was deliberate. This was only partly because I consider African education has too many detractors. It is also because I believe that the 'crisis' that many people identify arises in part from education's very success and from the disappointment of expectations that educational expansion inevitably brings in its train: 'more' means 'worse'; 'more' means less scarcity and therefore lower rewards. In some senses more means worse in the course of rapid educational expansion. When a system doubles or triples its size in only a few years, the average quality of teachers and buildings tends to decline, teachers tend to be less well trained and the average teacher is less experienced. It is quite possible that on average the ability of pupils to perform well in school also declines, regardless of whether classes get bigger and the system gets more impersonal, simply because more marginal populations are coming within the school net.

It is equally true that the expansion of education automatically reduces the 'premium' education bestows, whether in terms of social exclusivity or of a place well up the queue for good jobs or marriages. As much in London and Los Angeles as in Lusaka and Lagos, the social consequences of universalisation of education worry the socially more advantaged parents who would like their children to attend 'select' schools in the course of their preparation for further education and professional careers.

The universalisation and comprehensivisation of schooling can sometimes appear a threat to these concerns. As a result high-status parents may seek out more exclusive schools, often necessarily in the private sector or abroad, or pay for private coaching for their children. Certainly there is more to the quality 'crisis' in Africa than universalisation, as I will discuss. But I do believe that the 'crisis' is in part the direct and inevitable consequence of educational expansion and the recruitment to the school system of pupils more disadvantaged intellectually, physically, geographically, economically and socially.

It is also obvious, so obvious that I will not devote much space to it, that scarcity diminishes as supply expands. Any given level of education qualification appears to command an ever lower premium in the job market. In relation to any stated job, higher qualifications will be asked for by employers as the supply of candidates becomes more plentiful. Paradoxically, the message that reaches parents is not that schooling has lost its point as a result of the 'diploma disease'; rather the lesson many of them learn is that their children need *more* education if they are to get a job!

Unmotivated teachers

The economic constraints referred to above have bitten deeply into the real value of salaries of teachers and other education personnel. They are tempted to engage in other economic activities to supplement their income, 'moonlighting' by doing unauthorised supplementary work and — in urban areas particularly — drawing an increasing share of their income from private coaching. Absenteeism has become more widespread. In consequence regular teachers have in many instances become virtually part-time in their service, devoting much of their time to other economic activities in trading or farming and running private businesses.

Contemporary management structures in education are not always adequate to check this — the teachers normally cannot be removed or disciplined by school heads or local boards of management. They have thus become non-accountable to those most affected by a poor level of performance — parents and the community. There are widespread complaints that teachers no longer deport themselves with the same commitment to their jobs as hitherto. Alternatively qualified teachers may resign, causing high wastage rates and forcing governments which once seemed to be getting on top of their teacher supply situations to revert to the employment of untrained teachers. In Ghana for example, the proportion of untrained teachers rose between 1979–80 and 1982–83 from 44 per cent to 46 per cent at primary level, and from 28 per cent to 30 per cent at middle school level. In Botswana, the proportion has been falling but is still 31 per cent in 1984. In Zimbabwe 50 per cent of primary teachers were untrained in 1983.[13] Eicher cites figures of 61 per cent for Sierra Leone and 70 per cent for Chad.[14] In some special situations there is an outflow abroad to countries which offer better salaries for secondary graduate teachers and where demand has been high. Nigeria and Zimbabwe have both been recruiters from abroad. Many African universities have witnessed a serious outflow of senior staff to university posts elsewhere in the continent, to international organisations, or posts in the industrialised countries.

Erosion of public confidence

The squeeze on budgets also tends to result in allocations for books and materials being reduced more severely than other items. In any objective sense this represents an irrational development, since such materials represent an important support for teachers and constitute pupils' only survival kit if teachers are not functioning properly.

The result of these developments is a growing erosion of parental confidence in the quality of schools in the public system, and a decline in the respect in which teachers are held in their communities. Those well-to-do parents who can afford it exercise the alternative option of patronising private schools. They 'buy' an almost guaranteed place in the remaining good quality primary and secondary schools by sending their children to private nursery schools, preparatory schools, international schools and private tutors; all this in order to get high qualifying marks on the entrance exam.

At higher levels the wealthiest parents may even opt out of the local university system if they doubt its quality and find it prone to protracted closures, and send their children abroad for higher education.

However, the great majority of parents cannot opt out. They cannot afford to. Some may feel discontented with the local schools — they want more effective teaching, proper discipline and order, good examination results. Others are even less ambitious. For their families this is the first generation of schooling and they cling to the hope that comes from exposing their children to a new world of knowledge, to a different culture associated with paid jobs, a more sophisticated lifestyle and the ability to manipulate the modern world.

Given the problems of morale and resource shortage, the remarkable thing is the degree not only of tolerance but of active support that schooling continues to enjoy in Africa south of the Sahara. Despite all the criticisms of irrelevance and poor quality of the schools, parents continue in their hordes to patronise them. According to the recent *Summary Statistical Review of Education in the World* prepared by UNESCO's Office of Statistics for the International Conference on Education in Geneva in October 1984, first level enrolment in Africa was still increasing — by 2.4 million per annum 1970–75, 1.2 million per annum between 1975 and 1980 and by 4 million a year since 1980.[15] To be of any real interest these figures require disaggregation but they do appear to contradict suggestions made in the 1970s that demand for primary education in Africa was about to dry up.

Table 2: Average survival rates by region for cohorts starting first level education around 1980–81

Regions and groups of countries	Number of countries indicated	Percentage of 80/81 cohort reaching grade			
		1	2	3	4
Africa: Arab States	6	100	91	91	83
French-speaking	16	100	84	82	74
English-speaking	12	100	82	77	72
Portuguese-speaking	4	100	57	43	26
Total Africa	38	100	83	80	71
All developing countries	88	100	82	76	69
Europe	19	100	99	99	98

Source: *A Summary Statistical Review of Education in the World*, prepared by UNESCO Office of Statistics for the 39th Session of the International Conference on Education, October 1984, Table 17.

To be sure the picture is marred by the high incidence of early school leaving — a more accurate term than 'drop out'. This remains a major challenge and much remains to be done to eliminate it as Table 2 shows. At the same time it is unrealistic to expect that in the transition from an unschooled to a schooled society all those groups being brought within the fold of the school will at once be able to manage a full six- or seven-year primary course. It takes time for the household economy to adjust to the loss of children's services as child-minders and helpers in the home and on the farm.*

Meeting the challenge

These constraints and challenges — and I have deliberately been selective — amount to a situation where one could speak of education in sub-Saharan Africa being under siege. Africa must identify appropriate strategies to cope with this siege.

The two most pressing tasks if the siege is to be lifted are non-educational: to bring the rate of population growth to a more manageable level and to revitalise the economy. Internal policies and action and external assistance, particularly with resolving the indebtedness problem, are both called for. While both tasks are non-educational in the short-term, in the longer-term a fully relevant education would make its contribution to resolving them.

When we turn to educational strategies themselves as ways of overcoming the siege the three main possibilities would appear to be passive reaction, radical restructuring and planned improvement. I will dub these the 'sit-out', the 'break-out' and the 'work-out' options.

The 'sit-out' option

One approach is reacting by responsive adjustment, rather than by premeditated intervention, to successive pressures afflicting the system. One could argue that this is in fact the main strategy that African governments have pursued. Remarkably little study has been made of the processes of adjustment, of how the resource gap is actually handled: writings about the size of the problem and advocacy of alternative — often improbable — solutions, seem more plentiful. Observers with long memories cannot help reflecting that 20 years ago, when education systems were a third of their present size, treasuries and aid agencies were already claiming that 'the crisis' was imminent and that insoluble resource gaps were developing. But enrolment growth has continued and in some cases even accelerated, while tuition charges to parents have generally fallen.

How in the face of economic difficulty has it been possible to continue funding the education system?

---

* For this reason the use in these transitional situations of 'input-output ratios' (measured in terms of school years actually invested as compared with those needed for graduation) as an indication of system efficiency can be positively unhelpful. A country which puts only half its children through a full six-year course, leaving the other half totally unschooled, will score high. It will decrease its rating dramatically if it manages to get the remaining 50 per cent into school for an average of four rather than six years schooling in the first instance. Real and dramatic progress may earn a completely negative rating according to the input-output ratio.

Salaries have been allowed to decline in relative value so that teaching has become a depressed profession. The main symptoms have already been discussed. They are an unwillingness to enter teaching on the part of the best qualified graduates, heavy teacher turnover and wastage, high rates of teacher absenteeism, and 'moonlighting' by teachers. In some countries the qualification pattern of the teaching force has worsened, manifested on the one hand by a high number and proportion of unqualified teachers, and in other cases by a deliberate decision to recruit less highly qualified and paid teachers as a substitute for graduates or diplomates. Third, the class size has risen in some countries. Fourth, the length of the school term has been curtailed with schools starting late and finishing early, particularly those residential institutions where fewer days of school operation involve the saving of expenditure. It would be interesting to compare the actual number of school days per year in 1984 with what it used to be in 1964.

The point has already been made that the ability spread in schools may now be wider than hitherto. There is also the suspicion of qualitative erosion. It is sometimes alleged — though difficult to prove — that supposedly fixed standards have actually fallen and that attainment certificates in anglophone Africa represent a lower level of achievement today than they used to decades ago. The provision of books and materials is less generous than formerly. Transport for inspection and supervision is in seriously short supply.

In short, there are within an education system very many possibilities of subtle adjustment and dilution. The scope for qualitative erosion, without any direct challenge being made to the managers, has been considerable. The concerned professional is unhappy to see the erosion of standards. But it has often seemed in the past as if maintaining quality of education has been regarded as bringing less political reward than numbers of schools and teachers and particularly of enrolments. Is it still true even today that an attempt to climb back to former standards of provision, though laborious and time-consuming, would in fact be politically unrewarding? Or can public support for school improvement be marshalled, even though it demands more economic sacrifice?

The 'break-out' option

The second option might be described as the 'break-out' option, just as a besieged army might try to rush through the encircling forces. In education terms this might involve radical approaches and solutions, which involve redesigning the basic institutions of the school, the existing pedagogical organisation and the examination system.

The *school* can be (and is) criticised as being an institution which cuts pupils off from their traditional communities and, through its hierarchical system of grades and its formalised structure of teaching, often fails to produce genuine learning by the pupils. Individuality and creativity are suppressed in favour of rote learning, standardised content, artificial measures of achievement. The content of the curriculum is said to be theoretical and formal. Schooling is somewhat expensive because teachers are full-time and salaried and pupils have a full school day and five-day week. Radical alternatives could involve part-time instruction of students

100

either on the basis of a shorter day (or week) in formal schools, or else by using other religious and community institutions as providers of education. On the fringes of education systems, often by accident rather than design, some of these alternatives can be seen in embryo.

But whilst it is true that the closed nature of schools and the poverty of their material resources is a serious obstacle to learning, there is evidence from the public debates on the Zambian education reforms for example, that the notion of radical restructuring may not commend itself readily to parents. The school is an institution which is cheap to run and its standardised nature is a positive advantage in terms of equity and mobility of students and teachers. It is easily replicable as an institution, and it serves social functions of certification and custodianship of children which would be hard to replace. If schools have in a sense failed, it is arguable that it is partly because they have not been given a fair chance, with adequate resources or effective management.

Complete redesign of the traditional *pedagogy* and its *organisation* is sometimes advocated. An extreme model of the type of alternative solution that might be contemplated is exemplified by Project Impact in Asia. It includes the use of older students (rather like the former monitorial system) as a learning resource for younger pupils; voluntary and cheap assistance from the community to amplify teaching resources and reduce the number of paid teachers; extensive provision of materials and books for independent learning to supplement what the teachers themselves can do; and a range of different-sized physical spaces for learning. Clearly there are many ideas here which are pedagogically attractive, and although teachers and parents in Asia have not apparently seen Impact schools as preferable to the traditional schools, their objection may be more to the inbuilt dualism implied than to some of the innovations embodied in the model as such.

A quite different set of radical pedagogical reforms would involve substituting TV, radio and other mass media for traditional school inputs. Extreme versions of this option, using TV, have been tried and abandoned in Ivory Coast. Experience suggests that with younger learners the use of mass media can more usefully serve to enrich the work of teachers within the framework of the school system rather than to replace teachers. This neutralises their value as a cost-saving device. As an aid to self-learning by older out-of-school students at the upper levels of education they may have more to offer.

Finally *the examination system* is under fire. There is proper doubt as to what many of the examinations currently in use actually measure. The cramping effects of exams on the curriculum are much criticised, seeming as they do to shape the curriculum instead of being moulded to it. However traditional examinations do ostensibly provide an objective measurement, convenient as a criterion for job selection. This in the public view gives them a marked advantage over personal recommendation systems of appointment to jobs or admission to higher courses. Kinship and other social ties are recognised to be so strong that safeguards against them are vital. Although attempts have been made in some countries to supplement the evidence of written examinations with performance in community service or political commitment, it seems clear that the complete abandonment of examinations would be both technically and politically unrealistic. So the most attractive course must be examination improvement rather than replacement. Some pioneering work in Kenya has suggested that examinations can be a lever for bringing about curriculum reform rather than an obstacle to it.

Educational renewal: the 'work-out' option

Is there some middle way between passive reaction and radical restructuring, between 'sit-out' and 'break-out'? Can some middle way of purposeful educational renewal be worked out, confronting the surrounding problems and overcoming them by skill and will? There is some urgency about this, if Africa is not to succumb to another 'dark age' of dependency on others, for the gap in learning achievement between African pupils and students and those in industrialised countries could grow to virtually unbridgeable dimensions if the quantity and quality of resources available to African learners should lag further behind those in Europe and North America where there is increasing emphasis on both applying and learning new technologies in the education system. Priorities would seem to include:

Professional commitment and the restoration of morale

There is no short cut to restoring standards. The main task is surely to give teachers and students confidence in what they are doing. In the first instance this involves improved professional leadership and management of the teaching profession. The first challenge is to educational leadership to strengthen professionalism in education. This is needed at all levels, but most particularly perhaps the primary which is still regarded in too many countries as an area with no profile or expertise of its own, which can be run by subject specialists trained for secondary schools. The notion that promotion for primary teachers automatically lies in the secondary sector must be ended. On the management side prompt payment, a sense of fairness in postings and promotion, are all part of what is required. It is possible that new mechanisms of data storage and processing systems can help to achieve a speedier and more effective system for handling personnel work and payment of teachers. But equally important is the question of commitment and concerned attitudes on the part of managers which will show teachers that their interests are being protected and promoted. Improved teacher management must have high priority for reasons both of cost reduction and of effectiveness of the education system. But there is surprisingly little written about efficient operation of a teaching service commission in Africa, ways of improving the effectiveness of staffing sections and so forth.

Professional support

Support for teachers should go beyond the personnel function. A climate of professional ferment, excitement, experiment among teachers, is missing. There is a need to provide a multi-pronged programme to assist teachers with professional development and adequate resources to do their job. This involves proper advisory and supervision services through a local inspectorate or advisory cadre; the encouragement of professional meetings

102

and in-service training; the provision of opportunities for self-improvement through study programmes, possibly using distance teaching; creation of resource centres and facilities making it possible for teachers to engage in curriculum development and the making of low-cost teaching aids. Teacher associations can play a useful role in cutting down the isolation of the individual teacher. The articulation of teacher opinion on professional matters should be encouraged. Surely the whole area of teacher support should be a major priority for foreign aid, including recurrent funds for support of organisational expenses and travel in connection with teacher professional activities.

Teacher accountability at local level

Support for teachers must be balanced by greater teacher accountability. If teachers are to take pride in their work they must be properly supervised and managed at local level and have a sense of being responsible to an identifiable authority close at hand. Teachers in Africa have successfully campaigned for a unified system of education and for national managements negotiating with national teachers' unions. This brings many advantages over the former system of multiple managements and of a fragmented teaching profession but it has contributed to a situation where the local control and supervision of teachers has become weak. It is unlikely that effective education can be given unless teachers are in some sense accountable to their school head and beyond her or him to a local management committee on which are represented the interests of the community and parents most closely affected by the quality of a particular school. Decentralisation has its dangers: uninformed arbitrary decisions in which local politics play an undue part may make the lives of teachers miserable unless they are properly protected. But the need is evident to make teachers more accountable for their performance. As experience has shown, in Botswana for example, it is possible to combine local authority management of schools with national conditions of service for teachers. Below the district level, creation of local school boards and management committees is also necessary so that parental and community concern can be brought to bear on the management of schools and to give back to communities a sense of responsibility for schooling of their young people. Nigeria quickly recognised her initial mistake, when UPE was launched, of relieving local communities of the responsibility of school management and support. Community contributions for schools may be tapped more readily where institutions are community-managed. But I have the impression much more detailed work needs to be done on the nature and extent of community contributions and the variety of mechanisms which may be used to elicit a fruitful partnership between community and government.

Strengthening independent learning

One can look at this as 'pedagogical decentralisation'. On grounds of economy, on grounds of equity, on grounds of cost-saving, there is a strong case for providing students with improved possibilities for learning without total reliance on teachers. One priority is strengthening the learning resources within schools, colleges and universities through adequate provision of equipment, paper, books, libraries to support the work of regular teachers. An effort must also be made outside the schools to assist potential learners to undertake part-time study not only of academic kinds but also with an orientation towards the practical knowledge and skills required to earn a livelihood. African governments have done something — Zimbabwe is a notable example — to exploit the possibilities of supporting students through access to formal institutions in out-of-school hours. Library facilities, tutors, correspondence courses, distance teaching facilities can all be mobilised to support self-study by out-of-school learners but the full potential has yet to be exploited. I see this as another major priority for external assistance. Since so much 'material' assistance is required, much of it in the form of imports, one would expect it to appeal to aid donors. The learning resource famine in Africa may be less newsworthy than the food famine, but it may prove almost as destructive of Africa's future.

Cost reduction
There is surely great further potential for cost-saving measures. This is closely tied up with issues of decentralisation of management. There must be an incentive for heads of institutions and local administrators to bring about cost-savings. The issue here is really to align private interest with the public interest. Heads of private institutions often achieve a far higher productivity than the managers of public schools. The latter receive no credit for, or share in results of, economies achieved. Funds that are unspent tend to lapse, and monies saved revert to government. State school heads could frequently complete construction projects using direct labour at a fraction of the official tender prices. Staff overestablishment, resulting from poor organisation and supervision, is a major problem. It can probably only be tackled successfully if institutional managers themselves are provided with incentives to bring about a more economical use of teachers. The problem is worst of all in some higher education institutions where staff student ratios of between 1:4 and 1:8 are not uncommon as averages for whole institutions.

Improved planning and management of national systems
More work is needed — and donor support could be helpful — on improving basic data on the education system through the regular collection and publication of reliable statistical information. The development of management tools — resource allocation criteria, indicators of performance and cost effectiveness, formulae and norms — to assist better administration of the system should be a priority concern.

External assistance
This is mainly a province for other writers within the Conference. Outside resources can help African education to raise the siege which it faces. My own prejudices about the form those resources can most usefully take would put stress on materials (paper, equipment, books); multi-purpose facilities for teacher support and supervision (transport, resource centres); development of information statistics and management instruments that are most amenable to use and adaptation in the most flexible way by participants in education systems themselves, and which make the lightest

possible administrative demands on hard-pressed recipient governments.

It is simple to prescribe remedies for the educational ills of Africa: but so difficult to change the behaviours, resting on social values, that in the final analysis determine whether the remedies can be effective. African societies and cultures contain in abundance energies and creativity. The task is to try to release them in the interest of children and the schools. How can one strengthen the perception of, and commitment to, the public good as a counter-balance to the deeply-rooted web of personal and social obligations to particular groups of kin, fellow tribesmen or clansmen, community, neighbours? How can one ensure that the state, the government, the school are regarded as 'our' state, 'our' government, 'our' school instead of a source of patronage, power and resource for advancement of private networks of social relations? While education professionals have an important role to play, this task is one primarily for the national political leadership. Exhortation is not a sufficient answer. It has been tried and will be tried, but has limited effect. Personal example has more effect. But beyond personal example one needs to create systems of management and incentives which return to communities, teachers, parents and students greater control over the education process. How best can that be done? Here one must throw the ball back to political leaders. Their contribution at our Conference will be the most important of all.

References

1 UNESCO (1982) Conference of Ministers of Education and those Responsible for Economic Planning in African Member States. Harare 28 June–3 July 1982. *Final Report*, p. 39 (paragraphs 6 and 7 of the Harare Declaration). Paris, November 1982.

2 Submission to OECD Conference 1969 by H. Houghton, Deputy Chief Education Adviser, Ministry of Overseas Development.

3 UNESCO (1984). A Summary Statistical Review of Education in the World 1960–82. Paper prepared for 39th Session of the International Conference on Education, 16–25 October 1984, Table 21.

4 UNESCO (1984), Table 3.

5 UNESCO (1984), Table 1.

6 The World Bank (1984). *Toward Sustained Development in Sub-Saharan Africa: A Joint Programme of Action.* Washington DC: The World Bank, p. 9.

7 The World Bank (1984), Table 1.1, p. 10.

8 The World Bank (1984), pp. 29–30.

9 Unpublished study by the World Bank.

10 UNESCO (1984), Table 22.

11 UNESCO (1984), Table 5.

12 Unpublished study by the World Bank.

13 Material drawn from these countries' respective submissions to the International Conference on Education, Geneva, 1984.

14 Eicher, J. C., (1984) Educational Costing and Financing in Developing Countries: Focus on Sub-Saharan Africa. World Bank Staff Working Paper no. 655, p. 185.

15 UNESCO (1984), p. 16.

Education priorities in sub-Saharan Africa

Arthur T. Porter

Education is no longer perceived as a mere sector, divorced from other areas of a nation's activities. I recall the words of the President of Sierra Leone, Dr Siaka Stevens, when he opened the Conference on the Report of the Sierra Leone Education Review on 28 May, 1974:

> An apt designation for the report of the Sierra Leone Education Review might very well be 'All our Future'. All countries are dependent in the last analysis for their development and prosperity on their resources of trained manpower.

It is because of the centrality of education in all our activities that we seek to learn from each other how best 'education for all' can be provided in the context of our shrinking resources.

Before independence, the pattern of education in many of our countries was very narrow and circumscribed. In the former British colonies, it was mainly provided by the missionary societies and very much reflected the charity schools of nineteenth-century England. Nevertheless, it had come to be accepted as an important instrument for social and economic development.

By the time of independence, education had come to be regarded as the most important means by which the whole of society itself could be uplifted. There was a spirit of hope, of optimism, at what education could achieve. Universal primary education became a popular slogan for party manifestos. Education, to the politicians, was not merely a matter of filling gaps in the leadership cadre; it was not merely a matter of economics. It was almost a religion, a superstitious, if touching, faith in the magic of knowledge in itself. In this conviction, the governments were prepared to spend a great part, a disproportionate part, of their national income on education. They passionately believed not only that investment in education would pay off, but that it would also generate much needed employment. They even conceived it as a fundamental right of all citizens.

This mood was symbolised by two important UNESCO Conferences on African education held during that period, in the 1960s. At the 1961 Addis Ababa Conference, the African Education Ministers set themselves targets for educational expansion, one of the most important of which was the achievement of universal primary education by 1980. They were to reach this target by increasing primary school enrolments by 5 per cent each year. In the following year, in 1962, the Education Ministers met again, in Tananarive, to plot targets for the same period, that is, up to 1980, at the level of university education. Another UNESCO Conference, held in Lagos, in 1964, set a target of at least 200 scientific workers and university science teachers per million inhabitants to be achieved by 1980.

During the same period, the sixties, public expenditure on education continued to increase. It is estimated that it rose by an average of 12.5 per cent per annum as compared to 6.5 per cent in the industrialised countries

— a rate higher in the African countries than that of their budgets and much higher than that of the national income in each country.

Yet by the end of that decade it was beginning to be apparent that the results were not commensurate with the increased investments. The primary school rate of increase was only 1.5 per cent compared to the 5 per cent laid down in Addis. Equally significant was the rate of drop-outs. It was estimated that at the rate in the 1960s, two-thirds of the newest generation of young Africans would be destined for illiteracy. Clearly the battle was being lost even before it was begun.

The position in the 1980s is no less alarming. On top of the internal problems facing the system in each country are the external burdens arising from the escalating costs of crude oil and the global economic recession. Many countries are currently unable to meet their financial obligations due to an acute shortage of foreign exchange. Consequently, schools, among other institutions, are bereft of much needed funds for equipment and for the tools of the trade, with the inevitable effect of a deterioration in standards.

The facts are that the numbers of unskilled and illiterate people are increasing in spite of the serious educational efforts being made to overcome the problems. The statistics show that, notwithstanding the Addis Ababa resolution, fewer than 50 per cent of the children of primary school age do get the chance to enrol, on average. And of those who gain entrance large numbers drop out before completing the full school programme. There is also a corresponding imbalance in the number of girls enrolled in the system.

By 1973, an investment of $21 billion on public education by developing countries had reached less than one out of every three children of school age. Indeed as developing countries strained their own fiscal limits, the rate of growth in primary school enrolment began to decline. By the mid 1970s the rate of growth in primary school enrolment is said to have gone down from around 6 per cent per annum to about 4 per cent — a rate barely sufficient to keep pace with the rate of growth in the school-age population.

Given this situation, many countries are now experimenting with other approaches to education, variously referred to as non-formal or informal education. Even so, many countries in our region continue to face the twin problems of low levels of education for society in general and acute shortages of the needed manpower essential for economic growth and development. As our governments have tried, within the limits of their scarce resources, to respond to the demands for expansion of their education system, both the quality and the relevance of the education provided and the efficiency of the systems, have generally deteriorated.

It will be tedious and time wasting in a conference of this nature to attempt to document these general assertions or to illustrate them in detail. The facts are known to all of us and can be supported by the statistics of each of our several countries.

In Sierra Leone, for example, a review of the economy for the last ten years will indicate a condition of continuous crisis. The most serious manifestation of this crisis has been the adverse balance of trade position and the consequent depletion of the country's foreign reserves.

The mainstay of the Sierra Leone economy over the years has been the mining sector, particularly iron-ore and diamond mining. But this sector has been declining in recent years and there is little hope that it will regain its former buoyancy in the near future. Consequently, government's development strategy has been to develop an industrial sector based on the agricultural potential of the country. Towards this end, government, with outside assistance (particularly from the World Bank) has established what are called Integrated Agricultural Development Projects (IADP) in the different provinces of the country, whose objectives are to help farmers establish economic holdings of a variety of agricultural products by the provision of credit at concessionary rates and the provision of effective extension services. The projects are assisted by the Adaptive Crop Research and Extension (ACRE) project, with some US funding, and the Certificate Training Programme, with British inputs, at our Njala University College of the University of Sierra Leone.

One of the major constraints to the development of this sector, agriculture, and the linkage of the modern sector of the economy and the rural, has been the low level of basic education, particularly in the rural areas, which makes it difficult for farmers to take full advantage of the investments being made in the sector through the provision of credit, the supply of seeds, and the facilities for marketing. It is clear that on any analysis or calculation, improvement of basic education in the rural areas to ensure a strong foundation for development must be a priority area for education. This, however, must be read within the context of the earlier statement relating to the economy.

From what has been said above, it is equally clear that the economy is scarcely growing and per capita income is stagnant, if not declining. At the same time, the government is going through an extremely difficult financial situation. Thus its capacity to initiate any development policies requiring significant public expenditure in the near future appears to be seriously circumscribed by the financial constraint.

After the sharp rise in the enrolment ratio of the school age population from 14 per cent to 40 per cent between 1957 and 1970, the position has stagnated around the latter figure. During the same period, the quality of the teacher population has not only stagnated but declined. The publications of the Ministry of Education show the proportion of qualified teachers at the primary level dropping from 54 per cent in 1964 to 40 per cent in 1970 with no significant improvement since then.

At the secondary level, the enrolment ratio has been estimated at about 16.5 per cent, with wide regional disparities, the highest, in the Western Area, being 47 per cent and the lowest, the Northern Province, being 8 per cent. The sex differentials were also quite distinct, with an estimate of 23 per cent enrolment for boys and 10 per cent for girls.

Government policy, as stated in the National Development Plan, is to decelerate the expansion of secondary education while improving the quality and diversifying the content. This policy would appear to be justifiable in view of the recent evidence that secondary school leavers are finding it difficult to obtain employment.

Higher education is provided at the University of Sierra Leone which consists of two Colleges — Fourah Bay College in Freetown and Njala University College some 128 miles from the capital — and the Institute of Education.

There is no accurate information about the employability of graduates from the University, but there are increasing reports of graduates from the Faculty of Arts having difficulty finding jobs, though how far this is due to lack of opportunities as opposed to too high expectations is not clear. However, with the poor performance of the economy, the government's policy to decelerate secondary school expansion (which provided a major outlet for Faculty of Arts graduates as teachers) and the general prospects for employment, a strong case cannot be made for expansion of student numbers at the University, though there is an urgent need for a change in the mix, with more science-based entry than arts.

Sierra Leone, like many of our countries in sub-Saharan Africa, is predominantly rural with a small urban modern sector. The links between the economies of these two sectors are limited. The modern sector obtains a significant part of its consumption of foodstuffs from the rural economy, but little else, except, perhaps, firewood. Conversely, the modern sector supplies relatively few needs of the rural sector, textiles and cooking utensils being perhaps the main items.

It is in this context that the education system, briefly described above, must be considered. A characteristic of that system, as we all know, is that each level is structured as a preparation for the next level, not as an adequate exit point on its own.

Even so, as has been noted earlier, many who start do not complete the system: a high proportion drop out at the first, the primary, and others at the second, the secondary level, all with a sense of academic failure and no special preparation for the world of work.

Further, there appears to be little or nothing in the system which prepares its recipients for self-employment or to occupy risk-taking, decision-making positions in the economy. Instead, rigid adherence to the passing of examinations as the criterion of success implies conformity to work habits rather than scope for the individual initiative. More particularly, the present educational system, to the extent that it reaches the rural areas, is not related to the circumstances of rural life, nor oriented towards the possibilities of developing rural life patterns from the existing nature and level.

Thus, in making a case for expansion of basic or primary education as an area for priority, what will be required is, first, of course, the provision of facilities to reach an increasing number of the people. But equally important is the provision not merely of the addition of overtly rural or agricultural subjects to an already overburdened curriculum, but a more subtle process of changing the character of the subjects taught to give them a self-help orientation with a view to increasing the capacity and the desire of the recipients to initiate change in their subsequent lives.

The lack of contact between a mainly rural and small-scale economy and the inherited western nineteenth-century educational system, characteristic of most of our countries in sub-Saharan Africa, has already been noted. It is a fundamental problem which affects all development, and a solution of which must be a priority concern for education.

This misfit or lack of sufficient relevance between what is provided and what is needed, is true not only at the primary level but throughout the system. It certainly is true for technical education. In many of our countries, the courses provided are those intended to turn out western-style artisans, able to fit into a skilled work-force as urban wage-earners, even though an insufficient number of such jobs is available, while what is more needed is a steady supply of self-employed artisans with some business knowledge, able to seek out and develop for themselves business opportunities related in the first instance to agriculture; for example, the making and servicing of agricultural tools and equipment, motor vehicle and tractor repairs and services, maintenance of water and power supplies and such like. There is, admittedly, some of this going on today, but it is an unregulated process. It should develop further, giving the proper orientation in technical education.

Expansion and improvement of basic education and of technical training opportunities are, in my view, areas for priority in educational provision. And throughout the system there is an urgent need to ensure a better fit between the manpower demands of the economy and the products of the education system.

The economic forecast in many of our countries, certainly in mine, is, as has been indicated, not rosy. It is unlikely that there will be the needed funding available to finance the needed changes in the education system. And yet, unless the funds are forthcoming, and the education system changed, the expected returns to investment in other sectors of the economy will not accrue. It is to be hoped, therefore, that in this kind of impasse, aid, competent and adequate, will be provided to facilitate the needed changes in education, fundamental for economic and social development.

I have mentioned, and I hope made the case for, two areas which merit consideration for priority treatment, both quantitatively and qualitatively. There is a third which merits equal consideration, but from another angle of vision. I refer to the area of higher education. Sierra Leone regrettably does not regard development in this area as a major objective in its national development plan. My concern here is not to the need for a quantitative expansion of the student population nor to the accepted need for a better balance in the mix of students with more students in the sciences than in the arts.

I refer to the need to use the university more than is currently done, to educate the nation on the realities of living in a technological and scientific age. The university is the apex of any country's education system. Many of our countries have only one such institution within their borders; such an institution is surely expected therefore to provide the needed leadership to the whole system, and, equally important, to instil into its students, what ever their discipline, an awareness of the nature of the country's under-development, to infuse a spirit of self-reliance and a readiness and willingness to initiate and innovate.

Many of our countries, in my view, are missing out because they have consciously or unconsciously accepted outside judgements and assessments which negate the importance of the university as the capstone of the system for undertaking the needed research for the whole system from the angles of relevance and efficiency. We have come to see our universities too closely in terms of manpower development. The priority now is to see them more in their cognitive role.

We meet under the aegis of the London Institute of Education to look at our education systems and to examine what can be done in the context of a rising demand for education without a corresponding rise in the resources available. This Conference is sponsored and jointly planned by the Overseas Development Administration of the British Government and the University of London Institute of Education. Our governments, with assistance from donor agencies if forthcoming, should also commission our own universities to perform similar tasks for our respective countries.

I referred in my opening paragraphs to the Education Review conducted by the University of Sierra Leone, with assistance from the Carnegie Corporation of New York. The report was published in 1976. There is still no government policy statement on that report, but its policy recommend-ations have appeared in a number of government publications and others are still being discussed by the Ministry of Education. That kind of review should not be a once-and-for-all exercise. Universities should be supported adequately and competently to perform that role. The quest for a system of education and training which will serve the needs of, and relate as closely as possible to, the life and work of the people in each of our countries, must be a continuing endeavour, an unfinished business, and in the final analysis, a domestic activity, and somewhere — and I make a plea for this somewhere to be within the university — must be entrusted the task of undertaking such a review periodically and of monitoring progress during the years between one major review exercise and another. If our governments will set up such national mechanisms, then at the next Conference like this, we will have, readily available, exhaustive diagnoses of our individual countries' problems and the tried-out prescriptions, and the success rates of those used.

Philip Coombs, in his book *The World Educational Crisis* (1968), has a model of the impact of rising costs on the elementary school budget of a hypothetical developing country over ten years. The assumptions were conservative, yet they showed an increase in one case from $6 million to $14.5 million where student participation rate remained unchanged at 33 per cent, basic teacher salary levels remained unchanged and pupil-teacher ratio improved from 50:1 to 40:1. In the other case with the same assumptions except that the participation rate moved from 33 per cent to 50 per cent and the level of teacher salary rose at an average of 2.5 per cent per year, the total recurrent costs jumped from $6 million to $28 million. This was written in 1968 before the escalating oil prices of the 1970s and the present economic problems.

Each of us should try, if we have not already done so, some such run offs on the computer for our respective countries. In ten years from now, our countries will have to spend about five times the amount spent on primary education to be able to provide for half the number of children of that school age requiring education. The bill will have to be multiplied by ten if the aim is to achieve universal primary education.

This is a measure of the task facing us. A number of governments faced with this situation have turned to non-formal or informal education to provide additional resources. Innovative techniques (e.g. audio-visual, use of paraprofessionals) are increasingly being utilised to augment the traditional approach. But whatever the approach, whatever the inputs, there are certain problems relating to the efficiency or otherwise of what is being used. There are problems of class repetition and of dropouts from the system. It is said that, in the countries in our region, the typical pattern is for 15 per cent or more of enrolment in each class to be repeaters and for up to 50 per cent of all children entering to drop out before completing, with many not completing even the four years needed to obtain basic literacy and numeracy. And for those who complete, the average time spent in the six-year cycle is about nine years, that is, an additional three years of educational costs. In addition there are the hosts of problems arising from the dearth or inadequacy of data which can provide the necessary information for proper planning and decision-making.

Given all these problems, it will help to know what each country has done, what that country feels has been most helpful and successful in resolving some of the problems. Our task will next be to see how best these several successful experiments can be adapted to serve the needs of other countries.

Aid and outside assistance are important requisites, but they are not the panacea for all our problems. The fundamental requirement is a willingness and a commitment on the part of each country to put its education house in order so that it can serve the nation better. African governments must themselves accord priority to education, wholly and unreservedly. This commitment must involve a willingness to innovate and to provide the system with the means for such innovation.

I have referred to the need for adequate data and analysis. Equally, we need competent planning based on the data and the analysis, and planning which will be scrupulously and conscientiously followed. We now have planning units in many of our ministries of education, but I wonder how many ministries take them as seriously as they should. Indeed, how many of our governments pay more than lip-service to their national development plans!

I hope this Conference will do more than pay lip-service; I hope we will do more than pass resolutions. I hope that, as a result of our discussions and the sharing of experiences, we will evolve some practical mechanisms for monitoring those successful experiments which have occurred and for spreading this information and providing assistance as required to countries which may wish to adopt them. In this matter, no country is an island unto itself; we are all part of the mainland. We can assist each other through better concerted action.

The setting of education priorities is not a once-and-for-all action: it is an ongoing process to be reviewed periodically. I hope that this Conference will make some positive, lasting and practical contribution to this never-ending process.

112

Problems and prospects of aid to education in sub-Saharan Africa

Kenneth King

Recipient and donor perspectives on aid

A great deal more is known about donor perspectives on aid than recipient views. But in neither case is much written about the essence of the aid negotiation or the style and approach of the institutions that conduct it.

The most conspicuous absence in all the scattered literature on aid to education is any coherent account from the recipient perspective of how educational aid is perceived, negotiated, managed and reviewed. On the donor side, by contrast, there is immensely rich documentation of every stage of the aid negotiation from the original trip reports, feasibility studies, appraisal and consultant reports, pre-project drafts, final project summaries, review missions, evaluation and completion reports. On the other hand, despite this apparent overload of information on the side of the donors, they too seem to lack coherent accounts of what educational aid is actually about.

There is no scarcity of discussion about modalities, mechanisms or delivery systems for aid — how it should be programmed, sectoralised, packaged or projectised. Nor is there any shortage of changing rationales for types of education aid, for example, for high level manpower, nonformal education, or basic education. What does seem to be missing is an account of the assumptions that lie at the very heart of the aid process, and which may help to explain the enduring features of British, Canadian, French or German aid regardless of temporary changes in the delivery system.

It will perhaps be useful a little later to look at some of these temporary changes and current trends in the agencies, but it seems likely that in respect of these changing moods and priorities, agencies are very similar. Thus at much the same time all agencies begin to stress aid to the poorest, basic education, support of science and technology, etc. What is probably rather different and often undiscussed is the broader philosophy, style and approach to educational aid in the various bilateral and multilateral donors. It may be valuable to spend a little time on this before moving to the much more conspicuous problems and issues on the donor-recipient agenda.

Mapping the aided education system

What is really lacking on both sides of the aid fence are explicit and coherent representations of the education systems of Africa as currently and potentially affected by aid. That is to say that there is no shortage of data on what proportion of the development budget comes from external sources, or how many regular teachers and volunteers from abroad are present in the education and training institutions. But there does not seem

The author is indebted to Prakash Deshpande of the University of Pune, India (currently attached to the British Council, New Delhi) for a very valuable discussion of several of the issues in this paper.

to be an analytical account of what an educational system-as-aided looks like.

Planning for an aided educational system is obviously much more than presenting a shopping list of projects to various donors. Ideally it should involve an assessment of where foreign co-operation and advice is both necessary and acceptable, and to assess this satisfactorily, there needs to be a mature appraisal of the capacities of different donors, and behind the donors, some sense of the quality of the educational technology and experience of the particular countries involved. This local assessment of the education system as aided would need to analyse whether expatriates should play key advisory roles in teacher education, planning units, inspectorate, and curriculum development. Should they by contrast be restricted to specific projects which are perhaps experimental and are outside the educational mainstream? If expatriate teachers are present in significant numbers in schools, universities or polytechnics, should they, where possible, be restricted to line positions, and not be principals, directors, registrars and vice-chancellors? That is to say, is the local model of educational aid one which seeks to reduce the influence and visibility of the expatriates in the various projects sponsored by their countries?

These questions are worth asking since they begin to point to the outlines of the education system as aided. They indicate the kind of influence and authority that independent countries are prepared to allow to foreign technical assistance personnel. Thus, many countries will have expatriate heads of department in school and university, but not headmaster or principal. Many will have specialist inspectors and planners but not the chief inspector or the head of the planning unit. Doubtless the map of the aided education system will vary very greatly from country to country, and will contain many more features than the location of expatriate expertise. But even though such accounts do not presently exist, it seems likely that they would look rather different than the maps being used by the donor community.

The donor's map of the recipient's system

It is possible to reach approximations of the implicit educational 'maps' of the donor community by analysing the significance of the emphasis on multiplier effects by aid, constant reference to educational quality issues, the pacing and accounting of aid, responsiveness versus responsibility, and the insistence on more and more project justification data.

These maps, we have suggested, are not currently available for inspection, but some indication of their main features could be sketched out. The following characteristics are by no means common to all donors, since national and institutional traditions make a great difference to the final picture, but they will give some indication of the models of the education systems as aided that are implicitly being used.

Aid and the multiplier effect

There is a very strong tendency to look for situations in which the maximum impact can be achieved for the aid pound, dollar or franc. Sometimes, this is discernible in the desire for expatriate staff *not* to be in

114

routine line posts, but to be in positions where they can train trainers, curriculum developers, and influence policy. Sometimes this can be detected by the frequent use of the term 'key' personnel when the concern is with technical co-operation, likewise when the concern is with projects, there is commonly discussion of how the experimental project can have a policy impact by being replicated and generalised across the education system. Similarly with educational research support, there is an inclination to seek out 'research that will make a difference', or will somehow directly influence policy.

In these different ways it is clear that aid to education, by its very nature, must seek to do something that is not ordinary and routine but is influential and has policy impact. At this point it is worth noting that the model of education held by the donor may be at variance with the model held by the recipient.

Aid, educational quality and mismanagement

Although it is commonplace for donors to talk about emphasising quality as against quantity, what lies behind this axiom is a widespread feeling that education is being mismanaged. There are in fact very strong agency concerns about the decay of professionalism in the teaching force, decline of commitment in the inspectorates, curriculum development centres, colleges of education and even the universities. Added to this is a critique of the ministry or ministries of education as employing too many people who lack the relevant skills and commitment (this is part of a wider critique of the public sector). Finally there is an acute sense that appointments in the higher echelons of the education ministry and its major institutions have in some countries been politicised to a point where senior civil servants experienced in education have given way to political appointees often of very short duration. There has been a predictable collapse of civil service morale in the lower reaches and in the technical wings of the service as it has become clear progressively that technical knowledge is not particularly important to policy formation or implementation. Obviously this could not be a uniform condition across the many different education environments of sub-Saharan Africa. Rather what is being suggested is that some elements of the above inform the educational model of many donors. As a result, the search for impact and influence through the location of key technical assistance personnel takes on a special significance.

Aid, accountability and external control

The interest in accountability in recent years is further evidence of donors feeling that education somehow has got out of control. As a consequence donors increasingly construct aid packages in education that will survive the institutional drift and decay sketched above. The outcome is stricter deadlines, annual reviews and missions to check on progress, appointment of field co-ordinators 'to get things done', more careful attention to accounting, and more evaluation research. So, just as some agency initiatives underline the alleged incompetence of the teacher by being termed 'teacher-proof', others could be termed 'system-proof', so many are the checks and balances built in to ensure that the project proceeds according to order.

Donors' responsiveness versus responsibility

At the heart of the difference in the educational maps being used by donors and national governments is the distinction between the donors' responsiveness and their sense of responsibility. The notion of donors being responsive derives from their acknowledgement that the recipients are independent nation states which have their own coherent priorities to which donors can rationally respond. On the other hand, the honestly held ideal of responsiveness is coloured by the equally strong perception of educational mismanagement, politicisation and quantitative rather than qualitative priorities to which we have referred already. Consequently the ideal of responsiveness is tempered by a strong sense of responsibility both towards the taxpayers in the donor country and sometimes also towards the common man, the poor, the ordinary parent, the primary school teacher in the recipient country.

In crude terms, in the trade-off between sovereignty and accountability, it frequently transpires that the donor knows best, but the context of the dialogue requires that it continue to appear to be between professional equals. Responsiveness and flexibility on the side of the donor can readily result in *responsible interventionism* since ultimately the negotiation is loaded in favour of the aid-giver. Something of the complexity of the dialogue is revealed in these two quotations from different donors:

> However, the importance of paying sensitive attention to the recipient government's attitudes and policies need not imply a completely responsive posture, because there may be a lack of definition in the developing countries' own objectives in education. Thus there is continuing scope for discussion with countries to assist them in defining the area in which we would be ready to provide assistance under our own policies and in accordance with our own criteria, even where these may not appear initially to coincide with local ideas. How far it is possible to urge our views on governments is a matter of judgement which can only be determined in the light of relationships with a particular country.
>
> In relation to the recipient country the new type of agreements raise a fundamental issue related to the 'ethics' of foreign aid. . . . The issue is briefly this. Planning and follow-up of projects tend in practice to focus on matters of detail, matters which by both parties are considered to be of a technical rather than of a political nature. It follows that such problems can be solved by experts. Sector support agreements emphasise the aims and objectives of the sector as a whole and their relation to other sectors. In other words they look at priorities which make political considerations unavoidable. If this is what the dialogue should be about, sector agreements represent an improvement, if not, they have become a problem on both sides. If not handled with care they can easily be used as an excuse for more interference and control, and flexibility may create uncertainty instead of stability.

What both quotations reveal is the fundamental complexity of the aid dialogue, and, given the highly political nature of educational decisions, they also reveal how close to the local political nerve some aid negotiations may be.

Educational aid and educational information

Beyond the unevenness in the dialogue and the negotiation about aid, there is a further factor that distinguished the discussion of priorities between donors and recipients, and that is the increasingly sophisticated data base held by the major development assistance agencies. Some of the characteristics of this information are worth noting since they help to fill in the outline of these aided education systems.

First, donor agency representatives (whether headquarters or regional office staff) possess transnational information about education through working and advising on aid in a large number of countries. If, as is more and more the case, they come from research backgrounds in education or economics, they will be aware of the most publicised research findings on such matters as the impact of four years of primary education, the cost of a unit of university education over against a unit of primary education, the outcome of evaluations on diversified education at the secondary level, the present state of the debate on vocational training and so on. Thus when a scheme is, for example, put forward for the vocationalisation of the upper primary, or for the expansion of university education, there may well be a very firm view on the donor side about what is known already about such initiatives. (We are not concerned here about the validity of this knowledge, only about its likely impact in the negotiations.)

Second, the donor community possesses more and more knowledge about the particular country on which educational aid is being negotiated. As donors, for a variety of different reasons, have espoused sectoral aid to education or aid to a particular sub-sector of education and training, they have found it necessary to develop a knowledge base on the whole of the sector or sub-sector. Hence, it is now probably true to say that the best data bases on the polytechnic sector in country X, or the pre-school sector in country Y, or the technical and vocational training field in country Z are held by particular donor agencies who have made those areas their 'spheres of influence'. Sub-sector support to literacy by one donor or to the university by another, if extended over a ten-year period, produces a situation in which the institutional memory on literacy or university development in Africa may be more detailed in one of the OECD countries than in Africa itself. Hence the colonial tradition of having to study African education in London, Paris or Lisbon is to a limited extent continued through dependence on the data bases of the foundations, the multilaterals and the bilaterals, and of the very large numbers of Northern consultants who have assisted at various stages of the feasibility study, appraisal or evaluation of agency projects.

Third, there can at times be a correlation between the donor's relatively sophisticated data base for decisions and the recipient's less coherent analysis of their own education system. A good deal of the very scarce manpower in research and planning units in ministries is allocated to providing the various donors and their consultant teams with data sets related to their particular projects. For the reasons mentioned earlier, the assistance agencies wish to have more and more information on the entire sector in which their project or programme of work falls, hence the provision of project justification data can become a major preoccupation of the more talented people on the planning side of ministries.

It is equally common, however, for the visiting teams and associated consultants to get direct access to raw data, recent reports and government

117

commissions, even at a stage before these are known to educators and senior researchers in the country itself. The tight schedules of the visiting teams, and the close association between the data and the likelihood of project aid mean that facilitating the transfer of information to the donor becomes a high priority. It is increasingly common for ministry officials and planners to be formally attached to these evaluation and analysis missions, but they often do not have the advantage of the larger aid context in which the donor is working, the full-time commitment to complete the task, and often the access to the informal review sessions amongst the visitors in the evenings and weekends.

Hence a situation which, on the face of it, might offer local planners an insight into the preferences of donors and detailed data on different sectors, seldom works out in quite this way. The final analysis tasks and the report writing are often left to the visiting consultants and the aid team, and frequently take place outside the country. The outcome can be that the institutional memory of the ministry or planning unit is not necessarily developed by this frequent if irregular participation in servicing the data needs of the agencies. A major problem is that the country's top planners and civil servants in the ministry of education have not through this process built up a coherent picture of their education system as aided.

Educational aid in the absence of educational discourse

Despite the uneven distribution of information about education in sub-Saharan Africa between donor and recipient, there is a sense in which both parties lack essential knowledge about the very transaction in which they are engaged. On the one hand, the recipient is accepting the offer of aid to particular sections on the assumption that the donor has some comparative advantage in assisting that sector. But in many situations, the recipient has made no assessment of the donor country's claim to expertise in that particular sector. So the offer to improve primary school quality, the inspectorate, educational technology or whatever is taken for granted. There is seldom an attempt to assess in great detail what individual donor countries' own education systems are really like. Indeed, it could be argued that the image or representation of the donor's home education system in the eyes of the recipient is often distorted, as it was during the colonial era.

There is a further complication in the transmission of information about the education system of the aiding country; such information is mediated to the recipient by people who are experts on education in the developing countries, *not* on their countries of origin. In addition, the consultants or university departments most associated with the aid transfer as contractors are also likely to be known for their expertise on other third world countries. So the whole aid negotiation process may be carried out on the donor side by people who are primarily not knowledgeable about their own country's comparative educational advantage, and who indeed may know as much about Uganda or Mali as they do about the strengths and weaknesses of British or French secondary schools.

This lack of knowledge on both sides would not particularly matter if the donor was simply giving financial aid to support existing local structures, but very often the aid is given to transfer or implement a particular project,

118

for primary school improvement, vocational training, or decentralised management. So it does become important to know whether the 'export model' has any relationship to a well-tried system that the aiding country has grown up with, or whether it is an experimental model that perhaps makes eminently good sense to the aid community but exists nowhere in the form that is being suggested. In this connection Africa is now properly cautious about being an experimental station for notions that have been tried nowhere, since immense numbers of custom-made innovations have been associated with the continent.

The donor's representation of the aided country, despite all the data to which we have referred, seldom takes account of the operational limitations to reform within which the average ministry of education must perforce work. When the logic and discourse of donor and recipient proceed from very different sets of assumptions and of knowledge about each other's system, it is not surprising that an aid scheme that a donor believes will have a direct impact on primary school quality may appear to the recipient as a scheme that might make foreign aid personnel too visible or influential.

Co-ordinating country reports

In concluding this section on the donor and recipient's knowledge of each other's education system, we propose a mechanism for allowing a somewhat different discourse to emerge. Instead of the spate of individual agency reviews, appraisals, and sector reports which tie up top technical officers in ministries of education for a good part of the year, the aid donors might consider funding a single major OECD-style country review, for which the inviting country prepares in advance a major data set on its education system. On both sides of this review process major academic figures from the OECD countries and from the host country would be separately involved. The current burden on developing countries of servicing the information needs of the many donors in education could be significantly reduced through such co-ordinated country reports and technical co-operation reviews.

The resulting document (which would not be needed more than once every three or four years) would form the basis for individual aid negotiations. Such documents would have the advantage of becoming much more public and influential than the mass of grey material currently collected by agencies in their barrage of sector and appraisal missions, much of which is inaccessible both to the policy and academic communities in the countries from which it has been derived. On the recipient side, there would be some advantage in their having access to similar country reports done on the major OECD (i.e. donor) countries themselves. In cases where recipient countries have a relationship with a single major donor, a lot could be said in favour of a two-way dialogue or review commission to build up expertise on the donor country as much as on the recipient.

Finally reports which examined the education-environment-as-aided could be prepared for a number of countries. These would be concerned with the topography of educational aid in countries receiving considerable quantities from different sources. Instead of looking at the broad context of education in the manner of the country review, they would examine the role, scope and impact of education-related aid, pay particular attention to long-term projects, comment on major changes in aid policy as they affect the country, and note new aid projects. There would be something to be said for these technical co-operation reviews to be done by small groups of local experts from the region, with the option of calling in one or two scholars with broader experience of agency policies.

Such 'states of practice' reports of the education system as aided simply do not exist in any form today, but in some countries the range of different agency initiatives is such an important element in the development budget that they could perform a useful information and co-ordination role.

The suggestions made above may appear to increase the data requirements rather than reduce them. In effect, they seek to reduce the collection of similar education sector data by every agency that has a project of any size in the country, while acknowledging that agencies will still need to have technical discussions and detailed debate about their particular projects. The intention is also to separate the *general* analysis of the country's education system from the agency or agencies that seek to aid it, and encourage them rather to relate to a set of policy conclusions that result from country reports and country reviews in which national and foreign scholars and planners have been closely involved.

The anthropology of development assistance agencies

The anthropology of development assistance agencies has had virtually no attention, and yet understanding the national styles of the donors can be as important as analysing their data needs and programmes. Any move, such as has been suggested above, for co-ordination, has to take into account the very strong national pressures on bilateral donors. In regard to multilateral donors, it may similarly be true that regardless of the field of support their corporate style has a certain consistency that needs to be taken into account. National style is a very important factor in the bilateral aid process. It tends to remain constant whatever the content of the aid package may be, and it has very close connections with the donor's national education and training system.

Just as there was no single missionary type in colonial Africa but very different styles associated with the Basel, Lutheran, Anglican, Dutch Reformed and countless others, many of which were distinguished by the culture of the sending country, so the development assistance agencies tend to represent certain traits associated with their own countries. For instance, some of the following characteristics differ very markedly from country to country amongst the main donors:

1 A preference for identifying factors or variables that may make a difference across the whole range of Third World education systems as opposed to assuming that the mix of aid elements suitable for a particular country will likely *not* be transferable to others

2 A tendency to delegate very considerable powers to the local agency representatives, as opposed to various centralising tendencies

120

3 A tendency to invest in hardware (buildings, technology, textbooks, supplies) as compared with a confidence in software (people, co-operants, advisers, volunteers, teachers, local and overseas training, etc)

4 A preference for pilot projects, experimental models, research and evaluation-based strategies versus working through commonsensical assumptions that the problems are already only too clear, and require very ordinary forms of support

5 Differing assumptions about very many of the fundamental elements in the aid negotiation including the attitude to counterparts, openness of information, hire of locals as aid personnel (and on what terms), accounting, etc

6 Tendency to think of developing countries as fundamentally different kinds of societies from their own as opposed to being rather similar, and as a consequence different expectations about the rate of change anticipated, different time horizons, etc

7 Different expectations of what societies (including their own volunteers) can learn from each other across the North-South divisions

8 Different approaches to the role of education in development and to the very meaning of development.

Some of these tendencies are much more significant than others, but if they are taken in conjunction with some of the more general characteristics of the aid map as perceived by many donors, they present the recipient ministries with rather a formidable process of adjustment. The task of managing the aid portfolio when there are a large number of projects with different donors pursuing sometimes quite similar-sounding programmes with quite different styles of approach should not be underestimated. We shall suggest shortly that the adjustment to this spectrum of subtly different assumptions is not something that is only experienced by national ministries of education. It is also faced by university administrations and by research institutes dealing with many kinds of technical co-operation and research contracts. Compared with a research centre in the North which has at the most to deal with the funding culture of perhaps one or two countries besides the one it already understands, the research institute in the South has a task involving very considerable diplomacy, especially if it requires agency funding to support both its staff and its research programme.

In this situation, it is not surprising that the most economically dependent countries frequently have the greatest array of aid donors, and accordingly some of the greatest difficulty in aid absorption and aid accounting. It may sometimes simplify things if donors do not insist on seeing aid as discrete projects, each one timebound in a slightly different way. But on the other hand we have already noted that moving to a sector or programme approach does not necessarily simplify matters, but may put the local planning and accounting systems under even more pressure of responsibility than the one-off project.

Themes and issues in educational aid policy

Having suggested that the major problem about educational aid is that the educational maps and operating styles and assumptions of recipients and donors are seldom made explicit, and are not even coherently thought through, it may be useful to look in more detail at a number of particularly important themes and issues of which both parties have experience.

Civil service culture and the utilisation of manpower

Donor views about the increasing or continuing importance of expatriate manpower are inseparable from a more general critique of local civil service manpower, both of the professional and support staff. The concern of the 1980s is not so much with Africanisation but with the utilisation of the trained and localised manpower, both general and specialist, and in each case serious anxiety has been expressed by donors and recipients alike. Whether in the ministry, institute, college or school, there is a sense that the civil service infrastructure supporting the committed professionals has fallen away. This is not an outsider's view alone, for several governments have produced highly critical reports on their civil service culture, the delays in dealing with the public, the acute mobility problems, the almost complete breakdown of institutional memory in ministries and departments. There has been no research on the culture of the government office, but a case could be made that an increasing reliance on oral communication for many kinds of decisions has directly affected the institutional memory and in turn affected the role of personal assistants and secretaries. In addition, relationships within different strata of the civil service have been affected by the increase in mobility amongst those in positions of authority. The localisation of the inherited colonial civil services of France, Britain and other donors will eventually throw up different patterns of work and authority, but in this transitional stage, it is easy for outsiders to fail to analyse what is happening and why, and merely to dismiss the civil service infrastructure as incompetent and uncommitted.

Some of these features do however, directly affect the aid process. At the very point when agencies' activities are becoming much more information-intensive, they face a situation where the culture of literacy (in French and in English) is retreating in face of oral decision-making. This oracy is reinforced by the highly political nature of many education decisions, and the disinclination of junior officers to commit themselves to print when the views of their senior officers are unclear. The latter may react similarly in relation to the views of the politicians, particularly in situations where the prime minister or president is felt to be intimately connected with a particular reform or initiative.

The second manpower concern is with the selection, training and utilisation of specialist cadres in the education system, whether these are inspectors, planners, university economists, engineers, technical teacher trainers, etc. In far too crude terms, it is widely felt that training does not relate to utilisation — that planners don't plan, and inspectors don't inspect, and that high level technical skills are soon exchanged for administrative jobs. The emphasis in much of the first two decades of independence was with producing these cadres. Now the emphasis has

122

shifted to questions of utilisation, and these turn out to be connected with the wider culture of the civil service to which we have just referred.

The impact of these worries about under- (or non-) utilisation of expensively trained cadres has affected donors in different ways. One tendency has been to make the aid project 'administration-proof' which may mean hiving off more and more of the project into the control of the donor and those paid directly by the donor, whether local or foreign. Innoculating the project against the local problems can, in addition, mean requiring very firm reporting, frequent reviews to keep it in a healthy condition, and reliance on expatriate personnel. We shall note however that while this may produce results in the first instance, it can be counterproductive at the next stage.

A second tendency, related to the first, has been the re-emphasis on the need for donor-country manpower to remain in post. Technical co-operation personnel are seen by some donors to be essential for ensuring that a project succeeds. As donors become more and more aware of the complexity of objectives such as improving educational quality, it becomes clear to them that to guarantee impact there must be a co-ordinated project with a series of inter-related elements. In this way the project is insulated from the ordinary rough and tumble of life, and the expatriate personnel increasingly become the guarantors of its success. The recognition by one or two agencies that key expatriate manpower has been run down too rapidly is indicative of the tension between guaranteeing 'success' (at a cost that may be prohibitive) and the danger of connecting project quality with the presence of expatriate personnel.

The need for national training policies

In the new-found donor enthusiasm for human resource development planning, there has been insufficient attention by ministries to the articulation of national training policies.

It is symptomatic of these new concerns with manpower that many agencies are currently involved in rethinking their whole strategy of manpower development. The science of 'human resource development' is being dusted off in many agencies, and a great deal of thought is going into analysing its various forms, and in particular to exploring strategies for investing in scientific and technological manpower. The result of this rediscovery of human capital is taking different forms in different agencies. Some very useful work is being generated in this area, but it too is difficult to obtain. It is also difficult to sort out the various influences at work. Doubtless, one of these derives from the need to use personnel and train personnel more meaningfully in a situation where aid budgets are under attack. Another comes from the desire to achieve a measurable impact. But one area that is relatively little understood is the recipient philosophy on manpower development for the education system. Once all the initiatives of the donors have been added together (whether for training district or regional education officers, planners, curriculum developers, inspectors or whatever) what is left of the training policy of the ministry itself? Is it the sum of its aided parts? Or does it reflect a compromise between the ministry ideal and the reality of what could be negotiated externally and paid for locally?

Again, as an information task, it would be useful for one or two countries to map out the existing training, short course and in-service provision from external aid for ministry of education personnel at every level. The development of such a document could offer important insights into the totality of aid's impact on the national training provision. In some countries, the scale and scatter of the training provision, local and overseas, is so diverse that probably nobody has a picture of how the various parts might relate to a national strategy. Even if most of the agency training is project-related, the interesting question for the national government is whether it can be reconceptualised and made into something approaching a national education sector training policy.

From micro to macro projects, from quality to quantity

Aid has paid little attention to the experience of moving from micro education projects to macro generalisation. Micro projects in Africa have often been in areas untried in the country of origin. In basic education for example, it might be preferable to transfer tried working models to rural areas than 'appropriate' experiments, 'designed for Africa'.

This tension has been present throughout this analysis, and is inseparable from the process of educational aid (or indeed much other aid). In essence the dilemma is the following, and it becomes more pointed as agency funds shrink. In the face of an analysis about the consequences of rapid educational expansion, many donors conceive of their comparative advantage in terms of demonstrating quality improvement in some part of the system. To ensure a successful high quality project (given what has been said about the administrative culture) there is a temptation to insulate the aid project against failure by a series of co-ordinated inputs, including very close supervision, project-related training and often some kind of special status, through interministerial committees, incentives for participating schools and so on. Evaluation of the project when still aided is likely to confirm its success. But the very factors that ensured its success as a micro project ensure its failure when agency funds are removed. On paper the generalisation or replication of the project to other districts and provinces is assured. In reality, the micro project gradually returns to normality.

The classic dilemma of *how to prepare something special in an ordinary way* is at the centre of educational aid. For example, packaging or projectising aid involves focusing a whole series of aid elements on a single project. But the very coherence of the aid package can be its undoing, since this effectively makes it *the* Canadian, British, French (or whatever) project, with a term life of so many years.

A different way of looking at this same dilemma is to compare India with, say, Botswana or Mali. In the former, no aid agency could hope to have impact on all the inspectors, district education officers, etc, but in many African countries with only one university, one polytechnic, and one small national inspectorate, it is tempting for an agency to feel that it can directly shape the entire inspection system, vocational training sector, curriculum

124

development process or adult education organisation. All the key staff can be trained by a single agency. Thus a part of the appeal of Africa to aid agencies is precisely that the systems are still sufficiently small that it is possible to think strategically placed development aid can affect the whole system. In this sense, some micro projects do not have to be generalised laterally across the system but only generalised *longitudinally*, after the two years of training or curriculum development is complete.

But even though the key personnel in the administration of education seem numerically manageable for a single aid agency the reality is that a country of say 10 or 15 million people already has several thousand primary schools, and it is now several decades since an external agency felt it could directly influence events in the ordinary primary, or even secondary, school. Even those countries with the smallest proportion of children in secondary schools are too large for agencies to feel they can have direct impact on the whole. Hence, the process of influencing quality in the primary or secondary schools of a single country presents the same dilemma of the micro project and its extension to the whole system that we have discussed.

The result of the dilemma is that no agency any longer tries to indicate what an ordinary good quality primary school looks like as a functioning unit. Instead, the DEOs or the inspectors responsible for the system nationally are trained, or the headmasters are exposed to administration courses. But the ordinary primary school teachers seem now to be beyond the reach of aid; they have to be reached by the mysteries of the multiplier effect. The result of this judgement about impact is that no agency is responsible for assisting an ordinary good primary school in the rural areas.

If however the problem in many rural schools is low morale, heavy drop-out and repetition and poor examination success, agencies might usefully contribute towards morale and school quality by encouraging demonstration primary schools.

Arguably, what is lacking in a number of school districts is not more money for textbooks or a new curriculum, but some examples of what good primary education can be within the restrictions of the same budget. If it is worth taking headmasters to Europe to study the Scottish or Danish primary school, it might be more effective to have a handful of primary school teachers and headteachers helping to run demonstration schools in Africa. These could then be visited by ordinary teachers and in fact be a much more effective 'multiplier' than taking a few headteachers to Europe or America. Most countries already have a number of excellent rural primary schools without any expatriate primary teachers. In this situation, aid could make possible the sort of visits by other teachers in neighbouring districts and provinces that local budgets no longer allow. Alternatively, in districts or provinces that lack examples of good primary education, aid channelled through non-governmental organisations could provide the personnel to try running demonstration schools on the same budget as regular primary schools.

Reactions to this proposal from donors and recipients would reveal many of the issues about agency style and comparative advantage that we have referred to in the first part of this paper. Similar kinds of questions could easily be raised for sectors other than primary education.

From the donor perspective:

1 Basic primary education is frequently alleged to be the highest aid priority but there are no aid personnel in primary schools

2 Some aid projects are organised to *add* on to primary schools particular functions (e.g. environmental education, population education, distance education, computers in schools, polytechnical education), but virtually no aid project tries to improve primary schools by changing nothing except the school ethos

3 In essence agency strategies for school improvement are top-down — examining the levers for affecting primary school inspection, administration at the district or provincial level, or banking on the technologies of radio or teacher-proof curricula to reach children directly

4 The hesitations about having expatriates in primary schools mean that apart from the few short-term tours to primary schools in Europe and North America, the only examples of education as organised in the homelands are those available to the privileged city dwellers who attend the German, American or British schools or the French lycées, and none of these is basically intended to be a demonstration school.

From the recipient perspective:

1 Given the readiness to accept aid for primary school reform, new curricula, new delivery systems, teachers centres etc, would there be hesitations about demonstration schools in the rural areas (in contrast to schools for university staff children in the cities?)

2 If the acceptance of primary school aid assumes that the donor has a technology worth copying or adapting, then why not have the technology on view? There is perhaps a false assumption that an expatriate primary teacher trainer, or a trainer of trainers, or a primary adviser is a better multiplier than an ordinary primary school teacher in an ordinary school.

3 If national pride is not offended by accepting only top-level advisers for the primary sector, it presumably would be acceptable to have for example Scottish, Danish or Canadian teachers in primary schools provided they are given no greater resources than other voluntary service personnel.

4 If ordinary primary schools can become demonstration units through the addition of one ordinary working teacher or principal, well and good. If they can't, then this could point to the irrelevance of many of the much more expensive inputs, involving new technologies, delivery systems, new primary degrees, etc.

We have deliberately spent some time in examining the issue of micro to macro projects (and by implication the movement from quality to quantity) in respect of one of the favourite donor themes of agencies — the primary school sector. The discussion has been unavoidably complicated because the 'aid maps' and assumptions about this sector have not been clear or explicit. That is to say, the articulation of what donors should and should not directly seek to influence in primary education has not been clarified (for a good example, see the DAC note on 'Aid for Basic Education in

Rural Areas with special attention to Africa South of the Sahara', September 1984). Thus, it could be argued that countries such as Canada and Scotland with long and rich experience of running one-teacher schools in rural areas could

1 Transfer the technology at the same cost as in Canada or the UK, so that local teachers can see what is not present in their own small schools, or

2 Transfer the technology but keep the school equipment budget, etc, identical to the country receiving the technology.

Good arguments can be provided for either course.

In fact there is a lot of very muddled thinking about responsiveness and interventionism when it comes to transferring 'technology' in education whether software or hardware. This sometimes results in the developing country never seeing what the innovation or reform or ordinary system actually looks like in the country of origin. A perfect example of this may be taken from India in 1984 where the British computers-in-education project is being transferred without there being a single active, ongoing demonstration within India of how computers typically work in an English or Scottish upper secondary school. When the total cost of the project is considered (and the very real dangers of misunderstanding and distortion taken into account), it would have been extremely cheap to have had ordinary British staff working as teachers for two years or more in several demonstration schools. Without this, the project is going to go macro without any micro learning, and to go for quantity without any understanding of quality in the country of export.

Similarly, it could be suggested that, all over Africa, innovations are watered down or made 'appropriate' or cheapened to a point where they are either distrusted by teachers as 'designed for Africa', or have little influence because they are invisible. Yet the same agencies may expose local teachers and teacher trainers to education degrees overseas at relatively high cost.

Perhaps it is seen as something close to recolonisation to have expatriates teaching in primary schools, or a poor use of aid monies. Hence expatriates tend to be used in polytechnics and universities, and links are arranged between departments in Canada, Australia and Britain and departments in Africa at the university level. No one conceives of a link between primary schools in the North and the South. Yet arguably it could offer tremendous insights to both sides, and be invaluable as development education.

Finally, it would be useful to collect from a number of countries the record of what has been tried and what achieved. Agency style has predictably differed from donor to donor, but in general there has been more attention to innovating with something quite different (neither 'Northern' nor 'Southern') than merely improving what exists or demonstrating something that has been well proven in the country of origin. Ideally state-of-the-art pieces in the search for quality at the primary level would include both donor and host government initiatives.

Aid priorities and aid co-operation

Amongst donors, there are sufficient collaboration channels, but still negligible understanding of the culture and organisation of other agencies.

More thought needs to be given to structures for Southern participation in inter-agency dialogue, and more initiatives need to be taken in the South to pre-empt and complement these agency exchanges.

There are likely to continue to be tensions between the aid priorities of individual donors and forms of donor co-ordination. The separate traditions of donors, their preference for working in particular kinds of countries, and their sense of what they do best will tend to make it difficult to arrange much coherent co-ordination in individual countries. We have already suggested that there would be some value in donors co-operating in country reviews and technical co-operation reviews, but these were intended to reduce the basic information demands by agencies, and to increase their knowledge of who was doing what in educational aid. A number of further points can now be made about the relationships between aid priorities and aid co-operation.

Information exchange

There are already a number of existing co-operation channels through which the aid donors in education acquire information about each other's work. These would include the International Working Group on Education (IWGE) (formerly the Bellagio Education Group), the DAC of the OECD, the occasional inter-agency review seminar held by IIEP, specialist sector activities eg on the evaluation of technical and vocational training, one-off events like the ODA conference in December 1984, or the USAID – National Academy of Sciences aid priorities workshop in 1983. It is doubtful if more occasions or organisations need to be created to encourage exchange of information about donor activities, but a few comments may be made on the current situation.

Despite the Bellagio-IWGE group having met for seven or eight years, it is doubtful if donors know much more about how education aid is actually managed in Britain, Sweden, France or Germany now than they did in the early 1970s. This is because, although there is often a small show-and-tell element in these meetings, there is never any coherent attempt to explore in detail how education aid is managed in Canada, USA or the World Bank. There would in fact be considerable merit in arranging for workshops where the aid philosophy and practice of a particular donor would be on display, and time available to analyse in detail some of the largest or most significant new endeavours of the agency. For example, there is probably very little information amongst donors on USAID's very large recent initiative in primary education in several African countries, nor on CIDA's large new training and human resource programmes, nor on ODA's new approach to packaging a whole variety of hitherto scattered aid elements into a coherent project. Similar examples could be adduced from other agencies. This kind of workshop would be equally important for education planners and policy makers in developing countries who seldom get an opportunity to perceive the wider context in which a particular agency is operating and to understand the impact both of cuts and increased aid monies on agency styles.

Recipient countries have organised few meetings on education aid and research priorities to which donors have been invited. This has happened in Uganda in a rather restricted sense and in Zimbabwe in relation to university co-operation policies, but there would be much to be said in favour of regional or pan-African organisations inviting donor representatives to discuss a set of issues of critical concern in education. This can also be envisaged for education research groups which could follow the example set by Latin American centres in inviting the main donors to attend their seminars, rather than the other way round.

When a major new donor activity is initiated, whether in research, in review or in action, there may be value in other donors being involved from the outset. Even when there is a major new initiative to cut funds for education, opposing evidence from other agencies may be useful in making the case for education.

An international co-ordinating group such as IWGE should be able to convene a high-level workshop irregularly also when an issue such as the continuation of funding to UNESCO is at centre-stage. Arguably, an informal working group such as IWGE should play a role in relation to the present UNESCO crisis that could be extremely timely and ultimately influential.

One of the continuing problems with many of these informal inter-agency reviews of education in the Third World is that there is no obvious counterpart involvement from the developing countries. Representation tends to be by invitation, hence the impression may be given that developing countries have less to say about education priorities than the donors. We have already suggested that one response to this problem is for regional groups to organise similar meetings to which selected donors could be invited. But there may also be value in exploring other ways in which donors can receive rapid reaction and feedback about their projects, proposals and priorities for particular regions.

Political and professional priorities

Political and professional priorities need to be distinguished in both the North and South. The political priorities frequently complicate the negotiation between professionals, which is itself already marked by inequalities in information.

We have implied throughout this paper that it is useful to distinguish between several levels of priorities. First, the tradition, history and style of both bilateral and multilateral agencies tend to determine a particular way of doing business, and even the countries with which that business is done. Second, donor and recipient countries have at least two levels of priority — that determined by the broad politics of education, and that emanating from senior civil servants and planners in education. There is, thirdly, an area of priority-setting which tends to take place in international conferences, where the priorities are of a very different order than those to which we have just referred. The discourse on priorities in regional and international meetings tends to be a normative discourse, pointing to what is not in fact currently a priority but which perhaps ought to be in the eyes of national governments or of donors. Examples of such normative priority statements would be 'more aid to the poorest', 'more schemes for cost-recovery in higher education', 'less emphasis on high cost differential fees for foreign students', 'more rather than less aid to education' etc. Moreover in both donor and recipient countries, the programme personnel in the agencies and their opposite numbers in the ministries of education have their ongoing 'traditional' priorities constantly affected and interfered with for good or for ill by the political level, as well as by pressures for new priorities that emerge from other sources, usually in the North.

This last point is one that frequently upsets education practitioners and researchers in the South. At the level of axiom or rhetoric, a new aim for education will enter the discourse of seminars and workshops, and begin to become important for legitimating educational projects. The generation of these new legitimising frameworks for educational aid has been very little studied, but most developing country policy makers and researchers will recognise the phenomenon whereby a new phase suddenly encapsulates what appears to be a whole policy switch in aid. The problem is often that projects have to be reformulated to accommodate the new aid framework, but in many cases the change, though essential to project funding, does not greatly alter the traditional way in which the agency does its business. The other difficulty is that there can often emerge a consensus amongst all donor agencies about the new emphasis or new aid framework, so that at one level the donor community presents a united front.

Although we have implied that the emergence of these new Northern aid frameworks may often mean cosmetic changes in project development (and in agency styles), on other occasions, the change in the normative framework of aid actually requires new project components, or the abandoning of others. Hence an axiom like 'the universalisation of primary education in the context of the introduction of science and technology education' may remain at the conference level, but it may become also important to be able to show some curriculum intentions towards the new theme. Other examples come to mind in which notions such as 'community orientation to schooling', 'integration of education with productive work' and many others, at the very least, implied not just reformulation but a readiness to build into project proposals some scope for the field adoption of these components. Examples on the negative side might include the increasingly obvious consensus about boarding secondary schools and the pessimism about diversified secondary education.

Having distinguished political from professional priorities, we should recognise that these may be expressed at four different levels:

1 In the donor countries the *political* level which may be insisting on aid cuts, aid expansion, more or less aid to the multilateral agencies or the development banks, more or less emphasis on the trade implications of education aid, more or less tying of aid, more or less concentration of aid on particular sub-sets of countries.

2 The *professional programme* level in the donor countries, where under the shadow of the first level, hard choices on priorities need to be made in the context of aid cuts, and equally hard choices on new investments as aid budgets continue to rise in many countries. This level (with its associated academic colleagues and contractors) had a great deal to do with the formulation of new priority mechanisms and delivery strategies

for aid, but always within the culture of aid associated with that agency and country.

3 In the recipient countries the *professional programme* level, where perhaps the least is currently known about their own priorities for education since they are constantly at the interchange point between the priorities of the various donors and the priorities of their political masters.

4 The *political* level in the recipient countries, where (as in the industrialised countries) the locus of priorities lies not just with the minister of education, but with the treasury and frequently even with the president or prime minister.

There may be a tendency to give more attention to the professional programme level priorities, and within these to the improvement of mechanisms and strategies for aid. However, emphasis must be given to those priorities that go beyond the national boundary and the national political constraints, but which are finally vital to the maintenance of aid funds for education. Since the debate about priorities for educational aid in the context of plenty is very different from a debate about priorities in the context of cuts or of a retreat from education within the aid framework, it is important to stake out some agenda items that require comment and criticism. Some examples are noted:

1 What are the education priorities and policies of bodies like the AfDB?
2 Would it make sense to discuss an African agenda in education for UNESCO, and by implication comment on its current role and potential?
3 Are there satisfactory ways of monitoring what is happening to the education and training aid budgets of different donor countries? Given the extraordinary complexity of estimating the total human resource development budget, are there indicators of education aid commitments that could be used to put comparative pressure on agencies, such as league tables on fully-funded scholarships, level of commitments to the Banks and UN agencies?

Research and information aid to education

Strengthening the local research culture and planning capacity is central to improved discussion of priorities in education between countries. This is not a short-term project but involves long-term commitments by donors to policies that will eventually alter dramatically negotiations about education aid.

Throughout this paper, we have pointed to very specific research and policy information tasks related to making the aid process more coherent. Here we want to look at a small number of the most critical roles that research plays in affecting the climate of aid, as well as its particular direction. Generally the impact of education research on education policy is exceedingly indirect, and its role only too often is merely to reinforce a policy that has already been decided on other than research grounds. Nevertheless, a strong culture of research can become crucial to the maintenance and improvement of the operation of aid.

First, education research can be vital in confirming an aid direction desired by an agency, and even to maintaining the importance of the education sector within that agency. Research findings such as the one on the impact of four years of education on health, agriculture and fertility can prove vital in agencies that are looking for ways to justify continuing or increased expenditure on primary education. Such research findings play a greater role within the North, and are consumed more by the agencies whose ethos is very explicitly founded on strong data.

Thus paradoxically the professionals in many Northern agencies increasingly need research justifications for policies and projects to get these projects passed, and more broadly to argue for sector aid to education when faced with competing demands from agriculture, energy, water and health. It has to be acknowledged therefore that some research is sponsored by Northern agencies that may appear very exotic to the South and excessively sophisticated in its methodologies, but very often this is dictated by what we have called the culture of the agency and of the other disciplines within it. The status of education in the agency sometimes needs to be bolstered by highly persuasive arguments produced in the same medium as other investments. What this means is that national researchers in the North need for maximum impact to be aware of the kind of argument about education that would be powerful in the context and tradition of their own aid agencies.

Second, education research in many developing countries is still evolving its own culture, and in particular exploring its relationship with the policy process. The role of research and planning units in ministries of education is still very unclear, and there is little evidence yet of their creating a context for more informed decision-making or implementation. They are underdeveloped by three tendencies at the moment. On the one hand, they operate in what is still a very oral culture of decision making, and their literature is consequently consumed more by external donors (with their strong project-related data needs) than by their own top civil servants. In addition they function in a wider research environment where university research in education is regarded with suspicion, and hence there is a less fruitful interaction between the professionals in the education ministries in the South and their counterparts in higher education than there is in the often very influential exchanges between USAID and development researchers in the USA, or similar interactions in countries like Sweden, Canada or Britain. Lastly, research generated by Northern researchers is often more influential in African countries than local research. There is an aid dimension to this influence. Since Northern agencies require so much data, many Northern researchers find that, almost regardless of whether their work is related to the bilateral agency in their country of origin, they profit by association with that agency, especially if at some previous point they have been part of a team or consultancy group. This confusion of roles allows Northern researchers in some African countries to get privileged access to data that is often quite inaccessible to the local research community. The solution of this problem will not come by making life more difficult for expatriate researchers, but rather by the development of a local tradition of research that fits into and helps shape the evolving decision-making culture.

132

The challenge and difficulty of all this to the local research community cannot be exaggerated, but before assuming that it is yet another task of foreign aid to create a lively research community in education, it is important to allow for its emergence on its own terms. No doubt this can be encouraged by the direct funding of African researchers in ways that Canada's International Development Research Centre (IDRC) and the Swedish Agency for Research Co-operation with Developing Countries (SAREC) have done so much to explore. Also links and collaboration schemes can strengthen ordinary collegial access to findings in the North and the South. The experience of the Research Review and Advisory Group over the last several years suggests that in the face of the difficulties sketched above, the development of close informal associations between researchers and policy makers in the Third World can offer a mechanism for open debate on the issues. Provision for such groupings to develop their own research priorities in education is an important dimension of aid, though financially insignificant. Without abundant local expertise in educational evaluation, planning, experimentation and innovation both within and outside ministries of education, the dialogue and negotiation with donors will continue to be fundamentally uneven. The capacity to comment upon and critically appraise agency policies must be part of any mature definition of educational self-reliance, but this in turn is inseparable from the formation of a research culture that can appraise local directions in education policy. So long as the local evaluation of education and of education aid is reactive to other people's analyses of the problems, the dialogue will continue to be about someone else's priorities for the country.

Conclusion

By its very nature aid involves a tension between priorities of donors and recipients. Nevertheless, there are few donors who would not welcome the strengthening of the recipient capacity to set priorities, or to argue powerfully for counterpriorities to those proposed by the donors. This capacity, where it does not already exist, cannot be ordered up overnight, nor calculated in terms of numbers of masters or doctorates in educational planning. The development of a local research and planning culture, as confident as donors currently are about their insights, cannot be made part of a two- or three-year project. It requires long-term support to ministries and research centres, new and very flexible use of expatriate expertise in ways that do not turn local colleagues into 'counterparts', and exposure of national planners (through attachments and sabbaticals) to the ordinary work of the bilateral and multilateral donors. In this process, the maps of the education systems of both donors and recipients will become much clearer.

Meanwhile, out in the rougher world of primary schools, training colleges, polytechnics and universities, the best use of foreign money and people may become clearer when recipient governments are clearer about the comparative advantage of Britain, Canada, France or other donors in assisting them. In the pursuit of quality in primary and secondary schools, it may be necessary to explore very ordinary but perhaps unpalatable initiatives, such as the large-scale hiring of expatriates in secondary and primary schools, profiting from the experience of the voluntary services over the last two decades, as well as the expensive unemployment of schoolteachers in the North. Like the issue of research culture, the priority concern with teacher professionalism and morale has no overnight solution. Raising parental and teacher awareness of what constitutes good schooling involves very ordinary but complex things to fund, such as subject associations, school visits, school science competitions, and, most important of all, a sense that the inspectorate and local administration recognise and reward good schooling. Action on these fronts is extraordinarily hard for an external agency to fund since the need is less for hardware than for the skills and devotion embodied in people.

Finally, the case for more aid to education and training has constantly to be re-made and argued afresh, if indeed developing countries see this sector as continuing to be crucial for years ahead. The very success of so many countries in extending primary and secondary education quite dramatically may make it difficult to argue for increased aid. In the same way the existence of a single national university or polytechnic may make it difficult to argue for a second. One of the prime tasks is to review informally the rationales and logic of aid to education from the donor and recipient perspective, and to reach a common understanding about the unfinished business of development assistance. Such informal dialogue cannot alter radically the fundamental unevenness of formal aid negotiations. But if successful, it will offer fresh insights into the political and educational contexts of each other's priorities, and an appreciation of some of the basic contours and still uncharted areas of aided educational systems.

Aid to education

Dorothy L. Njeuma

Introduction

Before we go into a review of the aid process to education in the last decade in order to examine what prospects lie ahead and how external assistance to education in sub-Saharan Africa can be more fruitfully channelled and utilised, it may be useful to take a look back at how education has grown in our various countries, how much our achievement has cost us, and how resources, both national and external, have been allocated to various levels of education.

I am sure I shall be forgiven for drawing mainly on the Cameroonian example with which I am most familiar, in the hope that many of the patterns that will emerge and problems encountered in the financing of education in Cameroon will bear very close similarities with those of other countries in the sub-Saharan region.

Growth of education

At the Addis Ababa Conference of 1961, a number of goals were set for the development of education in Africa by 1980. It was envisaged that by that date, primary education would be free and compulsory, secondary education would be provided for at least 30 per cent of children aged 12–18 and that the rate of higher education would be at 20 per cent. Four years after 1980, many African countries south of the Sahara are far from meeting those targets, although great strides have been made and at great cost, in the last ten years.

In Cameroon at primary level for example, the number of children enrolled in primary schools has increased from 1 014 000 in 1973–74 to 1 564 000 in 1983–84, representing an increase in absolute numbers of 550 400 children (or 54 per cent) over the ten-year period. This represents an average rate of *scholarisation* of 74 per cent in 1983–84. This number of children was taught by 31 030 teachers in 30 325 classrooms, representing an overall average teacher/pupil ratio of 1:50 and an average classroom/pupil ratio of 1:52.

While these ratios seem generally acceptable by relative Third World standards, the situation in urban areas, with the phenomenon of rural exodus and the uncontrolled growth of urban centres, leaves a lot to be desired. In government schools in Yaoundé and Douala, Cameroon's largest cities, although the teacher/pupil ratio is 1:42, the average number of pupils to a classroom is about 1:140; most of the schools therefore run on a double-shift system.

Besides, a good 50 per cent of the teachers are unqualified. This factor, coupled with that of overcrowding, means that the efficiency of the system is rather low. Drop out and repeater rates are high (about 28 per cent on the average), and the average length of time a child takes to complete the six-year (or seven-year) primary school course is ten years.

Another element which comes into play to reduce the efficiency and

135

increase the cost of education is the state of primary school classrooms. About 50 per cent of the 30 325 primary school classrooms are constructed from non-permanent or semi-permanent materials which are forever getting destroyed during the heavy rainy season.

Enrolment in secondary grammar schools increased from 82 660 in 1973–74 to 216 000 in 1983–84, representing an increase of 135 340 (or 163 per cent) in ten years. In secondary technical schools, enrolment rose over the same period from 24 000 to 74 886, representing a nearly three-fold increase. On the average, 35 per cent of children finishing primary school can enter into secondary school, and the rate of scholarisation at secondary level is 26.7 per cent which is appreciable, though slightly less than the target set in 1961. A lot has been done to open new secondary schools, both on the part of government and by private individuals and religious bodies, especially since 1976.

At secondary level, the average teacher/pupil ratio is 1:30 and the number of pupils per class is 1:46. However, here again as at the primary level, the situation is catastrophic in large urban areas where ratios can be as high as 1:80 or more. In addition, there is an acute shortage of teachers in quality and in quantity, particularly in mathematics, physical sciences and technical education. Although there are 9381 teachers for the 285 000 pupils in secondary grammar and technical schools, giving the ratio of 1:30 indicated above, the majority (55 per cent) are underqualified or untrained, a factor which contributes to the inefficiency of the system; the failure and drop-out rates are fairly high (about 14 per cent) and examination results rather low (around 30 per cent on the average for end-of-course official examinations).

Despite the rapid increase in numbers of pupils at secondary level, it is worth noting the serious problems posed by the inadequacy of equipment for science laboratories in secondary grammar schools. The high cost of equipment for workshops has also kept the number of industrial technical schools rather low; most of the technical schools offer commercial education which is generally cheaper to provide and to manage. School libraries are largely absent and those which exist are poorly run.

It is at the tertiary level that there has been the most dramatic increase in student numbers. From about 5500 students in 1973–74 there were 12 200 in 1983–84, giving an increase of 122 per cent in ten years. Student numbers have tended to level off with the introduction in 1979 of measures to weed out students who fail more than once in each of the first two years of university. The emphasis also on science has meant that student numbers in the Faculty of Science have increased by almost 120 per cent from 1330 in 1979–80 to 2920 in 1983–84. This large increase has not however been accompanied by corresponding increase in classrooms and laboratories nor in the number of lecturers where progression was from 100 in 1979–80 to 116 in 1983–84. In spite of this shift of emphasis to the sciences, student numbers in the Faculty of Law still remain very high, with 43 per cent of students in the whole university system. Failure rate remains extremely high, especially in the Faculty of Science.

It should be noted, however, that among the specialized schools, enrolment at the Higher Teachers College (*Ecole Normale Supérieure, ENS*) has nearly doubled from 661 in 1978–79 to 1240 in 1983–84, a translation of government's concern to produce more qualified teachers for the secondary school system. However, the annual turnout of about 200 teachers from the ENS is still far below actual needs which stand at approximately 700 new secondary school teachers every year. The problem of attracting candidates of mathematics and physics into the ENS still remains acute, most candidates preferring to go to the Faculty of Science or even the Economics Department of the Faculty of Law if they fail to get into the specialized Schools of Engineering, Medicine or Agriculture.

The decentralisation of the University of Yaoundé by the creation in 1976 of four University Centres in Buea, Douala, Dschang and Ngaoundéré is worth mentioning here since, as we shall see later, this has had a very significant impact on the distribution of investment to the various levels of the educational system.

To the 12 000 students in university in Cameroon, one should add at least another 5000 who are studying abroad, particularly in France, Britain and the United States. This would put the total population of Cameroonians in higher education at about 17 000, which is about 7 per cent of the enrolment at secondary level.

In general, of about 4000 pupils who graduate from secondary schools every year about 3500 or 87.5 per cent succeed in entering the specialized schools or faculties of the university system. This rate is very high and far exceeds the target of the Addis Ababa Conference of 1961 for enrolment in education at tertiary level. But the relevance of training at this level to the needs of the job market poses serious problems. The University of Yaoundé turned out 1121 graduates in 1982–83, 602 from the Faculty of Law and Economics, 330 from Arts and 189 from Science.

Financing of education: the national effort

While Cameroon has not yet attained universal primary education, it has made considerable strides in enrolment at primary, secondary and tertiary levels. This rapid increase in pupil and student numbers has certainly exceeded the means available to provide adequate staffing, infrastructure, equipment and funds for running costs. In this section, we shall look at the national effort made towards what has been achieved. The objective is not only to assess the volume of this effort in relation to the total financial and human resources required, but also to provide a yardstick by which to measure the external assistance that Cameroon has received over the years to supplement its own effort in the development of its educational system.

Cameroon has always devoted a considerable part of its financial resources to education. In the first three years of the 5th Five-Year Development Plan from 1981 to 1984 for example, education represented 18.2 per cent of national budget. In actual figures, this represents a sum of 225.2 billion FCFA out of total government expenditure of 1240 billion FCFA. Of this sum, recurrent expenditure accounted for 168.3 billion FCFA (that is, 74.7 per cent of total expenditure) as against 56.9 billion FCFA (or 25.3 per cent) on capital investment.

An analysis of government's recurrent expenditure on education in these three years shows the following:

Primary and Secondary Education: 130.5 billion FCFA (77.5%)

Higher Education: 37.8 billion FCFA (22.5%)

In other words, although enrolment in higher education constituted only 0.6 per cent of total enrolment in the educational system, it consumed 22.5 per cent of total recurrent expenditure in this sector.

Further analysis of recurrent expenditure on primary and secondary education from 1981 to 1984 reveals the following:

Salaries: 103.1 billion FCFA (86%)

Running costs: 9.6 billion FCFA (8%)

Maintenance of buildings: 1.3 billion FCFA (1.1%)

As much as 86 per cent of recurrent expenditure went to pay teachers' salaries. Eight per cent was devoted to running all services and schools, and only 1 per cent was used to maintain all administrative and school buildings. Without counting administrative services, less than 10 per cent of the budget was supposed to run and maintain 4300 primary and nursery schools, 321 secondary grammar and technical schools and 19 teacher training colleges. Needless to say that it has been difficult to run these services and schools efficiently on the meagre funds available. Whereas demand is high for boarding schools, the high cost of maintaining such schools in these times of accelerating inflation and high cost of living has actually led to the closure of dormitories in many schools. By far the greatest problem affecting the management of schools has been the absence of vehicles; even where they have been available, maintenance costs have been high. Considerable sums of money were spent on the construction of new schools and classrooms, but these rapidly became dilapidated due to shortage of maintenance funds.

As far as capital investment goes, expenditure on education has also been very high, representing 12.4 per cent of all government investment in the period from 1981 to 1984. Of the sum of nearly 57 billion FCFA spent on capital works in the education sector over that period, 50.6 per cent went to higher education. This is a reflection of the rapid expansion of higher education, especially since the mid-1970s, and the need to provide more adequate infrastructure (classrooms, libraries, laboratories, halls of residence, dining facilities, etc). This left 18.4 per cent to be spent on general secondary education, where expansion has also been considerable. Only 5.2 per cent was devoted to technical education, despite government's desire to improve on this sector of education. Also, only 10.8 per cent of capital expenditure on education went to primary and nursery education, which caters for the greatest bulk of children (84 per cent) in the formal school system. Investment on teacher-training for primary level represented only 1.9 per cent of total capital expenditure on education.

These proportions reflect more the internal social pressures on the system rather than the relative priorities of government in each sector. At secondary level, for example, there are considerable social pressures to expand on general education, which people consider more prestigious, than on technical education on which the nation's technological development so much depends. Since foreign aid donors have appeared more inclined to invest in technical education than in general education which is considered to produce job-seekers rather than job-creators, government has tended to

138

leave the development of this sector to foreign aid.

In higher education, besides the pressures to provide better facilities for the ever increasing numbers of students entering the faculties (and here again, foreign aid donors are not keen on developing general university education), the decentralisation of the University of Yaoundé by the creation of four new university centres has required considerable investment on the part of government.

Taking into account the need to develop other vital aspects of the economy such as agriculture, road infrastructure and to provide social amenities such as health care, water, electricity, housing, etc, it is clear that government cannot invest more in education without sacrificing these sectors. In fact, without development in these areas, it will be difficult for education to really develop, especially in qualitative terms. The tendency for teachers to concentrate in urban centres is a reflection of the real problems they encounter in rural areas whose access is not only difficult, but where basic facilities such as primary health care, reasonable housing, potable water, electricity, etc, are grossly lacking.

Yet because of the importance of human resources to general development, government cannot do otherwise than spend considerable sums of money on education. In fact, it is only in recent years that capital investment on road infrastructure (14.6 per cent) has exceeded that on education (12.4 per cent). 10.9 per cent of capital public investment between 1981 and 1984 has gone to agriculture, while the development of health services has had only 4.4 per cent and mines and power 4.7 per cent.

According to the fifth five-year development plan, an estimated total sum of 202 billion FCFA was to be spent as public capital investment to meet the needs of the education sector from 1981 to 1986 as follows:

Primary education 65 billion FCFA (32.2%)
General secondary education 22 billion FCFA (10.9%)
Technical education 31 billion FCFA (15.3%)
Teacher training 9 billion FCFA (4.5%)
Higher education 61 billion FCFA (30.2%)
Equipment 14 billion FCFA (6.9%)

If the plan were to be implemented according to schedule, a total of 121.2 billion FCFA should have been allocated to education by the end of the third year; as can be seen, the actual funds available have been only 47 per cent of the target and some of the proportions have been reversed, secondary education taking the lead behind higher education at the expense of primary education and technical education.

Financing of education: foreign contribution

While external assistance to sub-Saharan Africa was geared in the 1960s towards the development of human resources, much external aid went into the education sector, particularly to institution-building. It is thus that in the case of Cameroon for example, substantial sums of bilateral and multilateral aid went into the construction of institutions such as the University of Yaoundé, the School of Administration and Magistracy, etc. Aid in the form of scholarships to train Cameroonian personnel abroad as well as technical assistance personnel to run the institutions which had been set up was also very substantial.

In the latter part of the 1970s, however, and with the complications of geographical and adverse climatic factors, attention has been focused rather on the development of agriculture in order to improve on the acute food situation as well as on the so-called productive sectors to boost the economies of sub-Saharan countries of Africa. The education sector has therefore attracted less and less external aid.

Capital investment

Even so, external assistance to education in Cameroon in the last decade, though relatively small, has been quite significant. The volume of direct external assistance to education in Cameroon in the period from 1974 to 1984 can be set at about 50 billion FCFA, excluding the cost of technical assistance. The form of aid provided has consisted of contributions to capital works, equipment, book donations, refresher courses, short study trips, scholarships and technical assistance and has come from bilateral and multilateral sources.

Aid in the form of direct external contribution to capital works and equipment has covered, in descending order of the volume of funds spent, higher education (with emphasis on agricultural education at tertiary and secondary level), teacher training, general secondary education and technical education. Such funding has financed a total of 58 projects, 42 of them from subventions and loans from the World Bank.

Considering that this assistance actually spans a period of 21 years from 1969 to 1990, it can be seen that it averages about 2 billion FCFA per year which, though small compared with national investment in education in the three years from 1981 to 1984, has contributed substantial inputs into the system in terms of badly needed infrastructure and equipment.

While the emphasis placed on agricultural education is understandable, it has however proved disappointing that aid donors have not been as forthcoming as was expected in their assistance to technical education and especially to the training of teacher trainers for this sector. Negotiations have often been very long and drawn out, some aid donors making it abundantly clear that their intervention would be contingent upon contracts being awarded to specific firms from their countries, on the use of imported building materials and even upon substantial modifications to local training programmes.

Most of the aided projects have been initiated by Cameroon and then submitted for external financing. However, a few have been initiated by aid donors; while these latter projects do fall within Cameroon's priorities, sometimes emphasis has not been quite judiciously placed.

Most of the bilaterally-aided projects comprise substantial components of technical assistance which, in most cases, has been provided by aid donors, even where local manpower which is substantially cheaper has sometimes been available.

In certain cases, even where projects have been initiated by Cameroon, important local factors, especially demography, have not been taken into consideration. School enrolment, for example, has often been very highly

140

underestimated, so that infrastructure proves inadequate before it is even put into use (for example, a full cycle four-year secondary school is planned for 320 children, whereas actual figures are around 1000 at least).

Sometimes, projects have taken much longer to realise than envisaged, because of the unavailability of appropriate land to house projects and administrative red tape. This has sometimes led to periods of loan disbursement being overly extended, with increased costs especially to the recipient country. Fortunately, these drawbacks have been realised and are gradually being corrected so that loan agreements are signed only after land is actually available and preliminary architectural studies effected.

A few externally-funded projects have comprised manpower training components which have been incorporated early enough so that local human resources are available to run the projects soon after they are realised. Some of these have even included the provision of recurrent costs in terms of vehicles, equipment and personnel to run the projects in their initial stages, as well as follow-up.

Unfortunately, however, some projects have no built-in component for the development of appropriate human resources. Such projects have proved difficult to run once completed and to produce the desired impact.

Fortunately for Cameroon, we have had little or no conflict between aid donors as concerns their participation in assistance to education even where several aid donors have contributed to the same institution. This has been mainly due to the co-ordination of all external assistance by one single ministry — that of Planning and Regional Management. Aid donors usually send out several preliminary missions to discuss projects with all the ministries concerned before agreement is actually reached. In most cases, the periodic synthesis reports of the World Bank have served as very useful sources of information to many aid donors in Cameroon.

Technical assistance and scholarships

Out of a total of about 650 technical assistance personnel in Cameroon, 371 or 57 per cent are in education, the majority coming from countries with which Cameroon has traditionally had close diplomatic links. Of this number, 153 or 41 per cent are involved in the teaching of mathematics and science subjects, 138 or 37 per cent in technical education, and the rest distributed over language teaching (especially English and French, the official languages of Cameroon, as well as German, Spanish and Arabic).

There is no doubt that this assistance, though small in relation to our needs, is essentially in those vital areas where qualified staff is in short supply. However, it also happens that in these particular areas donors also have staff shortages. This sometimes makes it difficult to recruit technical assistance personnel. Sometimes, personnel already recruited turn down their offers of employment abroad at the last minute, although donor countries always do all they can to find suitable replacements. Sometimes also, it has happened that donor countries withdraw some of their personnel at short notice and in areas on which they themselves decide.

While technical assistance is useful, the high rate of turnover of such personnel creates problems of discontinuity within the system. Most of such staff come out for short tours of two or at most four years. They have

141

to leave just when they are becoming familiar with the system.

The inclusion by some donors of counterpart training in their technical assistance programmes is highly appreciated, as this contributes significantly to building up local manpower through a multiplier effect. However, the need for teacher trainers, especially in mathematics, the sciences and technical education remains very great, especially in the effort to improve on the teaching of these subjects at secondary level and to develop local teacher training institutions at tertiary level. Yet many aid donors seem reluctant to venture further or to support these areas which we consider vital for Cameroon's industrial and technological development. Negotiations for assistance in this sector are very long and drawn out and do not seem to generate as much interest as would be expected unless aid donors see the direct benefit that they can derive from such investment.

The number of foreign scholarships from which Cameroon benefits has dwindled very significantly over the years. This reduction can be largely accounted for by the creation of more institutions for specialized training locally. The number of foreign scholarships awarded to Cameroon annually stands currently at about 45. This number is no doubt very small, compared with the number of Cameroon-sponsored students abroad. Actual offers of scholarships exceed this figure; but most times offers are received so late that closing dates are difficult to meet.

Most aid donors tend to restrict offers of scholarships only to areas for which no local institutions exist. Yet the need is felt to train more personnel than the present capacity of many local institutions, and also to benefit from the experience of more developed countries through training abroad. The result is that the number of students abroad on national scholarships is increasing, at a time when developed countries are adopting more protective policies that make foreign students, especially those from developing countries, pay fees that far exceed those of home students. From 425 students sponsored abroad by the Cameroon government in 1979–80, there were 620 in 1981–82 and 1087 fully sponsored and 285 partly sponsored in 1984–85. When to the excessively high fees are added the high cost of living abroad and unfavourable exchange rates, the financial burden becomes really tremendous and sometimes prohibitive.

Perspectives

From the foregoing, it is clear that while considerable progress has been achieved in education in Cameroon, a great deal still remains to be done.

With the high rate of population growth in many sub-Saharan countries, problems of education are compounded further. Cameroon, for example, given its present rate of population growth, will count 14 million inhabitants by the year 2000. Of this population, and even without arriving at free and compulsory education, there will be 2 915 000 children in primary school. Even if we maintained the teacher pupil ratio at 1:50, we shall need 29 020 more teachers and at least an equal number of classrooms, without even replacing the currently unqualified teachers and temporary classrooms.

At the level of general secondary education, there will be 786 000 pupils, requiring 11 400 new teachers and as many new classrooms, without mentioning libraries, laboratories and equipment.

In technical education, there will be about 222 000 pupils, requiring 4920 new teachers and classrooms, plus corresponding workshops, libraries and equipment.

At university level, there will be at least 22 000 students, which is almost double the current enrolment.

At primary and secondary levels alone and at present costs, a total sum of 305 billion FCFA will be needed between now and the year 2000 to build classrooms only, without considering laboratories, workshops, libraries and equipment, or an average of 19 billion FCFA per annum. Almost 2000 additional primary school teachers and about 1000 new secondary school teachers will be needed every year if the present standards already described as inadequate are to be maintained.

At the level of the university, current capital expenditure per annum will have to be at least doubled, thus placing annual total capital investment on education at about 37 billion FCFA.

The challenge is indeed enormous, and this simply to maintain standards at their current levels of inefficiency! How much of this funding can we ourselves really afford and how much can we reasonably expect from aid donors especially at this time when the spectre of hunger and poverty looms every year larger over most of sub-Saharan Africa and when the attention of aid donors is drawn more and more to other vital sectors of our ailing economies?

If present trends should continue, it would appear that we shall have to depend mostly on our own resources to finance our educational needs and select specific areas to which external aid to education should be channelled to maximise benefits.

Conclusion

The case of Cameroon is not at all unique in sub-Saharan Africa. Most of our countries spend nearly one-fifth of their national budgets on education. While substantial progress has been achieved in the education sector, a great deal still remains to be done. The huge portion of our resources spent on education is clearly largely inadequate to meet needs which remain enormous at all levels of the system. This makes it difficult to establish priorities because every level of education appears to carry the same relative importance. Even where priorities are established, they cannot be respected because of internal pressures and attitudes.

With the need to develop other vital areas of our economies, we can hardly afford to spend more on education without jeopardising overall development. While external aid to education is significant, the tendency is towards its reduction in favour of other sectors that are more directly productive. Assistance towards institution-building, especially in mathematics, the sciences and technical education on which our industrial and technological development depends, seems difficult to negotiate.

Yet, in the face of galloping population figures, substantially increased financial resources are needed to maintain present standards in education which are far from satisfactory. The indications are that African countries will have to depend largely on their own resources to finance education, and select specific areas to which external assistance should be channelled.

Notes for working group discussion

Theme I: Education priorities

A. Background to the discussion: the effect of current demographic and economic realities on the policy and practice of education

Educational priorities need to be set and educational decisions taken in the light of critical problems facing nations in Africa under the shadow of a world economic recession. Pressures derive from:

1 *Numbers* School-age populations are fast rising and distribution between rural and urban areas changing. School enrolments show dramatic increases in response to demands for mass education.

2 *Demand* Public demand for education, and for certificates and diplomas at various levels, continues to rise and becomes increasingly out of step with the ability of the public education system to provide it. There is increasing concern over standards and over the mismatch between qualifications and employment requirements.

3 *Finance* Economic realities and rising numbers and demands place enormous pressure on government financing of education. The education sector may be under pressure to maintain its current share of national budgets in competition with demands from other sectors. Within education, there are mounting pressures to do 'more' with 'less' — to increase provision and hence to reduce unit costs; to share costs of education with communities; and to accept increased private financing of education services.

4 *Economic Policies* In the face of recession and world economic trends, many governments have announced policies and priorities with far-reaching effects on the provision and content of education.

B. Areas for discussion

1 Priorities, levels and approaches

a *Levels of formal education* Given resources available, current political and economic realities, lessons gained from experience in the last decade, and probable development trends, how far should current investment in education at different levels in the formal system be sustained? What changes in emphasis need to be made? Where and how can cuts effectively be applied, or alternative patterns and structures considered:

   i in basic or universal education
   ii in upper primary or junior secondary education
   iii at secondary level
   iv at tertiary level
   v in teacher education?

These notes were prepared by the Conference organisers as a background to the discussions on each theme. They were not intended as an agenda, but merely as an aid for chairmen and working groups in pointing to some of the timely and important issues.

b *Sectors: formal and non-formal education* Given the altered perceptions of the role of education, rapid changes in society, in the nature of knowledge and in occupational structures, and swift advances in technology, it is possible to argue for greater sustained investment in non-formal education. But how far is this desirable, acceptable or possible?

c *Quality of education* To what extent should investment be maintained in the provision of means and machinery to determine, plan and monitor appropriate content for education?

d *Relevance and terminality* How far is education conceived as a means to promote opportunity and mobility, and how far as a means of efficiently fitting leavers to meet identified needs in the economy?

2 Improving efficiency

Systems are under great pressure to sustain or increase educational provision, to improve its quality and, at the same time, to reduce gaps between official provision and actual practice, to modernise and update systems, and to reduce inequitable gaps in the provision and content of education. But they must also contend with shrinking resources, and little prospect of greater or even current levels of investment per capita. Is it possible that challenges may at least partly be met by making inefficient systems of education more efficient? The issue of efficiency inevitably opens up debate on how far radical innovations should be contemplated and how far they would be absorbed.

Structure, organisation and management

a Can greater efficiency be achieved
  i through more effective use of staff and facilities
  ii through improving systems of supervision and support
  iii through promoting ideas and practices of accountability
  iv through more efficient use of instructional time; leading to possible savings of hours, days or even years of schooling
  v through greater decentralisation?

b Such discussion may lead to consideration of more radical alternatives such as
  i examination of the length, pattern and function of mass education
  ii reassessment of the present separation of formal and non-formal systems and examination of ways in which the two could be integrated with periods of full-time and part-time education commonly combined
  iii significant policies in the devolution and decentralisation of educational management.

c What information exists and would need to be gathered to inform decision-making in this area? Do examples of such practices exist? Can working models be effectively established and monitored?

Teachers and alternative delivery systems

a Can greater efficiency be achieved
  i through better and more economical patterns of training and deployment of teachers

ii through use of teachers' aides, peer teaching, parental and community involvement

iii through some involvement of educational technology and mass media (bearing in mind, however, the failure of past attempts to *replace* teachers by technology, rather than *assist* them)?

b Such discussion may lead to consideration of radical alternatives in
   i the structure and pattern of teacher education proposed, for example for shorter initial training cycles
   ii the whole approach to pedagogy and school organisation.

c What information exists and would need to be gathered to inform decision-making in this area? Do examples of such practices exist? Can models be effectively established and monitored?

Content and assessment

a Can greater efficiency be achieved through
   i better selection and prioritisation of education content
   ii the 'pruning' of educational content at all levels, including university level
   iii the use of different modes of education — formal and non-formal — to teach content for which they are best fitted
   iv more efficient use of assessment systems to raise quality?

b The discussion may lead to consideration of more radical alternatives such as
   i fundamental reviews of the content of education at school level
   ii reviews of the whole pattern and basis of assessment and certification
   iii reviewing the fundamental purpose and hence content of tertiary education.

c What information exists and would need to be gathered to inform decision-making in this area?

The financing of education

a The group may wish to consider educational financing side by side with the issue of increasing efficiency through the sharing and apportioning of responsibilities for the provision and management of education.
They also need to consider
   i Whether measures are available to shift the burden of educational expenditure from central public funds more directly on to the consumers of educational services? Is such a shift desirable? Does it lead to savings through more rational and efficient expenditure? Does it make the provision of education more responsive to demand? Does it lead to greater inequality in favouring those individuals or communities best able to pay some of the costs?
   ii Whether there are other forms of funding available, and what are the benefits and disadvantages of alternatives?
   iii Whether the taxation system is in need of reform in order to generate more funds, or to distribute the burden more appropriately?

b What information exists and needs to be gathered to inform decision-making in this area?

146

Theme II: Aid to education

1 The record of aid assistance and lessons gained from experience

It may be valuable to consider very briefly how focuses and rationale of educational assistance have changed over the past decades, hopefully for the better:

a In relation to allocation of *priorities to sectors* of education — primary, secondary, tertiary and non-formal

b In relation to *focus and purpose of aid* — the development of key manpower, emphasis on planning systems and content of education, promoting innovation

c In relation to the *type of aid* provided — capital inputs, technical assistance, training, co-operative loans, project loans vs sectoral loans; hardware vs software

d In regard to *relations between donors and recipients* and the nature of the negotiation process

e In relation to *links* between aid to education and other development aid.

What are the most significant lessons gained from experience?

2 Responses to priorities identified

a Given identified priorities and recognising that the aid process is better able to assist in some areas than others, is a change of emphasis in the amount of aid provided desirable or, indeed, possible between sectors or levels?

b Within levels and sectors identified — universal primary education, diversified secondary education, tertiary education — in what way is the aid process best able to make a contribution?

c What role can the aid process have in relation to priorities identified for improving the efficiency of education: for providing innovative alternatives, for changing patterns of education financing? Is there a role for the aid process in clarifying alternatives; identifying, organising and monitoring working models; planning; training?

d Do the identified priorities in Theme I raise any fundamental issues about the nature and purpose of aid — in relation to its role either in maintaining the current models and systems, or changing them? In what way can aid be provided so that it decreases rather than increases dependency?

3 The aid process: where and how can aid be best directed?

a To what extent and in what circumstances should overseas aid now seek to finance recurrent as opposed to capital investment costs of programmes and projects? How can the realities of the relationship between capital and recurrent costs be better realised?

b In particular, is specific help needed in the provision of materials of education for schools — books and equipment for example — but if so, how does this affect long-term provision of materials?

c What are priorities for technical co-operation and training, and are the new patterns desirable or possible?

d In relation to supply of technical assistance, is there a right balance between short-term personnel who are meeting immediate needs and long-service personnel who are experienced but represent a setback to localisation policies? How are projects best localised?

e What possibilities exist of helping NGOs with official aid?

4 The aid process: the nature of aid negotiations and agreements

a What 'strings' are legitimate in aid agreements in terms of conditions imposed on recipients? How can agreements be better negotiated to achieve greater flexibility, yet ensure original purposes are maintained? To what extent do recipients actually welcome conditionality?

b What are the advantages or disadvantages of 'packaged aid' — in terms of projects, institutional links, or in other forms?

c How can agencies and recipients assess appropriateness of time-scales in relation to programmes and projects?

5 Improving communication among all those engaged in the aid process

a Is it possible for more information about policies and priorities to be made widely available from aid agencies?

b How can dialogue between donors and recipients best be structured so that the perceptions of each can be modified with subsequent implications for the flexibility of plans and proposals?

c In respect of 'packages' funded by more than one donor, how best can co-ordination take place: by prior co-ordination among donors? Or by negotiation initiated by recipients? How do recipients view policy dialogue with donors: are donors perceived as bringing valuable insights from other education systems?

6 Improving the information base on which aid decisions can be taken

a Is it necessary or possible to improve awareness by all partners in the aid process of the policy concerns which shape proposals and of the operational constraints which exist in implementing them?

b What policies are necessary and desirable towards research and data gathering? How far should donors initiate and support research, and of what kind?

c How far is information available on local grassroots initiatives, local perceptions, and local realities of implementation? Could the aid process help to make such information available?

d Should there be more monitored experimentation funded by donors in innovative pilot experiments, or has there been too much in the past?

Aid to education in Africa: analysis of provision and policies of selected aid agencies

Ian Clifton-Everest

The evolution of donor policy

The following analysis draws on both internal policy statements of donor agencies as well as those of the government to which donors are answerable. Within the last ten years, most agencies have produced policy documents specifically on aid to education. Further policy information is contained in general reporting and publicity material. This has been used to fill certain lacunae. Insofar as possible, the same conceptual tools and loose framework are used in the analysis of every donor. However, some gaps in the information are inevitable because the review of documentation was by no means comprehensive. In addition it has to be borne in mind that policy does not always prescribe on exactly the same issues and some apparent lacunae may be intrinsic in the nature of policy itself.

Canadian International Development Agency (CIDA)

CIDA was created in 1968 with the objective of 'facilitating the efforts of the people of developing countries to achieve sustainable economic and social development in accordance with their needs and environments. . . .' This objective was to be pursued with the broader aim of 'contributing to Canada's political and economic interests abroad in promoting social justice, international stability and long-term economic relationships for the benefit of the global community'. Prior to 1968 a programme of official Canadian assistance was operated by its Economic and Technical Assistance Bureau. The programme for Commonwealth Africa began in 1959 and for francophone Africa in 1961.

Reflecting the spirit of the times in which it was conceived, CIDA's policy has always put strong emphasis on both social development and returns to the individual. Although value is attached to economic development, and mention is quite openly made of possible spinoffs for the Canadian economy, CIDA describes its motives as humanitarian, political and economic, in that order.

In its *Strategy for International Development Co-operation, 1975–1980,* CIDA laid strong emphasis on the notions of basic needs and Third World self-reliance. Within its policy framework, educational activities were to be

This is an edited version of two sections of a longer paper prepared by Ian Clifton-Everest for the Conference. It should be read with two caveats in mind. Firstly, it makes no attempt to provide an exhaustive description of aid agency policies. It deals only with seven agencies, two multilateral and five bilateral, and there is no discussion of voluntary agency aid to education. Secondly, this paper in no way represents an official view of aid agency policies. It is offered in this report as it was at the Conference, as an attempt to synthesise valuable information about policies and priorities, and in the hope that its existence, and even its shortcomings, may inspire others to seek to expand and improve upon the information it contains.

supportive of those in other sectors and this was to be achieved by taking a country approach to planning assistance. In pursuit of this policy in individual countries, importance was attached to:

1 The collection of basic information relating to education (this should include manpower requirements and learning needs, as well as the existing educational provision)

2 Adaptation of educational institutions to accommodate indigenous systems of learning, to be more problem-centred, flexible in meeting changing learning needs

3 The evolution of a basic first cycle education, universal in its coverage, supportive of rural development, and the satisfaction of other basic needs and rights.

In addition, this document placed considerable stress on the use of Canadian human resources to provide training in nonformal education, vocational education and educational technology, including mass media. Wherever possible, such training should be provided in local institutions.

In 1980, CIDA restructured the organisation of its assistance programme so as to focus impact on three main sectors: food and agriculture, energy, and human resources. The effect of this was to strengthen the broader human resources orientation of CIDA's educational programmes.

In its 1984 policy paper, *Elements of Canada's Official Development Strategy*, CIDA reaffirmed its commitment to the world's poorest, and to the marginal groups that are bypassed by economic growth, pointing out the potential they offer for contributing to the well-being of the population as a whole. At the same time it stressed the importance of creating capacity for development, noting that:

> only by improving the well-being and abilities of its people can a Third World country ensure that development will be indigenous, will serve national goals, and will reduce dependence upon foreign assistance and technology.

One of the more fundamental notions underlying CIDA's policies is that of resource sharing. Assistance essentially means sharing Canadian expertise and technological know-how with developing countries, and a key consideration in policy formulation is the nature of the resources that are available. At the same time, there is sensitivity to the dangers of systems transfer, and great stress is placed on the importance of supporting indigenous development. CIDA links educational assistance to a distinctive concept of human resource development which emphasises people as 'both the means and the end of development'. The application of this policy is particularly well illustrated by its Kenya training programme.

Under current policy, 80 per cent of CIDA's resources are concentrated on low-income countries, and 40 per cent on African countries. Thirty per cent of CIDA's bilateral aid is channelled through NGOs in keeping with its policy of fostering links between individual institutions in Canada and the developing world. Such links are also considered as the most effective way of ensuring that aid reaches the poorest sectors in developing countries.

150

West German Agency for Technical Co-operation (GTZ)

GTZ was created in 1975 as an independent, but government-owned, enterprise under contract to implement the technical co-operation programme of the Federal Ministry for Economic Co-operation. Although the Federal Republic's current policies on aid to education in developing countries date only from 1971, its programme of aid in Africa originated in the early 1960s. Its earlier programmes were concerned primarily with institution-building in the tertiary sector. Although it pledged to support development in the primary sector too, it encountered difficulties in establishing the necessary working relationships to launch a programme in this area.

According to GTZ's publicity material, its aim is to 'promote economic and social development in Third World countries' and priority is given to 'fighting mass poverty by satisfying basic needs'.

The policy document on education and scientific aid adopted by the Federal Republic in 1971 drew heavily on the United Nations proposals for the Second Development Decade. Education is seen as having a vital role to play in promoting 'the improvement of living conditions of people in developing countries'. This it can do by activating 'the will for and ability to undertake self-help for innovation, for social integration, and for political involvement of large sections of the population . . . and more equitable distribution of social opportunities'. To this end, priority is given to the development of functional basic education and further occupational training, with special attention to those who cannot readily be reached by the formal system. Specific mention is made of the need to create an interface between the formal and non-formal systems. A further area of strategic concern is the promotion of training that will strengthen support services, not only in education, but also in agriculture, trade and industry, and health. Here it argues that universities and other tertiary institutions can be helped to develop a vital training function. To further the role of education in promoting 'social integration and political involvement', GTZ proposes to support leadership training for those who exercise influence over current socio-political problems.

Like CIDA, GTZ is highly sensitive to the dangers of 'systems-transfer' or the imposition of ill-adapted educational models from donor countries. It lays heavy stress on the need for careful research to establish local needs, and methods for supporting the evolution of indigenous systems of education.

In its more recent policy statements, *Promotion of Basic Education* (1981) and *Promotion of Education and Science* (1982) the commitment to functional basic education and vocational training, and to educational research is reiterated. Well-targeted functional basic education is, however, given the highest priority. An overall strategy is to promote the evolution of an educational infrastructure in developing countries with capacities for teacher training, production of teaching aids and educational planning. In this respect, there is perhaps some likeness with CIDA's policy of promoting capacity for development. Stress is also laid, however, on the need for built-in flexibility and capability to adapt and respond to changing demands at different stages in the country's development.

151

German development policy is firmly rooted in notions of human rights. Education contributes to the attainment of such rights by providing occupational and other functional skills that enable individuals to meet their basic needs.

Swedish International Development Authority (SIDA)

SIDA's programme of aid to education stretches back into the First Development Decade when the agency was active in promoting vocational training, women's education and teacher training — as well as some primary and secondary school construction. At the beginning of the 1970s, it too produced a major policy document: *Aid and Education* (1972). In this it proposed that:

> The aim of education should be, on the one hand, to attain a more even distribution of knowledge, proficiencies and resources and to promote economic growth, and on the other, to enable people to gain a livelihood and to have an influence on their living conditions.

This double aim can be referenced to a duality of notions underlying Swedish development policy as a whole. The aim is to promote on the one hand the development of social, economic and political systems, and on the other the well-being of individual people. Within the broad framework of policy on education, priorities for support can be ordered thus:

1 non-formal education, elementary education, vocational training and supplementary vocational training, including agricultural training and training of teachers and administrators within these fields

2 secondary education, especially in science, technology and agriculture, training of secondary school teachers and administrators

3 tertiary education.

Certain target groups, namely those that are socially, economically or geographically marginal, are singled out for special attention, and stress is laid on the need for realism in developing truly functional forms of education for them. Thus, the document says:

> In the long view, it should be possible to provide many with work within a growing industry, but for a long time to come in developing countries it will be agriculture that offers most opportunities for employment. ... It is in the community outside the school walls that the great fights for knowledge exist.

In 1978, Parliament declared that Swedish development co-operation should be directed towards (1) economic growth, (2) economic and social equality, (3) economic and political independence, (4) development of democracy in society. Against this background, SIDA's 1982 paper, *Assistance in the Field of Education,* stresses the need to promote systems of education that serve the mass of people rather than a small élite. Education, it argues, not only has to be functional, but also 'related to knowledge and levels of technology existing in society and its prevailing norms and values'.

SIDA's policies, like those of CIDA and GTZ, reflect concern about systems transfer and cultural imperialism. While its approach to development co-operation is one of resource-based aid, it recognises that considerable care is needed in sharing Sweden's resources, both

152

technological and human, with developing countries. A key consideration must be the ability of a recipient country to meet the maintenance costs of a technological innovation. Within the field of education, it considers that the most readily transferable technologies are the production-oriented ones, such as those involved in the printing of books and other teaching materials.

SIDA insists that its approach to development co-operation is, in essence, a responsive one. Thus, while within the framework of its policies it has its own priorities, the priorities of the recipient country are seen as paramount. In keeping with this principle, SIDA's policy documents are highly explicit on matters of problem analysis, on definition of objectives and methods of collaboration, but they avoid pronouncing on matters of development strategy, which it regards as the sovereign concern of the recipient country.

In 1983, the Swedish Minister for Economic Affairs wrote;

> Sweden is a small country with limited resources and this means that our contribution can only be marginal. To ensure that our international assistance is put to the best possible use, we are compelled to limit both the number of countries with which we co-operate and the number of fields in which we engage. We concentrate mainly on a relatively small number of countries whose development policies and goals are similar to our own.

United Kingdom Overseas Development Administration (ODA)

ODA was created in 1966 (then known as the Ministry of Overseas Development) against the background of the United Nations declaration of the first Development Decade, and prior to 1970 sought to continue policies of funding expatriate teachers and other resource personnel, as well as giving a high priority to strengthening the capacity of tertiary institutions to train higher cadres of administrators, professionals, scientists and technicians.

In 1970, the British government issued a White Paper on *Aid to Education in Developing Countries* which reviewed focal problems and British aid strategies, and strongly reaffirmed its belief in the strategic importance of education in economic and social development. It also pointed to a number of considerations that should guide future policy:

> Every country has to ask itself such questions as how much education should be provided, and what kind? What should be the dominant objectives? What are the rights of the individual to education compared with the needs of the country and its economy? How is the country concerned to import what it needs in the way of educational philosophy, methods and media without undermining or impairing its own culture?

These concerns with balancing the rights of the individual against the needs of the nation-state were central to the theme of the paper. In addition, the paper alluded to the looming problem of unemployment in the modern wage sector; the need to focus education more on problems of rural development; and the need to address the geographical imbalance in the distribution of resources favouring urban areas. If education was to assist the process of social and economic development, it needed to be reoriented towards manpower requirements. This depended not only on

153

new curricula, but also on strong educational administration capable of directing the change. To achieve the aims of decreased intervention but greater effectiveness, it proposed to redeploy a large part of educational aid going to teacher supply, particularly to the primary sector. Eventually teacher supply was to be restricted to upper secondary English, science and mathematics, and the bulk of aid was to be concentrated on improving administration and support services.

A further White Paper in 1975 contained the Government's formal commitment to focusing aid on the world's poorest, and outlined the measures it proposed to take to achieve a reallocation of aid. However, while accepting the need to ensure that aid benefits the poorest sections of the community within recipient countries, the paper avoided specifying any strategies, considering these to be a matter for the national policies of recipients. However, the paper is notable for arguing that non-formal education should not be assumed to be the obvious device for improving the lot of the poor. While it may be important, it is not a panacea and there is a danger of it evolving into a substitute, and second class, education.

In the 1982 edition of its pamphlet *British Aid to Education in Developing Countries*, ODA says:

> British aid to education in developing countries emphasises the developmental role of education in relation to manpower needs and both social and economic growth. Emphasis is placed on the multiplier effect of aid to education and on assistance to selected key points in the education system of each recipient country. . . . The ODA has no universal response and no universal priorities (except possibly the teaching of English) in the process of assisting developing countries.

In a way that is reminiscent of SIDA's policy, it goes on:

> In seeking to relate inputs in the field of education, as in other fields, to the overall strategy of aid to each individual country, it is necessary to take account of national priorities of the receiving countries in the context of manpower and other planning geared to the promotion of economic and social development and to the relief of poverty.

Since 1983, manpower training has become an even more central element in British aid policy, particularly in Africa. Building on strategies proposed by the World Bank in its recent strategy paper for *Accelerated Development in Sub-Saharan Africa* (1981), the aim is to assist in improving return on investment by focusing on the functioning of key operative institutions and providing training in policy analysis and administration.

The 1984 edition of the pamphlet *British Aid to Education in Developing Countries* points out that ODA's policies on educational aid are supportive of this broader human resources development strategy. And at the same time, on a country-by-country basis, the policies are guided by the principle of achieving rational and efficient investment in the education sector. Thus it is noted, for example, that they take account of the 'accumulating mass of research that indicates the high economic (not to mention social) return achieved by investment in primary or some form of basic education'. Both the 1984 information pamphlet and ODA's 1984 *Education Sector Policy Paper* emphasise that overall, policy is highly pragmatic and is based on the principle of bringing British resources in education to bear on the agreed needs of developing countries. From ODA's perspective, these needs have to be seen in terms of the general efficiency of the educational system as a whole; more specifically, they are judged in terms of manpower requirements and improved social conditions. Within this broad framework, ODA currently sees a number of priority areas for its future assistance:

1 Training, especially in the specific skills of planners, administrators, managers, inspectors and advisers in education, both in Britain and in the developing countries.

2 Support for ELT, with increasing emphasis on ESP and English for non-Commonwealth countries.

3 Pre-vocational, vocational and technical education of various kinds and at various levels, including training in agriculture, in industry and in management: in this there is scope for the use of ESP.

4 Support for elements of formal education at all levels from primary to tertiary, and with special reference to the 'developmental' role of such education. In this regard, support is given to the selective initial and in-service training of teachers, and the training of teacher educators against a background of the continuing but diminishing provision of expatriate teachers and educationists in these fields. There is also room for the implementation of curriculum reform towards locally defined goals.

5 Encouragement of co-operation between tertiary level institutions in Britain and in developing countries.

6 Experiment and innovation in non-formal education and in the border-zone between formal and non-formal education, particularly in the training of trainers and group leaders, and in the design of low-cost equipment for functional literacy.

7 Co-operation in the application of appropriate distance teaching techniques and in the production of materials and programmes in both formal and non-formal education.

8 The provision of books and related materials to school classrooms and to the libraries of key institutions; assistance to the development of library services.

9 Research in education directed to the solution or illumination of problems of special interest in the aid programme.

10 The evaluation of aid to education in all its forms.

United States Agency for International Development (USAID)

USAID was born in 1961 to a long line of predecessors. Under the United States Foreign Assistance Act of 1961, USAID was to seek to promote world economic development and international stability with a view to protecting social justice, freedom and peace. Within this policy context, USAID's programme of assistance to Africa during the 1960s was based on a principle of reinforcing the viability of newly independent nation states. Within education, this was taken to mean assistance in creating manpower required by vital administrative, managerial, and technological institutions. USAID's policy was to encourage the provision of such assistance through existing links between institutions in the tertiary sector in the United States and in developing countries.

The 1970s however, saw strenuous efforts to redirect USAID's assistance away from support for the tertiary sector and the creation of high level manpower, towards reform and expansion of elementary and non-formal basic education, the introduction of a more appropriate educational technology, and systems of mass communication. John Hannah, then Administrator of USAID, commented:

> General social progress cannot be achieved by a small élite commanding a huge constituency of illiterate and disoriented people. Success in development requires that at least the majority of people be supplied with knowledge and the opportunity to participate to some reasonable degree in economic, social and political activity.

A strategy involving three elements was proposed for tackling this task of mass education:

1 Exploring the potential of educational technology

2 Fostering experimentation in the field of non-formal education

3 Encouraging research and experimentation in the use of educational finance.

A commitment to mass basic education and the creation of productive skills among rural families and the urban poor was also written into the Amendment of the Foreign Assistance Act in 1973.

By the mid-1970s, USAID had an impressive list of criteria for the provision of aid to education. Among the principal criteria listed by John Hilliard, then Director of the Office of Education and Human Resources, in a paper in *Prospects* (1974), were the following:

1 functionality

2 expansion

3 researching disadvantaged groups

4 internal efficiency

5 improving articulation between levels and subsectors

6 improving content and methodology

7 extension into areas of health, population, etc.

8 more efficient use of resources

9 better institutional involvement in education for development.

The creation of a division of education and human resources in USAID in the late 1970s reflects the growing concern, held in common with CIDA, ODA and the World Bank, that the education programme should be more centred on human resource needs, and that education should more thoroughly permeate activities in other sectors.

USAID's 1982 policy paper on *Basic Education and Technical Training Assistance Strategy* adopts a human capital perspective, but along with the World Bank, places its main emphasis on the efficient use of resources in education in developing countries. While there is still a commitment to extending coverage, and achieving greater equality of opportunity, it is argued that these will follow quite naturally from the more efficient use of resources. The document advocates a number of ways of improving efficiency. Apart from increasing capacity for policy analysis, planning and administration, other measures mentioned are: privatisation and encouragement of market mechanisms, decentralisation so as to achieve more needs-focused administration and support services, and a greater appreciation of the labour market in educational planning and in training.

In its *Basic Education and Technical Training Assistance Strategy* paper, USAID's Africa Bureau emphasises that research on resource utilisation must be a key element in any attempt to implement this policy. Wherever possible, training should be organised regionally or on a country basis, and should be a collaborative exercise with counterpart trainers from both the United States and recipient countries. There is, moreover, a need to accept the long-term nature of the training commitment.

United Nations Childrens Fund (UNICEF)

UNICEF was created in 1946 to continue the relief work with children undertaken in the post-war period by the United Nations Relief and Rehabilitation Administration (UNRRA). According to the United Nations General Assembly Resolution 57(I), the residual assets of UNRRA, supplemented by voluntary contributions of governments and individuals, were to be used by UNICEF for 'supplies, materials, services and technical assistance . . . for the benefit of children and adolescents' and 'to assist in their rehabilitation' and for 'child health purposes generally'. Although a small amount of assistance was provided outside Europe in 1948 (notably in Asia, the Middle East and North Africa), it was not until 1953 that, by General Assembly Resolution 417 (V), the efforts of UNICEF were formally redirected to the developing countries, including East and West Africa.

In 1961, its Executive Board made it legitimate for UNICEF to assist education programmes at both primary and secondary level, and between 1961 and 1968, expansion of primary education became a key element in UNICEF policies. In 1968 however, a joint UNICEF/UNESCO review recommended that assistance should be refocused on educational planning, curriculum reform, teacher training, strengthening of inspectorates, and action to improve internal efficiency. Programming moreover should be such as to support the development plans of individual countries, but at the same time, stress should be placed on innovative, pump-priming and promotional roles of UNICEF.

Following a further review in 1972, new policy guidelines were issued focusing assistance on primary and non-formal basic education for children and adolescents of underprivileged groups. Emphasis was placed on the importance of nutrition education as well as education for parenthood. The agency's policies on non-formal education were further elaborated by the Executive Board in 1973. Non-formal education should provide a package of basic essential learning that would help children to earn a living, raise a family and take part in the development activities of the community. The

157

delivery system should lie at grassroots, mobilising and capitalising on the interests and energies of the people involved.

The basic services approach that was endorsed by the General Assembly in 1976, and infiltrated the policies of many other donors, crystallised gradually from field experience. Educational services were to be evolved simultaneously with, and in support of, other services, guiding their development, and ensuring their effective use.

In 1980, the Executive Board urged UNICEF to 'continue to follow a comprehensive approach to meeting the learning needs of children using both formal and non-formal approaches'. It was now stressed that an important element of the comprehensive approach should be the dissemination of relevant information to parents, families and communities. To support this, educational components, including literacy activities, should be built into such services as child health, sanitation, water supply, nutrition, child care, and women's programmes.

The 1984 document *Profile on UNICEF Co-operation in Education* says:

> The rationale for UNICEF co-operation in education lies in its obligation to collaborate with developing countries in planning and implementing comprehensive programmes for meeting the needs of survival, growth, and welfare of children.
>
> The basic services approach that emphasises popular participation, cost-effective methods, appropriate technologies and special efforts to reach disadvantaged groups is taken as the guideline for UNICEF Country Co-operation Programmes. In pursuit of this policy, technical support to educational services is essential, and UNICEF continues to be committed to curriculum reform, development of teaching aids and textbooks, teacher training and retraining, strengthening of management and planning capacities, and the improvement of monitoring and evaluation.

UNICEF's global policies on education have to be understood in the light of the dual nature of its broader role which on the one hand is to protect children, and on the other to 'enable children to develop their full potential and become productive members of their society'. UNICEF's commitment to education springs in part from its perception of education as a human right. However UNICEF's concerns also embrace broader matters of international development and it argues that 'the development of children is an essential step in the development of peoples, and therefore in the development of countries'. Elsewhere it writes: 'UNICEF believes that it is important that decision-makers recognise the link between programmes benefiting children on the one hand and economic and social progress on the other'.

Another strategy fundamental to UNICEF's policies is that of 'advocacy'. Given the limits of its resources, the best way in which it can promote the welfare of children is by innovative examples, consciousness-raising, and stimulation of local initiative. At the same time, far from encouraging the follies of blind enthusiasm, UNICEF stoutly defends careful and realistic planning of services for children that are sustainable within the economic means of the country, and its aim is to angle its assistance so as to support the gradual evolution of services in tune with the country's broader social and economic development.

158

The World Bank: International Bank for Reconstruction and Development (IBRD)

The World Bank was created in 1945. By its Articles of Agreement, it was authorised to provide investment capital to support projects 'for productive purposes, including the encouragement of the development of productive facilities and resources in less developed countries'. It was not, however, until the creation of the soft-loan affiliate, the International Development Association (IDA) in 1960 with the purpose of promoting 'higher standards of living and economic and social progress in the less developed countries', that the World Bank committed itself to lending in the education sector. Finally concluding that education was not just a 'basic human right', but 'could pay great economic dividends especially in the less developed countries', the Bank made its first loan to education in 1962. The President's Memorandum in 1963, however, stipulated that 'the Bank should finance part of the capital requirements of education projects designed to produce trained manpower of the kind and in the numbers needed to forward economic development. This means concentrating on both vocational and technical education and training at various levels, and general secondary education'. Although normally only buildings and equipment would be financed, technical assistance would be provided through the IBRD/UNESCO Co-operative Programme and through the IIEP. Throughout the 1960s however, such restrictions were gradually relaxed, as teacher training, supply of books, and even primary education came to be considered legitimate areas of support.

In July 1970, the President recommended to the Executive Directors that:

> We should continue to emphasise projects which, like vocational training, produce trained manpower directly, but we should also consider for financing other types of project which should have important long-term significance for economic development.

He argued further that the scope of projects considered should be broadened, and projects should be selected on the basis of the needs of educational systems as a whole rather than by designating *a priori* areas of eligibility.

The World Bank's first *Education Sector Policy Paper* in 1971 concluded that, following the 'needs' principle, technical, agricultural, improved secondary education, and teacher training would continue to provide the bulk of projects. There would nevertheless be a need to concentrate resources more in the agricultural sector that had been neglected at the expense of the modern sector. New areas for investment would be non-formal training and measures to improve the effectiveness of educational systems: curriculum reform, development of mass media, programmed learning, and management studies to improve the planning and control of education.

The Presidential Address of 1973 that heralded a refocusing of the Bank's lending on basic needs and the problem of the world's poorest had rapid repercussions on educational policy. While a major emphasis of the 1974 *Education Sector Policy Paper* continued to be manpower requirements,

159

there was a new concern with education as a right — particularly for those who had been excluded from social and economic progress. Key themes of the document were a minimum basic education for all and equalised educational opportunity. To achieve this, priorities would have to differ from country to country. Within a number of countries the focus should be on primary and basic education rather than on higher education which produces a 'small and intensively trained élite'.

The 1980 *Education Sector Policy Paper* reaffirmed the commitment to universalising basic education and placed emphasis on the need to develop low-cost systems that are effective in reaching less accessible sectors of the population. The paper argued that the choice of basic education as an area for investment can be justified on the grounds of its very high rate of return in those countries where coverage is not universal. Such returns however depend not simply on providing people with employable skills but also with a certain political and organisational capacity that enables the poor and marginalised to make their voices heard, secure their own rights, and participate in the development process.

Running parallel with the Bank's policies on investment in educational systems and services, are its policies on human resource creation. Investment here is seen as essential both for maximising returns on its own capital investment and for promoting economic growth more generally. The Bank's investment policy is to include a human resources development element in all its projects through programmes of project-related training. A major thrust of the Bank's policy on human resource development that has been taken up by other donors is the creation of capacity for rational investment strategies through policy-analysis, improved administration and organisational methods. Training in these areas is seen as central to the Bank's lending strategies for African countries and the intention is to provide support for it at the stage of needs analysis and project design.

The concern with rational investment is no less strong in the education sector than in others, and through its support for improved planning and organisation, the Bank's aim is to achieve greater efficiency both internal and external, and to reduce costs. This concern with cost reduction is one that the Bank appears to share with USAID and ODA in particular. The Bank argues that, bearing in mind factors of social demand, as well as those of manpower requirements, this proposed improvement in efficiency is best achieved through conventional systems of schooling at both primary and junior secondary levels rather than through non-formal education programmes or diversified secondary educational schemes.

Forms of assistance and their organisation

Aid is usually provided in a variety of forms under a number of separate schemes that are sometimes administered by independent bureaux of the same agency. Recipients need to understand how much is available, of what kind, through what channels, and the latitude of its use.

The brief agency profiles that follow have been constructed under far from ideal conditions and with very inadequate information; the scantness and superficiality with which they treat key aspects of agency operations are

160

only too well recognised. They are however an attempt to present some basic facts that would enable both recipients and donors to gauge the kind of support needs that individual agencies can most readily meet.

Canadian International Development Agency (CIDA)

CIDA provides both technical assistance and capital aid to education. Slightly more than 50 per cent of CIDA's capital aid is tied to the procurement of Canadian goods. Capital aid will not normally be provided for construction projects, and policy favours the development of local industries for the production of educational materials. Recurrent costs will be met where absolutely essential, and the principle of local cost financing is also accepted.

Training scholarships are provided, but only project-related training is supported, and policy favours the provision of this in local or regional institutions. Recently CIDA has decided to reverse its former policy and increase the amount of training provided within Canada.

Most experts financed by CIDA are employed directly by Canadian organisations under contract. CIDA provides short pre-service training courses for its experts during which they have the opportunity to discuss possible roles and working methods with officials from developing countries.

Following a recent reorganisation, CIDA's assistance is now administered on a geographical rather than sectoral basis. An aid framework specifying allocations to geographical areas is established by Parliament. Individual country allocations are determined at ministerial level on the advice of the Development Policy, Planning and Co-ordination Division within CIDA. Sectoral priorities are decided by the country programme team following discussion with the government in the recipient country. All country programmes are expected to have some educational component, linked in part to other CIDA funded projects.

A small fund of $5 million is made available to High Commissions and Embassies in recipient countries for funding non-recurrent projects of local NGOs. A substantial proportion of CIDA's assistance to education is provided through NGOs, such as the Association of Canadian Community Colleges, the International Development Office, and the World University Service.

German Agency for Technical Co-operation (GTZ)

Although GTZ provides both technical assistance and capital aid, technical co-operation is seen as being focal to GTZ's development work which is based on the principle of collaboration between institutions in the Federal Republic and in the recipient country. Some capital aid is needed to service this. Further capital aid is provided in the form of programme aid which is support for projects in which GTZ is not a co-partner. Most of the Federal Republic's capital aid, however, is provided by a separate institution in the form of loans.

Training supported by GTZ is exclusively project-related. The non-academic training is run by the German Foundation for International Development (DSE) and the Karl Duisberg Society. Both individualised training programmes and courses are provided for top level specialists

161

including managers, planners and middle-level technicians. These may be organised either in the Federal Republic or in a developing country. The programme of courses is designed on the basis of actively researched needs as well as received requests. Project-related training may also be provided in universities and polytechnics in the Federal Republic. In the former case it is organised through the DAAD (Deutscher Akademischer Austauschdienst) and in the latter, through the Central Placements Office.

In addition to the project-related training supported by GTZ, a large fellowship programme is funded through the Federal Republic's Foreign Ministry. Fellowships may be awarded for initial or further training of nationals of developing countries either in the Federal Republic, in third countries, or in their own country.

In practice, the system of *sur place* and third country fellowships is largely limited to Africa and to academic study – although an attempt is being made to diversify it. The fellowship scheme is intended to help meet manpower requirements of developing countries and the Federal Republic lays down guidelines for areas of study to be supported in each country. These are notified to the West German Embassy which handles applications.

Experts supported by GTZ may either be under direct contract, or employees of institutions in the recipient country. In the latter case support is provided through salary supplementation. Experts may also be people on secondment from institutions in the Federal Republic. As a point of policy, experts are expected to work with counterparts.

While GTZ is under contract to implement all the assistance programmes of the Federal Republic, it considers itself to have focal areas of expertise. Such areas related to education are:

1 Promotion of industrial and vocational training
2 Integrated education for rural and urban masses
3 Institution building in universities: engineering and applied science

GTZ is a semi-autonomous institution with its own board of directors. The Federal Ministry for Economic Co-operation decides with GTZ's advice, which projects GTZ should implement, and provides money on a project-by-project basis. The Federal Republic's policy is to respond to requests for assistance rather than to solicit them. Justification for a project is sought, however, within a plan for development of the sector as a whole. The principle of co-operation requires that there be an institution from the recipient country that has clear responsibility for project management.

GTZ is organised on a sectoral rather than a geographical basis. While mechanisms exist for intersectoral co-ordination, there appears to be no country-level planning.

In addition to implementing the Federal Republic's official technical assistance programme, GTZ has a small fund of its own with which it can carry out projects not exceeding DM100000 in cost. These do not require the approval of the Federal Ministry for Economic Co-operation, but have to be cleared with the embassy in the recipient country. GTZ will also provide technical services against payment from other donors or recipients.

Swedish International Development Authority (SIDA)

SIDA provides by far the greater part of its assistance in the form of capital aid, and 70 per cent of this is untied. However, SIDA follows a resource-based approach to foreign aid, and to this extent procurement of Swedish goods and products is encouraged. However, within education the emphasis is on setting up local capacity for production of materials and equipment, with SIDA providing basic plant and technology. Capital is mainly used for school building, teacher aids, school furniture and teacher training.

SIDA's support for training is largely restricted to the needs of its own projects. Wherever possible, training will be provided in the country of origin, but where no training facilities exist, the location will be chosen that can best meet the needs, although because of language problems this is seldom considered to be in Sweden itself.

During the 1970s SIDA began to reduce its supply of experts to the field as part of a broader non-intervention strategy. This policy however has now been reversed in the light of demand from recipient countries. Experts may serve either in executive line functions or as advisers. Short-term consultants are also provided. Expertise is also provided by volunteers, who are engaged by those NGOs to which SIDA provides support. (Thirty per cent of SIDA's aid is channelled through NGOs.)

SIDA is a semi-autonomous statutory agency. Although it is responsible to the Ministry of Foreign Affairs for implementing the bilateral component of Sweden's development co-operation programme, it has its own board of directors composed of representatives of the different political parties and non-governmental organisations. The aid framework, in the form of allocations to a select group of countries, is made by the Swedish Parliament with SIDA providing advice. Sectoral allocations are made internally on the basis of a country's development plan and discussions with its government's representatives. Most assistance is provided on the basis of sectoral agreements. Under these, funds are provided to support the implementation of a number of projects or programmes included in the national development plan. The use of funds may be prescribed in varying degrees of detail, but in most cases funds can be moved from one project to another making for greater flexibility in start-up order. They may also be reallocated to new projects with the agreement of both recipient and donor following annual reviews.

United Kingdom Overseas Development Administration (ODA)

ODA provides support almost exclusively in the form of technical co-operation. Capital aid constitutes not more than a few per cent of total aid provided to the sector. Capital aid in general is approximately 77 per cent tied. For the sake of convenience, ODA includes in its definition of technical co-operation some capital support items such as books and certain media materials.

Training is supported through a fellowship scheme. The majority of fellowships are provided for study in Britain, but study in a country of origin or in a third country is also supported in certain circumstances,

163

including where this proves cheaper. In the case of third country training it is also a condition that the host country be itself aid-worthy. The policy is to concentrate third country training in certain specialised regional training centres. In so far as possible, training resources are deployed so as to assist the development of the manpower required by key development projects. In any case, subject eligibility is prescribed on the basis of an assessment of the manpower needs of each recipient country, and in education, awards may be in the formal, non-formal and technical fields.

Experts supported by ODA may be either technical co-operation officers under contract to ODA itself, or employees of the government, or some other institution in the recipient country. In the latter case, support is provided by salary supplementation. The policy is to increase the amount of assistance provided by people on short-term secondment from institutions in the United Kingdom. Experts may either fill executive line positions, or they may act as advisers, or they may fulfil consultancy functions. ODA also provides support to a number of British volunteer services.

ODA is a branch of the United Kingdom Foreign and Commonwealth Office administering both bilateral and multilateral components of the British aid programme. A framework for the bilateral programme specifying allocations of both capital aid and technical assistance to the various country programmes and to a number of functional programmes and institutions is agreed at inter-ministerial level. Within country programmes, allocations to different sectors are made by ODA on the basis of its own country analyses and discussions with the government of the recipient country. Manpower reviews are also carried out by ODA in major recipient countries, and the results of these are also taken into consideration in allocating technical co-operation resources between sectors. The decision as to what form technical co-operation should take in the education sector rests largely with the recipient government. The government may, for example, trade salary supplementation against fellowships, or KELT. However, the particular form in which technical assistance is provided is expected to seem rational within the terms of manpower needs. It is, moreover, policy to 'package' or 'projectise' aid so that technical assistance serves a definite objective within the country's development strategy. Certain forms of technical assistance are provided outside country-programme allocations under functional schemes. These include in-country educational seminars run by visiting experts, and the Commonwealth Scholarship and Fellowship Plan. Such schemes are administered on ODA's behalf by the British Council. The fixed resources are allocated largely on a first-come first-served basis.

In addition to administering certain functional schemes of technical assistance for ODA, the British Council runs its own small programme of technical assistance financed by the ODA. Through its Higher Education Division it provides consultative services and short-term support to institutions of higher education as well as assistance to libraries and information services. Its TETOC (Technical Education and Training Operations and Consultancies) Group provides consultative services in the field of technical and vocational education as well as advice on the procurement of British resources to meet support needs. Much of the assistance is provided directly by staff of British Council missions, but special budgets exist to support technical assistance to higher education and technical training. The technical assistance resources of the British Council are also administered on the basis of country allocations.

United States Agency for International Development (USAID)

USAID provides assistance to education through three bureaux working somewhat independently, and each with its own budget.

These are the Regional Bureau for Africa, the Bureau for Technical Assistance, and the Bureau for Science and Technology. The Regional Bureau for Africa in particular provides substantial capital assistance as well as technical assistance for the education sector. The Bureau for Technical Assistance has a special commitment to long-term projects in human resources development, while the Bureau for Science and Technology is more concerned with agricultural education.

Support for training in the United States is largely restricted to the graduate level. There is an emphasis on regional training coupled with an attempt to strengthen specialist regional centres in Africa. In addition, large field missions organise and even run local training projects recruiting their own experts from the United States or elsewhere to service them. These are regarded as bilateral projects however, and United States experts are counterparted by local professionals. Experts and trainees may be financed either from project accounts or from sectoral functional accounts.

The United States Senate approves an aid programme which specifies not only country allocations, but the activities they are to fund. Despite the extent to which the use of funds is prescribed, however, field officers are left with considerable latitude in deciding how and in what form the aid programme should be implemented.

United Nations Childrens Fund (UNICEF)

UNICEF provides assistance in the form of funds, supplies and technical co-operation. The amount of assistance provided to education in the form of supplies is on the decrease, and by far the greater part of aid is financial. It would perhaps be wrong to call this capital aid, since UNICEF's objectives are primarily advocacy and catalysis rather than investment. Within clearly specified limits, UNICEF is willing to meet recurrent costs and local costs.

Stipends are provided to trainees either in terms of specific training projects, or to meet manpower needs of other UNICEF projects. Within education, most trainees receiving stipends are teachers. Most training is organised locally, but some is provided by regional seminars and study tours.

Some advisory services are provided by UNICEF's own staff. Support may be provided by other experts as well, but UNICEF favours the use of national or regional expertise wherever possible. Most experts function as trainers, but consultants and advisers are also provided to assist in needs identification, programming, project design, and project execution.

Rolling five-year plans specifying budgetary targets for each recipient country are approved annually by UNICEF's board, which is composed of representatives from both donor and recipient countries. Country targets

165

are decided mainly by level of development, but any current country crisis is also taken into consideration. UNICEF's board is also responsible for committing funds annually for country programmes. These programmes, usually covering a period of about three years, are drawn up collaboratively by national officials and UNICEF staff, on the basis of the recipient's development plans. An attempt is made to ensure that planning within the various sectors concerned with the welfare of children is co-ordinated, so that programming inputs into sectors can be achieved simultaneously. UNICEF's board approves programmes and commits funds annually. Funding is usually within 25 per cent of the country target. Where programme requirements exceed the target figure, funds are committed for the core, or most urgent projects, and the remaining projects, known as listed projects, are put forward to potential donors for supplementary funding.

By far the greater part of technical assistance is supported out of country programme funds, but advisory missions for needs identification, programming and project design may be supported from a special inter-regional fund for project preparations. Local UNICEF offices also contain valuable advisory resources. In addition, they play an important backup role to projects, providing administrative assistance and organising the flow of resources. They have a major responsibility to ensure that UNICEF assistance is supplied when and as needed.

World Bank: International Bank for Reconstruction and Development (IBRD)

The World Bank provides almost all assistance to education in the form of investment capital; technical co-operation accounts for less than half of one per cent of total lending. Recently the Bank has agreed to provide certain re-current cost financing. It has also accepted the need to meet certain local costs.

Training may be supported out of project loans to the extent that it is needed to support human resource requirements. The Bank attaches considerable importance to this.

Project loans can also be used to finance experts required for purposes of needs identification, project planning, implementation, and training. Wherever possible the Bank favours the procurement of local expertise for these purposes, but it accepts that this is frequently not possible. Much support is provided through the World Bank/UNESCO Co-operative Programme. In addition, UNESCO and World Bank staff are available themselves to help with needs assessment and the formulation of project proposals. In 1982, this support capacity was strengthened by placing a number of new personnel in advisory positions in the field. Where large amounts of expertise of a specialised nature are required at the planning stage, these can be financed from the Bank's project preparation facility. The use of United Nations Development Programme pre-project finance facilities is encouraged, however, to the extent that these are now available.

At the planning level, the basic structural divisions within the World Bank are sectoral rather than geographical. There are annual targets for lending within sectors. Educational activities however can be financed not only through education sector loans, but also through urban and rural development projects, and through the project-related training component of any sector.

166

Bibliography: main sources

Canadian International Development Agency

CIDA. *Annual Aid Review*. 1982.

CIDA. *Elements of Canada's Official Development Assistance Strategy*. 1984.

CIDA. *Mandate and Objectives*. 1984.

CIDA. *Strategy for International Development Co-operation, 1974-1980*. 1975.

West German Agency for Technical Co-operation

DSE. *The Education and Scientific Aid Programme of the Federal Republic of Germany*. 1971.

GTZ. *Co-operation with Developing Countries*. 1978.

DSE & CDG. *The Federal Republic of Germany's Training and Advanced Instruction Programme for Experts and Executives from Developing Countries*. 1981.

GTZ. *Promotion of Basic Education*. 1981.

GTZ. *Bildung und Wissenschaft in der Technischen Zusammenarbeit mit Entwicklungsländern*. 1982.

GTZ. *Promotion of Education and Science*. 1982.

GTZ. *Activities: Documentation on German Technical Co-operation in General Education*.

GTZ. *Key Services* (undated).

GTZ. *Technical Co-operation Programmes of the Federal Republic of Germany* (undated).

Swedish International Development Authority

SIDA. *Aid and Education: Policy and Programme*. 1972.

SIDA. *Factsheet: SIDA's Organisation*. 1981.

SIDA. *Sector Support Agreements – the Swedish Experience*. 1981.

SIDA. *SIDA's Assistance in the Field of Education*. 1982.

SIDA. *Sweden and International Development Co-operation*. 1983.

SIDA. *Swedish Bilateral Assistance to Education – Scope, Direction and Current Issues*. November 1984.

United Kingdom Overseas Development Administration

HMSO. *Overseas Development: The Work of the New Ministry*. 1965.

HMSO. *Overseas Development: The Work in Hand (Cmnd. 3180)*. 1966.

HMSO. *Changing Emphasis in British Aid Policies: More Help for the Poorest (Cmnd. 6270)*. 1970.

HMSO. *Aid to Education in Developing Countries*. 1970.

HMSO. *British Aid to Education in Developing Countries*. 1982.

ODA. *British Overseas Aid*. 1982.

ODA. *British Overseas Aid*. 1983.

HMSO. *British Aid to Education in Developing Countries*. 1984.

ODA. *Education Sector Policy Paper*. 1984.

United States Agency for International Development

USAID. *AID Assistance to Education: A Retrospective Study (Report Prepared by Creative Associates Inc.)*. 1981.

167

USAID. *Policy Paper: Basic Education and Technical Training Assistance Strategy.* 1982.

USAID. *Africa Bureau Development Management Assistance Strategy.* 1984.

USAID. *Agricultural Education and University Building in Africa: A Development Strategy.* December 1984.

United Nations Children's Fund

UNESCO. *Co-operation with UNICEF: Joint Recommendations to the Director General of UNESCO and the Executive Board of UNICEF.* 1972.

ECOSOC. *Flow of External Aid to Education at the Primary School Level and to Non-Formal Education, and UNICEF Participation.* 1977.

ECOSOC. *Assessment of the Application of UNICEF Policies in Education.* 1980.

ECOSOC. *An Overview of UNICEF Policies, Organisation and Working Methods.* 1983.

UNICEF. *A Profile of UNICEF Co-operation in Education.* 1984.

UNICEF. *Moving Towards Universal Primary Education and Literacy. A Report Prepared by the UNICEF-UNESCO Joint Working Group.* 1984.

The World Bank: International Bank for Reconstruction and Development

World Bank. *Annual Report* various years, 1975-1983.

World Bank. *Review of Bank Operations in the Education Sector* (Report 2321). 1978.

World Bank. *Education Sector Policy Paper.* 1980.

World Bank. *Accelerated Development in Sub-Saharan Africa: an Agenda for Action.* 1981.

World Bank. *Review of Training in Bank-Financed Projects* (Report 3834). 1982.

World Bank. *Study of the Bank's Lending Strategy in Education and Training in Sub-Saharan Africa.* (undated).

World Bank. *World Development Report.* 1984.

World Bank. *Toward Sustained Development in Sub-Saharan Africa: A Joint Programme of Action:* 1984

A Bibliographic note on educational assistance

Ian Clifton-Everest

I The status and purpose of aid policies

There is little documented discussion on donor policy. However, in 1979 the World Bank took the unusual step for a donor agency of placing its draft policy document for the educational sector before the international community for critical comment. The discussions that followed examined, with various degrees of thoroughness, the different dimensions of policy outlined above. A number of critics queried whether, in prescribing on the objectives of education and the strategies that should be used in achieving these, the Bank's policies went beyond their legitimate realm of jurisdiction. [1, 2] Other critics queried the effectiveness of the strategies themselves, and the development models on which they were based, pointing for example to shortcomings in traditional manpower planning methods [3, 4] and the limits of education as a tool for popular mobilisation. [5] Others criticised the narrowness of the Bank's objectives in education, in its concern with economic development, at the expense of development of other kinds. [6, 7]

Attention was also drawn to what was seen as a fundamental inconsistency between the Bank's declared policies, and its mandate and broader interests as a financial institution. [7, 8] This raised queries as to whether the Bank's policies were really just a statement of the kind of development strategy it would like to see implemented, rather than those it would be willing to actively support. [9] The tendency to make generalised prescriptions about the needs of underdeveloped countries was challenged by more than one commentator. [6, 7] A further issue of discussion was the wider impact that donor policies have on education in developing countries. Some argued that such policies have an impact far out of proportion to the amount of actual aid provided. [10, 11, 12]

It is perhaps regrettable that in these discussions of policy, the viewpoints of the recipients themselves have been poorly represented.

References

1 Ahmed, Manzoor. World Bank Assistance in Education. *Prospects* 11.1, 25–35, 1981.

2 Hurst, P. Aid and Educational Development: Rhetoric and Reality. *Comparative Education* 17.2, 117–125, 1981.

3 Psacharopoulos, G. The World Bank in the World of Education: Some Policy Changes and Some Remnants. *Comparative Education* 17.2, 141–146, 1981.

This bibliographic information derives from Ian Clifton-Everest's paper for the Conference. There are three sections, the first two on donor policy and technical co-operation. The last is a more substantial review of studies on aid to education in developing countries.

4 Bacchus, K. Education for Development in Underdeveloped Countries. *Comparative Education* 17.2, 215–227, 1981.

5 McLean, M. The Political Context of Educational Development: A Commentary on the Theories of Development Underlying the World Bank Education Sector Policy Paper. *Comparative Education* 17.2, 157–162, 1981.

6 Williams, P. Education in Developing Countries: Halfway to the Styx. *Comparative Education* 17.2, 147–156, 1981.

7 Fernández. M. The World Bank and the Third World: Reflections of a Sceptic. *Prospects* 11.3, 294–301, 1981.

8 Carnoy, M. International Institutions and Educational Policy: A Review of Education-Sector Policy. *Prospects* 10.3, 265–283, 1980.

9 Phillips, H.M. Criteria and Methods of Generating Education Co-operation Projects for External Funding. *Comparative Education* 17.2, 195–205, 1981.

10 Spaulding, S. Needed Research on the Impact of International Assistance Organisations on the Development of Education. *Comparative Education* 17.2, 207–213, 1981.

11 Dias, P.V. L'Influence des Organisations Internationales sur les Réformes Educatives: le Tiers-Monde. *Education Comparée* 20, 67–69, 1979.

12 Benveniste, A. Le Rôle des Organisations Internationales dans la Planification des Technologies Educatives dans les Pays du Tiers-Monde. *Education Comparée* 20, 37–41, 1979.

II Technical co-operation

Attention is drawn to the findings of a recent high-level meeting of the Organisation for Economic Co-operation and Development (OECD) Development Assistance Committee [1] and the proceedings of a meeting entilted 'Experts in Africa' [2] held in Britain in 1982. A paper presented at the latter meeting [3] reviews current practice in the use of experts.

A recent article by Hyung-Ki Kim [4] reviews many of the issues in improving the transference of newly acquired skills to the work situation, and Lackey,[5] Ogranovitch [6] and Defore [7] provide interesting examples of models for developing training programmes. The studies of Eisemon,[8] Viallet [9] and Di Rosa [10] look at the problems of educational transfer from a somewhat different angle. A study of third country training including appraisals from the point of view of both donors and recipients was recently made by O'Brien.[11] More general evaluations of technical assistance are those of Bok,[12] Honadle *et al.*,[13] Michelwait *et al.* [14] and Brown.[15]

References
1 OECD. Development Assistance Committee. *Development Co-operation: Training Assistance.* Paris: OECD, 1982.

2 Stone, J.C. (ed.). *Experts in Africa.* Proceedings of a Colloquium at the University of Aberdeen. Aberdeen: University of Aberdeen, 1980.

3 Stutley, P.W. Some Aspects of the Contemporary Scene, in Stone, J.C. (ed.). *Experts in Africa.* Proceedings of a Colloquium at the University of Aberdeen. Aberdeen: University of Aberdeen, 1980.

4 Hyung-Ki Kim. Lenders, Borrowers and Educational Development. *Prospects* 13.4, 439–447, 1983.

5 Lackey, A.S. A Proposal for Improving Development Training. *Community Development Journal* 16.1, 2–10, 1981.

6 Ogranovitch, S. How to Design an International Training Programme. *Training and Development Journal* 34.8, 12–15, 1980.

7 Defore, J.J. Co-op Programmes in the Development of International Technical Manpower. *Engineering Education* 67.8, 741–800, 1977.

8 Eisemon, T. Educational Transfer — Implications of Foreign Educational Assistance. *Interchange* 5.4, 53–61, 1974.

9 Viallet, F. Exporter de la Formation Après Quelques Précautions. *Education Permanente* 54, 41–53, 1980.

10 Di Rosa, P. Le Point de Vue de l'Exportateur. *Education Permanente* 54, 33–40, 1980.

11 O'Brien, C. and J. Jacobs. *Third Country Training: An Evaluation Report to the United Kingdom Ministry of Overseas Development,* 1977.

12 Bok, D. Technical Assistance Abroad. *Human Rights Quarterly* 6.1, 40–55, 1984.

13 Honadle, G., Gow, D. and Silverman, J. Technical Assistance Alternatives for Rural Development: Beyond the By-pass Model. *Canadian Journal of Development Studies* 4.2, 221–240, 1983.

14 Michelwait, D.R., Honadle, G.H. and Barclay, A.H. Rethinking Technical Assistance — The Case for a Management Team Strategy. *Agricultural Administration* 13.1, 11–22, 1983.

15 Brown, A. Technical Assistance to Rural Communities — Stop-Gap or Capacity-Building. *Public Administration Review* 1, 18–23, 1980.

III Studies of aid to education in developing countries

Two of the most comprehensive studies of aid to education in developing countries are those by Phillips[1] and Parkinson.[2] Both review the policies and work of major donor agencies and contain several recipient country case studies. Phillips makes, in addition, a detailed appraisal of various forms and functions of educational aid drawing from this some prescriptions for the future. Both studies were completed a decade ago, and a further one on their scale is now timely.

Critical analyses of the programmes of individual donor agencies have been few and far between. Two earlier ones that might be mentioned are those of Baudouin[3] on the World Bank, and La Brousse[4] on French bilateral aid. Two more recent appraisals of the Bank's programme are those of Schechter[5] and Aklilu and Heyneman.[6] Attention should be drawn to the comments of Lux[7] and Goldschmidt[8] on the German Federal Republic's programmes. Berman[9] has provided a provocative and controversial analysis of the work of the programmes of several large non-governmental agencies.

A number of appraisals have been made of aid to specific areas of education. Pierens,[10] Tribe,[11] Heller[12] and Moock[13] have examined the role of aid in higher education and Mayburn[14] has reviewed programmes of support to science education. These might be taken together with articles by Reiff,[15] Weiland,[16] Phillips,[17] Adiseshiah,[18] Mackinnon[19] that analyse critically some of the more general problems in international co-operation for educational development, and with the frank appraisals by Hurst,[20] McLean,[21] Carnoy,[22] Fernandez,[23] Saraf[24] and Dias[25] of what donor agencies can realistically be expected to contribute to educational development.

Case studies of aid to individual recipient countries are also small in number. Sifuna[26] and Lillis[27] have recently provided them for Kenya, and Goranson[28] one for Tanzania. Mention should also be made of a valuable series of reviews published by SIDA[29] on their own programmes in African countries. Several of these contain unusually frank appraisals of what has been achieved, and report shortcomings as well as successes. Outside of Africa, of interest are those of Chiappo[30] on Peru, and Castaneda[31] on Guatemala.

On the issue of interagency co-ordination a review of various administrative approaches to providing sector support is contained in a recent Annual Report of the OECD Development Assistance Committee.[32] A recent document by Bellander and Gustafsson of SIDA[33] contains a detailed description and critical appraisal of the agency's own experience of sector support agreements. An approach to sector support based on strengthening the recipient capacity for planning and administration is described by Ireton and Sandersley in ODA's Annual Report for 1982.[34]

Two works of special note because they have been made by recipients themselves are the Zambian Ministry of Education evaluation report of Zambia's World Bank Education Project[35] and Diambomba's[36] article on aid to educational research. The former is a particularly honest analysis of shortcomings in both project design and implementation. A recent paper by Ishumi[37] reflects the degree of concern felt by many recipients to improve the opportunities for a frank and honest contribution to the evaluation exercises of projects funded by external donors.

A number of 'dossiers' on aid to education contained in *Prospects*[38] contain a useful miscellany of papers on aid processes, policies and practice.

References

1 Phillips, H.M. *Educational Cooperation Between Developed and Developing Countries.* New York: Praeger, 1976.

2 Parkinson, N. *Educational Aid and National Development: An International Comparison of the Past and Recommendations for the Future.* London: Macmillan, 1976.

3 Baudouin, D.E. *La Banque Mondiale et l'Aide à l'Education: Analyse Critique de la Politique Suivie par la Banque Mondiale.* IIEP Occasional Paper. Paris: IIEP, 1970.

4 La Brousse, A. *La France et l'Aide à l'Education dans Quatorze Pays Africains et Malgache: Politique Entre 1959–1970.* IIEP Occasional Paper. Paris: IIEP, 1971.

5 Schechter, M.G. Assessing the Impact of Intergovernmental Organisations: The Case of the World Bank and Non-Formal Education. Paper presented at the Annual Conference of International Studies Association, Cincinnati, Ohio, March 1982.

6 Aklilu H. and Heyneman, S. Education for National Development: World Bank Activities. *Prospects* 13.4, 471–479, 1983.

7 Lux, M.J. Mitwirkung der Bundesländer an der Zusammenarbeit mit Entwicklungsländern, Dargestellt am Beispiel des Landes Baden-Württemberg. *Zeitschrift für Verwaltungslehre* 72.1, 35–48, 1981.

8 Goldschmidt, D. Zusammenarbeit in Bildungsforschung und Bildungsplanung zwischen Entwicklungsländern und der Bundesrepublik Deutschland. *Bildung und Erziehung Stuttgart* 31.1 70–78, 1978.

9 Berman, E.H. Foundations, United States Foreign Policy, and African Education, 1945–1975. *Harvard Educational Review* 49.2, 145–179, 1979.

10 Pierens, P. Problèmes Actuels et Perspectives d'Avenir de la Coopération Inter-Universitaire. *Revue de l'AUPELF* 47.2, 149–164, 1980.

11 Tribe, D.E. Patterns and Problems in Development Assistance for Higher Education. *Journal of Tertiary Educational Administration* 5.1, 43–52, 1983.

12 Heller, B.R. Selected Problems of International Cooperative Education: The U.S.A. as Sender and Receiver of Study Abroad Students. *Journal of Cooperative Education* 20.3, 41–52, 1984.

13 Moock, J.L. and Peter R. Moock. *Higher Education and Rural Development in Africa: Toward a Balanced Approach for Donor Assistance.* New York: Afro-American Institute, 1977.

14 Maybury, R.H. *Technical Assistance and Innovation in Science Education: A Critical and Comparative Appraisal of Five Projects for Science Education Improvement.* New York: Wiley, 1975.

15 Reiff, H. International Co-operation in Education with the Least Developed Countries. *Prospects* 13.4, 449–458, 1983.

16 Weiland, H. Bildung in Entwicklungsprojekten: Ein Ungenützter Freiraum für Reformen. *Bildung und Erziehung Stuttgart* 33.5, 467–474, 1980.

17 Phillips, H.M. Criteria and Methods of Generating Education Cooperation Projects for External Funding. *Comparative Education* 17.2, 195-205, 1981.

18 Adiseshiah, M.S. From International Aid to International Cooperation: Some Thoughts in Retrospect I. *International Review of Education* 25.2, 213–230, 1979.

19 Mackinnon, A.R. From International Aid to International Cooperation: Some Thoughts in Retrospect II. *International Review of Education* 25.2, 231–247, 1979.

20 Hurst, P. Educational Aid and Dependency. Paper presented at the Seminar on Foreign Aid for Education, Nordic Association for the Study of Education in Developing Countries. Oslo, September 1983.

21 McLean, M. The Political Context of Educational Development: A Commentary on the Theories of Development Underlying the World Bank Education Sector Policy Paper. *Comparative Education* 17.2, 157–162, 1981.

22 Carnoy, M. International Institutions and Educational Policy: A Review of Education-Sector Policy. *Prospects* 10.3, 265-283, 1980.

23 Fernández, M. The World Bank and the Third World: Reflections of a Sceptic. *Prospects* 11.3, 294–301, 1981.

24 Saraf, S.N. *Education in the 1980s. World Bank Perspectives: The Myth and Reality.* IIEP Occasional Paper. Paris: IIEP, 1980.

25 Dias, P.V. L'Influence des Organisations Internationales sur les Réformes Educatives: le Tiers-Monde. *Education Comparée* 20, 67–69, 1979.

26 Sifuna, D.N. Kenya: Twenty Years of Multilateral Aid. *Prospects* 13.4, 481–492, 1983.

27 Lillis, K.M. Comparative Processes of Secondary Curriculum Innovation in Kenya. Paper presented at the Seminar on Foreign Aid for Education, Nordic Association for the Study of Education in Developing Countries. Oslo, September 1983.

28 Goranson, U. *Development Assistance to the Education Sector in Tanzania Since Independence.* Dar es Salaam: Tanzania, Ministry of National Education, Department of Planning, 1981.

29a Engquist, O., Jiven, L. and Nyström, K. *Education and Training in Sri Lanka.* SIDA Education Division Document No. 1. Stockholm: SIDA, 1981.

29b Agrell, J.O., Fägerlind, I. and Gustafsson, I. *Education and Training in Botswana 1974–1980.* SIDA Education Division Document No 2. Stockholm: Swedish International Development Authority, 1982

29c Carr-Hill, R. and Rosengart, G. *Education in Guinea-Bissau 1978–1981.* SIDA Education Division Document No 5. Stockholm: Swedish International Development Authority, 1982.

29d Johnsson, A.I., Nyström, K. and Sunden, R. *Adult Education in Tanzania.* SIDA Education Division Document No 9. Stockholm: Swedish International Development Authortiy, 1983.

29e Gumbel, P., Nyström, K. and Samuelsson, R. *Education in Ethiopia 1974–1982.* SIDA Education Division Document No 11. Stockholm: Swedish International Development Authority, 1983.

29f Fägerlind, I. and Valdelin, J. *Education in Zambia: Past Achievements and Future Trends.* SIDA Education Division Document No 12. Stockholm: Swedish International Development Authority, 1983.

29g Johnston, A. *Education in Mozambique 1975–1984*. SIDA Education Division Document No 15. Stockholm: Swedish International Development Authority, 1984.

30 Chiappo. L. *La Cooperación Internacional en Educación: Estudio de la Experiencia Peruana.* Paris: UNESCO, 1979.

31 Castañeda, E.A. *International Cooperation in Education: The Guatemala Experience.* Paris: UNESCO, 1979.

32 OECD. Development Assistance Committee. *Development Cooperation: Use of Various Forms of Non-project Assistance for Longer Term Development and Emergencies.* Paris: OECD, 1982.

33 Bellander, L. and Gustafsson, I. *Sector Support Agreements: The Swedish Experience.* Stockholm: Swedish International Development Authority, 1981.

34 Ireton, B.R. and Sandersley, G.P. *British Overseas Aid.* London: Overseas Development Administration, 1982.

35 Zambia. Ministry of Education. *Evaluation Report of the Zambia World Bank Education Project.* Lusaka: Ministry of Education, 1977.

36 Diambomba, M. Research and External Aid: A Review from the Recipient Side. *Prospects* 11.3, 352–359, 1981.

37 Ishumi, A.G. Foreign Aid to Education in Developing Countries: The Significance of Local Initiatives in Education and Innovation. Paper presented at the Seminar on Foreign Aid for Education, Nordic Association for the Study of Education in Developing Countries. Oslo, September 1983.

38 See *Prospects* 4.2, 1974; 5.4, 1975; 6.1, 1976; 6.2, 1976; 6.6, 1976; 13.4, 1983.

Appendices

List of participants
(designations as at time of Conference)

Ato Abdul Menan Ahmed
Permanent Secretary
Ministry of Education
Addis Adaba
Ethiopia

Dr Manzoor Ahmed
Senior Education Adviser
UNICEF
United Nations
New York
United States of America

Dr Aklilu Habte
Director
Education and Training Department
Education Policy Division
International Bank for Reconstruction
and Development
(The World Bank)
Washington D.C.
United States of America

Dr S C Aleyideino
Director
Institute of Education
Ahmadu Bello University
Zaria
Nigeria

Mr Nahas Angula
Secretary of Education and Culture
SWAPO of Namibia
Luanda
Angola

Professor Henry Ayot
Professor of Education
Kenyatta University College
Nairobi
Kenya

Mme Simone Ba
Directrice
Ecole Normale Supérieure
Nouakchott
Mauritania

Mr Charles Bassett
Vice President
Canadian International
Development Agency
Hull, Quebec
Canada

Dr Herbert Bergmann
Acting Head
General Education Section
Deutsche Gesellschaft für Technische
Zusammenarbeit (GTZ), GmbH
Bonn
Federal Republic of Germany

Professor Lalage Bown
Director
Department of Adult and
Continuing Education
University of Glasgow
Scotland

Mr Ian Buist
Under-Secretary
Africa Division
Overseas Development Administration
London
England

Mr Ahmed Bushra Ibrahim
Educational and Cultural Attaché
Sudan Embassy
London
England

Dr Trevor Coombe
Lecturer in Educational Planning
Department of Education in
Developing Countries
University of London Institute
of Education
London
England

Dr Philip H Coombs
Vice Chairman
International Council for
Educational Development
Essex, Connecticut
United States of America

Mr M D Francis
Education Adviser
Overseas Development Administration
London
England

Alhaji Yahaya Hamza
Co-ordinating Director (Education)
Federal Ministry of Education, Science
and Technology
Lagos
Nigeria

Mr Hugh Hawes
Reader in Education
Chairman
Department of Education in
Developing Countries
University of London
Institute of Education
London
England

Dr Paul Hurst
Senior Lecturer in Education
Department of Education in
Developing Countries
University of London Institute of
Education
London
England

Dr Roger Iredale
Principal Education Adviser
Head
Education Division
Overseas Development Administration
London
England

Mr Arthur Kambalametore
Principal
The Polytechnic
Blantyre
Malawi

Dr Kenneth King
Reader in Education
Department of Education
University of Edinburgh
Edinburgh
Scotland

His Excellency Mr B K Kipkulei
High Commissioner of the
Republic of Kenya
Kenya High Commission
London
England

Hon Joseph R L Kotsokoane
Minister of Education, Sports
and Culture
Maseru
Lesotho

Dr Kevin Lillis
Lecturer in Education
Department of Education in
Developing Countries
University of London Institute
of Education
London
England

M Yaya Mede Moussa
Directeur de l'Institut National pour la
Formation et la recherche en Education
Port Novo
Peoples' Republic of Benin

M Jean Ménéchal
Sous-Directeur adjoint des
Infrastructures et de l'Industrie
Coopération de Développement
Ministère des Relations Extérieures
Paris
France

Hon Kebatlamang Morake
Minister of Education
Gaborone
Botswana

Hon Kebby Musokotwane
Minister of General Education
and Culture
Lusaka
Zambia

Hon Dr Dzingai Mutumbuka
Minister of Education
Harare
Zimbabwe

Hon A A N' Jai
Minister of Education, Youth,
Sports and Culture
Banjul
The Gambia

177

Hon Dr Dorothy Njeuma
Vice Minister of National Education
Yaoundé
Cameroon

Mr Kieran J O'Cuneen
Regional Training Adviser
European Development Fund
Harare
Zimbabwe

Hon Professor Isaac Newton Ojok
Minister of Education
Kampala
Uganda

Mr Dennis Okoro
Assistant Director of Education
Planning and Development
Federal Ministry of Education,
Science and Technology
Lagos
Nigeria

Dr Cynthia Perry
Chief
Education and Human
Resources Division
Bureau for Africa
United States Agency for
International Development
Washington D.C.
United States of America

Dr Arthur Porter
Formerly Vice-Chancellor
University of Sierra Leone
Freetown
Sierra Leone

Dr Ralph Romain
Education Adviser
Education and Training Department
Education Policy Division
International Bank for Reconstruction
and Development
(The World Bank)
Washington D.C.
United States of America

Mr Joseph Rugumyamheto
Director of Manpower Planning
Ministry of Labour and
Manpower Development
Dar es Salaam
Tanzania

Dr Pierre T Seya
Education Expert
African Development Bank
Abidjan
Ivory Coast

Mr Tony Somerset
Lecturer in Education
Department of Education in
Developing Countries
University of London Institute
of Education
London
England

Dr Beryl Steele
Education Adviser
Overseas Development Administration
London
England

Mr Jakes Swartland
Deputy Permanent Secretary
Ministry of Education
Gaborone
Botswana

Miss M A J Swinley OBE
Controller
Africa and Middle East Division
The British Council
London
England

Hon M Iba Der Thiam
Ministre de l'Enseignement Supérieure
et de l'Education Nationale
Dakar
Senegal

Dr Carew Treffgarne
Lecturer in Education
Department of Education in
Developing Countries
University of London Institute
of Education
London
England

Professor Kankam Twum-Barima
Formerly Director
Institute of Statistical, Social and
Economic Research
University of Ghana
Legon
Ghana

178

Professor Asavia Wandira
Vice-Chancellor
Makerere University
Kampala
Uganda

Mr Peter Williams
Director
Education Programme
Human Resource Development Group
Commonwealth Secretariat
London
England

Mr Lennart Wohlgemuth
Head
Education Division
Swedish International
Development Authority
Stockholm
Sweden

In attendance

**Overseas Development
Administration**
Rt Hon Timothy Raison MP
Minister of State for Foreign and
Commonwealth Affairs
Minister for Overseas Development

Sir Crispin Tickell KCVO
Permanent Secretary

Mr R A Browning
Deputy Secretary

Dr D G Osborne
Head of Eastern and Western Africa
Department

Mr P G Scopes
Education Adviser

Mr D G Camps
Principal
Education Division

**Department of Education and
Science**
Hon Peter Brooke MP
Parliamentary Under-Secretary of
State for Education and Science

The British Council
Sir John Burgh CB
Director-General

Mr R E Cavaliero
Deputy Director-General

Mr D Beard CBE
Assistant Director-General

Voluntary Organisation
Mr Frank Judd
Director
Voluntary Service Overseas
London
England

Conference officers

Chair
Asavia Wandira
Philip Coombs

Lead speakers
Theme I
Arthur Porter
Peter Williams

Theme II
Dorothy Njeuma
Kenneth King

Respondents to lead speakers
Theme I
Isaac Ojok
Kankam Twum-Barima

Theme II
Dzingai Mutumbuka
Aklilu Habte

Working groups
Group 1
Yahaya Hamza Chair Theme I
Paul Hurst Rapporteur Theme I
Cynthia Perry Chair Theme II
Herbert Bergmann Rapporteur Theme II

Group 2
Kebby Musokotwane Chair Theme I
Trevor Coombe Rapporteur Theme I
S C Aleyideino Chair Theme II
Trevor Coombe Rapporteur Theme II

Group 3
Yaya Mede Moussa Chair Theme I
Carew Treffgarne Rapporteur Theme I
Manzoor Ahmed Chair Theme II
Lalage Bown Rapporteur Theme II

Group 4
J R L Kotsokoane Chair Theme I
Kevin Lillis Rapporteur Theme I
Jakes Swartland Chair Theme II
M D Francis Rapporteur Theme II

Steering Committee
(responsible for preparation of Conference)
Hugh Hawes (Chair)
Roger Iredale
Peter Williams
Beryl Steele
Kevin Lillis
Derrick Camps
Carol Coombe (Conference Secretary)

Index

This index covers all parts of the volume except the following: abbreviations (pp.1-2), suggestions for further reading (pp. 22-23), notes for working group discussion (pp. 144-148), bibliography (pp. 167-168), references (pp. 169-170, 170-171,172-175), and lists of participants and Conference officers (pp. 176-180).

Common abbreviations are not spelled out in the index. Readers are referred to the list on pp. 1-2.

The letters f, n and t after page references in the index refer to figure, note and table respectively.

research requirements 117, 131-132, 151, 155

sectoral programming, 28, 84, 86, 88, 162, 163, 164, 166

structure, 87-88

superior information capability, 51, 60, 85, 113, 116-118

support for NGOs, 150, 161, 163, 171

technical assistance personnel, 59, 60, 115, 122, 123, 133-134, 140, 141-142, 150, 153, 157, 161, 162, 163, 164, 165, 166, 170

See also Education; Information; Training; *individual aid agencies*

Aid management, 53, 65, 71

continuity, 72, 73, 74

diplomacy, 121

donor withdrawal or substitution, 72

efficiency, 18, 66, 71-77, 121, 122-123, 141, 155, 156-157, 158, 159, 160

evaluation, 72, 155, 170, 171, 172

lessons from World Bank experience, 56

project control, 72, 85, 122-123, 124, 141, 162

project implementation, 74, 141, 166, 172

project preparation, 64, 65, 71-72, 85, 140-141, 166, 172

See also Educational management; Educational projects

Aid priorities, 113

and donor co-ordination, 127-129

and human rights 152, 153, 158, 159, 160

as 'hard choices', v, ix, 32, 34

'basic needs' approach, 149-150, 151, 152, 157-158

human resources development approach, 56, 74-75, 123, 150, 153, 154, 155-156, 159, 160, 164, 165

internal and external agendas, 34

political vs. professional, 63, 129-131

research requirements 54, 56,131-133, 150, 151, 157

responsive to recipients' priorities, 19, 28, 53, 54, 63-64, 66-71, 73, 84-85, 88, 116, 127, 153, 154, 162, 163, 164, 166

support for economic and social development, 153, 154, 159

support for poorest and marginal groups, 150, 151, 152, 154, 156, 157-158, 159-160

support for self-reliant development, 150, 151, 152, 153

See also Educational priorities; *individual aid agencies; individual education sectors*

Aklilu Habte, 33, 41, 47, 48, 54, 56, 70, 76, 77

Aleyideino, S.C. 19, 50, 78

Anglophone countries, 60, 79, 99t, 100

Angola, 6t, 8t, 16t

Arab states, 99t

Asia, 13, 14f, 46, 94, 101

Association of African Universities, 78

Basic education, 30, 39, 44, 67, 77

and social mobility, 38

and urban populations, 38, 39

as aid priority, 54, 55, 66-69, 110, 124-125, 150, 151, 156, 157, 160

clientele, 39-40

concept, 34-35, 36, 54-55, 66, 67, 109, 151

content, 37-39, 44, 55, 66, 67, 69

co-ordination between formal and non-formal, 35-36, 38, 41, 43, 66, 67, 109

costs, 36, 37, 44

international meetings, 77, 126

leadership development, 44, 70, 103

management, 36, 41

'national centres of primary pedagogy', 44

organisation, 36, 41, 66, 67

priority for rural development, 108, 109, 150

qualitative requirements, 39, 40-43

role in women's development, 35, 58, 66

resources, 35, 37, 41

usable research required, 44

universalisation, 69, 150, 160

See also individual education sectors

Bassett, Charles, 33, 58, 79

Bellagio Education Group (former) *See* IWGE

Benin, 6t, 8t, 16t, 45

Bergmann, Herbert, 55

Botswana, 6t, 8t, 10, 16t, 17n, 36, 95, 97, 103

Bown, Lalage, 40, 66

Brain drain, 31, 97

British aid programme

Foreign and Commonwealth Office, 164

Ministry of Overseas Development (former), 105, 153

See also British Council; ODA

BREDA *See* UNESCO

British Council, vi, 113n, 164

Higher Education Division, 164

TETOC, 164

See also British aid programme; ODA

Buist, Ian, 28, 57

Burkina Faso, 6t, 8t, 16t, 17n

Burundi, 6t, 8t, 16t

Cameroon, 6t, 8t, 16t, 28

educational expansion 135-136

financing education, 137-142

future educational needs, 142-143

technical assistance and scholarships, 141-142

Canadian aid programme

Association of Canadian Community Colleges, 161

High Commissions and Embassies, 161

International Development Office, 161

World University Service (WUSC), 161

See also CIDA

Caribbean (region), 93

Carnegie Corporation of New York, 111

Central African Republic, 6t, 8t, 16t

Certification

and employment, 9, 26, 97

linked to passivity/dependency, 9

social demand, 9, 92

Chad, 6t, 8t, 16t, 17n, 58, 97

CIDA, 151, 152, 156

education policy, 149-150

forms and organisation of aid, 160

human resource development programmes, 128, 150

private, 96, 98, 104, 126
problems of reform, 15, 38, 46, 102
public attitude toward, 9, 25, 26, 38, 42-43, 44, 46, 105
qualitative achievements, 92
rates of return, 95-96, 149, 154, 160
regional programmes, 20, 44, 47, 49, 65, 70, 76, 77, 78-79, 87
resource centres, 67, 70, 102, 103, 104
resource gap, 29, 41, 44, 91, 93, 98, 99-100, 106, 110, 143
science and technology, 23, 25, 39, 109, 110, 136-137, 142, 152
self-help, 81-82, 84, 109
social demand, 10, 12, 19, 20, 26, 30, 33, 53-54, 63, 67, 80, 92, 95-96, 98, 160
structures, 84, 95
'under siege', 22, 33, 99, 104
See also individual education sectors
Educational administration *See* Educational management
Educational costs, 20, 41, 111, 112, 135
affordable basic education advocated, 37, 160
and rates of return, 95-96
high unit costs, 47, 48, 94
impede universalisation of secondary education, 94-95
of expanding non-formal education, 36
reductions proposed, 35-36, 100-101, 104
Educational finance
alternative sources, 20, 32
and educational policies, 28-29
budget restrictions, 19-20, 28, 31, 32, 35, 41, 44, 94, 95
capital investment, 20, 28, 137, 138, 139
community contribution, 20, 35, 82, 96
donor role, 20-21, 28, 63, 68
high budgetary allocations, 24, 30, 47, 94, 106-107, 137-138
research, 156
unavailable for innovation, 86
Educational management
accountability to community, 82, 83, 84, 97
and national development, 29, 49, 84
as aid priority, 49, 59, 64-66, 104, 115, 152, 155, 156-157, 158
building capacity, 48-49, 50, 51, 56, 64-66, 71, 115, 157
community responsibility, 103, 104
consultants as catalysts, 65
decentralisation, 103, 104, 157
efficiency, 49, 64-65, 107, 115, 122-123, 155, 156-157, 158, 159
field support systems proposed, 65-66, 67, 70, 82, 113
personnel systems, 66, 101, 102, 103
political involvement, 41, 49, 115, 116
redefinition needed, 64-66
strengthening professionalism, 101, 102
See also Aid management; Educational quality; Information; Training
Educational materials, 49
as aid priority, 68, 70, 103-104, 151, 153, 155, 158, 159
production, 68, 70, 102, 153, 161, 163

shortage, 15, 20, 41, 42, 68, 97, 100, 107
Educational planning, 19, 34, 49, 71, 81, 114, 122, 129, 133
as aid priority, 59, 64-66, 104, 151, 155, 157
as service to aid agencies, 117-118, 119-120, 121, 132
data collection, 49-50, 56, 62, 71, 104, 112
for aided systems, 114
integral part of management, 49-50
political involvement, 57
research role, 132-133
skill requirements, 49-50
status, 50, 112
See also Educational management; Information; Training
Educational policies
African control, 50
and educational finance, 28-29
in 1960s and 1970s, 19
role of aid in formulation, 73, 115, 116
Educational priorities, v, ix, 15, 20, 21, 37, 43
a priority area for discussion and training, 64
and educational needs, 32-33, 34, 143
and problems of implementation, 15, 28, 43, 64
and resources, 28-29, 31, 32, 110
as 'hard choices', ix, 27, 28, 32, 33, 34, 80, 130
as proposed by Roger Iredale, 83-84
as proposed by Arthur Porter, 108-111
as proposed by Peter Williams, 101-105
Conference preferences, 29-30, 44, 45, 47, 48, 58, 64, 80
continuing process, 112
differences between countries, 5, 28, 32
factors influencing Conference discussion, 7, 27-29, 32-34, 56, 58, 80
'five major issues', 80
in relation to other priorities, 28, 30-32, 35, 63, 84-85, 131-132, 138-139, 143
influence of international conferences, 129-131
need for clearer definition, 63-64
negotiable with aid agencies, 29, 33-34, 43, 59, 62-71, 85-88, 116, 129-131, 133, 134, 139
not differentiated by African governments, 33, 34, 63, 116, 143
outcome of political process, 28, 63, 116, 129-130
political vs. professional, 129-130
See also Aid priorities; Information
Educational projects, 49, 51, 65, 71
as legacy of past policies, 53-54
complementarity between projects and sectors, 74
expatriate participation, 123
experimental imports, 61, 114, 115, 118
generalising innovative projects, 123-127
justifying project priority, 63, 64, 84-85, 117-118
management, 71-72
project aid vs. sectoral support 116
regional projects and programmes, 78
reviews of long-term projects, 119-120

184

31, 69, 74, 123
  See also Training
Hurst, Paul, 63

Ibrahim, Ahmed Bushra, 76
IDA *See* World Bank
IDRC (Canada), 133
IIEP *See* UNESCO
Illiteracy *See* Literacy and illiteracy
IMF, 17n
India, 58, 124, 127
Industrialisation, 37, 39
Information
  about communities receiving education, 60
  and research, 50, 86, 131-133
  co-ordination of country documentation, 61,
  119-120
  data needs for planning and management,
  50-51, 60, 61-62, 85, 104, 112
  exchange across development sectors, 74
  improving information systems, 61-62, 150
  'maps' of African and donor systems, 59, 61,
  72, 113-116, 119-120, 121, 122-124, 126,
  133, 134
  management information systems needed, 21,
  30, 50, 104
  needed for education and aid policy, 56, 59-
  61, 67, 84, 128-129, 131-133, 160
  personnel information systems, 101
  sharing among African countries, 43, 51, 95,
  112
  sharing among donors and aid partners, 61,
  77, 79, 121-129
  training needs, 62
  universities as key centres, 48
International Conference on Education (39th
Session), 92t, 98, 99t, 105
IWGE, 77, 128, 129
Iredale, Roger, v, 33, 80
Ivory Coast, 6t, 8t, 13, 16t, 101

Jefferson, Thomas, 31

Kalahari Desert, 6
Kambalametore, Arthur, 45, 46, 51
Kenya, 6t, 8t, 10, 13, 16t, 65-66, 70, 94, 95, 102,
150, 172
King, Kenneth, 28, 33, 53, 63, 73, 81, 85, 113
Kotsokoane, Joseph, 28, 45

Latin America, 13, 14f, 45, 93, 94, 129
Lawton, Denis, v
Lesotho, 6t, 8t, 16t
Liberia, 6t, 8t, 16t
Libraries, 104, 136, 138, 155, 164
Lillis, Kevin, 52n
Literacy and illiteracy, 81, 82, 112
  adverse effect of population growth, 11, 91,
  92, 107
  as aid priority, 41, 45, 155, 156, 158
  challenge of development-related literacy, 12
  'culture of literacy' declining, 122
  functional literacy, 45, 155
  literacy central to basic education, 34, 39, 66,
  68, 158

measures of literacy, 43, 68
post-literacy materials, 41
  See also Basic education
Lomé Convention, iii

Madagascar, 6t, 8t, 16t
Malawi, 6t, 8t, 16t, 83
Mali, 6t, 8t, 16t, 36, 94
Manpower, 85, 86, 107, 109, 110, 122-123, 141
  See also Human resource development;
  Training
Mao Tse-Tung, 22
Mauritania, 6t, 8t, 13, 16t
Mauritius, 6t, 8t, 16t
Mede Moussa, Yaya, 36, 38, 45
Missionary societies, 120
  See also NGOs
Mozambique, 6t, 8t, 16t, 18, 58
Musokotwane, Kebby, 5, 39, 51, 57
Mutumbuka, Dzingai, viii, 22, 29, 35

Natural resources education *See* Agricultural
education
NEIDA *See* UNESCO
NGOs, 125, 133, 149n, 161
  aid support to local NGOs, 161
  and co-ordinated education programme, 15,
  29
  demonstration schools, 125
  educational experience, 134
  role in non-formal education, 12, 29, 35, 84,
  87
Niger, 6t, 8t, 16t
Nigeria, 6t, 7, 8t, 13, 16t, 95, 97, 103
N'jai, A.A., 17, 42, 46
Njala University College (University of Sierra
Leone), 108
Njeuma, Dorothy, 28, 31, 44, 52, 75, 84, 135
Non-formal education, 107
  approaches to skills training, 45, 46, 82,
  110
  as aid priority, 87, 150, 151, 152, 155, 156,
  159
  as part of basic education, 34, 38, 41, 43, 66-
  67, 109
  as supplement to formal provision, 111-112
  enhancing human capacities, 12
  for survival and development, 13, 15, 20, 32,
  38, 40, 45, 157-158
  links with formal education, 36, 41, 43, 44,
  45, 67, 81, 82-83, 87, 109
  not a panacea, 154
  representation at Conference, vi
  universities' role, 48
  See also Agricultural education; Basic
  education; Extension; Skills training
North America, 102

OAU, 7, 15
  Lagos Plan of Action, 15, 18n, 21n
  1985 economic summit, 18n
ODA, iii, v, 70, 76, 77, 108, 128, 156, 160
  and British expertise, 87, 88
  as joint Conference organiser, v, vi, 80n, 111,
  128

awards and overseas students' fees, 75-76
Commonwealth Scholarship and Fellowship
Plan, 164
education policy, 84, 88, 153-155
forms and organisation of aid, 28, 84, 86,
163-165
policy documents, 153, 154, 167
Indian schools computer project, 58,127
Joint Funding Scheme, 87
KELT, 164
manpower reviews, 86, 164
Principal Education Adviser (Roger Iredale),
ix, 80n
See also British aid programme; British
Council
OECD, 77, 105, 117, 119
DAC, 77, 126-127, 128
policy documents, 126, 170
Ojok, Isaac, 46
Okoro, Denis, 9

Parents, 66, 116
attitudes to school and students, 26, 31, 36,
42, 43, 96, 98, 99, 100-101, 134
élite response to democratising education, 96,
98
financial support and responsibility for
schools, 20, 82, 96, 103, 105
participants in non-formal education, 158
Perry, Cynthia, 37, 40, 47, 55, 69
Phelps-Stokes Commissions (1920, 1924), 38
Phillips, H.M., 54
Population
and employment, 30
Conference discussion, 9, 12, 30-31, 81
ecology and food production, 10, 12-13, 30,
37
education, 58, 74
effect on illiteracy and enrolment rates, iii, 11,
19, 30, 42, 91, 94, 107, 142
structure and growth rates, iii, 7, 8t, 9, 10-12,
18, 19, 20, 30, 42, 80, 93
urbanisation, 7, 10, 25, 135
See also Education; Sub-Saharan Africa
Porter, Arthur, 32, 42, 45, 47, 68, 83, 106
Primary education, 40, 92, 98, 99, 133, 135,
160
aided demonstration schools proposed, 124,
125-127
as aid priority, 54, 55, 66-69, 125-127, 151,
152, 157, 159
as part of basic education, 34, 36, 40, 54, 66,
109
Canadian, 126, 127
Danish, 125, 126
deformalisation, 36, 43, 45, 66, 67
generalising innovation, 125-127
linked with rural development, 55, 109
necessity of re-orientation, 42, 109
Scottish, 125, 126, 127
strengthening professionalism, 102, 125-
126
unit costs, 35, 94
universal, 11, 91, 94-95, 96, 103, 106, 111,
137

See also Basic education; Schools
Project Impact, 101
Public services, 80
'civil service culture', 121-122, 123
decline, 18, 21, 115
staff development needs, 21
See also Governments, African; Training
Pupils *See* Students

Raison, Timothy, iii, 88
Research
as educational management tool, 49
as aid priority, 44, 51, 86, 111, 115, 120-121,
129, 131-133, 151, 155, 156
research culture and education policy, 132-
133
demystifying, 86
developing indigenous capacity, 51, 86
influences on aid policies, 131-133
institutes and university systems, 47, 50, 121
international agencies (IDRC and SAREC),
133
networks on education, 50, 132-133
on agriculture and natural resources, 13-14,
15, 19, 48, 70
on aid process, 131
on appropriate pedagogy for basic education,
44
on development needs, 71
on educational diagnostic and monitoring
instruments, 44
on school quality, 49, 65-66
on schools and communities, 62
See also Information
Research Review and Advisory Group (RRAG),
133
Romain, Ralph, 33, 51, 63
Rugumyamheto, Joseph, 31, 56
Rural conditions
agrarian base of African economies, 7, 13, 19,
31, 37, 39, 108
food production decline, 10, 13, 14f, 15, 38,
80
unequal rural/urban development, 7, 14, 18,
109, 135, 139
urgency of ecological problems, 9, 16, 38
See also Agricultural education; Food;
Population
Rwanda, 6t, 8t, 13, 16t
Ryrie, Sir William, v

SADCC, 79
Sahara *See* Sahel
Sahel, 10, 12, 37, 78
SAREC (Sweden), 133
Scholarships and fellowships, 65, 76, 77, 140,
142, 161, 162, 163
See also Students; Training
School inspectorate *See* Educational supervision
School leavers
employment and training, 9, 19, 31, 41, 45,
55, 58, 108, 109
Schools, 9, 10, 20, 62, 66, 100, 126
advantages, 101
as 'necessary evil', 26

Prepared by the Overseas Development Administration and the Central Office of Information.
Printed for Her Majesty's Stationery Office by Robendene Ltd., Amersham.
Dd 738229 C25 2/86